Seashells
of the
Egyptian
Red Sea

Seashells
of the
Egyptian
Red Sea
The Illustrated Handbook

Mary Lyn Rusmore-Villaume

The American University in Cairo Press
Cairo   New York

Photographs Copyright © 2008 by Mary Lyn Rusmore-Villaume
Illustrations by Ahmed Gheith

Dar el Kutub No. 3132/07
ISBN 978 977 416 096 7

Dar el Kutub Cataloging-in-Publication Data

Rusmore-Villaume, Mary Lyn
        Seashells of the Egyptian Red: The Illustrated Handbook / Mary Lyn
    Rusmore-Villaume.—Cairo: The American University in Cairo Press, 2008
        p.   cm.
        ISBN 977 416 096 7
        1. Shells—Egypt   I. Title
        594

1 2 3 4 5 6 7 8 9 10 11 12   12 11 10 09 08

Designed by Sally Boylan/AUC Press Design Center
Printed in Egypt

Dedicated to my parents

Jay T. Rusmore and Jean E. Rusmore

in gratitude for their enthusiastic support and encouragement
of all my interests and efforts in education and natural history,
and for sharing with me their deep love of all nature

Contents

Acknowledgments

Without the generous and untiring assistance of many people I could never have written this book. Henk Dekker of the Netherlands assisted me with the identification of a great many species, especially those published only in scientific journals. He also read several versions of the manuscript and reviewed the photographs. His photographic memory, kindness, and patience are remarkable and I am truly grateful. Graham Oliver of the National Museum and Galleries of Wales separated and identified many apparently identical bivalves. He also read the initial bivalve manuscript and offered many important suggestions. He has been one of the best teachers I have ever had and I am deeply appreciative. For encouragement and use of facilities I am grateful to Rob Moolenbeek of the Zoölogisch Museum Amsterdam, and to his entire family for their hospitality. Henk K. Mienis, Curator of the National Mollusc Collections at the Hebrew University of Jerusalem and Tel Aviv University, Israel, contributed much information on the presence of species in the Gulf of Aqaba. Ed Heiman of Israel has been very encouraging, and his journal *Triton* has provided much useful information on shells from the Gulf of Aqaba. Bob van Syoc and the California Academy of Sciences provided encouragement and use of their facilities.

For assistance and hospitality I am happily indebted to Anna Holmes and Harriet Woods of the National Museum and Galleries of Wales. I extend my warm gratitude to Mr. and Mrs. Dekker of Winkel, the Netherlands, for their repeated hospitality. I thank Amelia MacLellan of the Natural History Museum, London, and Virginie Héros and Rudo von Cosel, Musée Nationale d'Histoire Naturelle, Paris, for special assistance with the tellinid *Pseudometis dubia*. Solly Singer of Israel provided helpful information on the Epitoniidae and Fissurellidae. Dr. Mohamed Abou Zeid of al-Azhar University contributed advice and encouragement. Dr. Mahmoud Hanifi of Suez Canal University loaned me his copy of *Red Sea Shells* (Sharabati, 1984) and really got me started on the unique shells of the Red Sea. Dr. Richard Willan of Darwin, Australia, contributed greatly to the process of determining that I had found a previously unknown species of *Gari*.

For their friendship, companionship, hospitality and specimens I am grateful to Henk Dekker, Barbara Fudge, Eva Montville, Pam Piombino, Nancy Ramadan, Barbara Rusmore, Kaki Rusmore, Myrette el Sokari, Pam Sparr, Bob and Amy van Syoc, and Nate Villaume. Pam Piombino became my field assistant and helped in countless ways. Special thanks are due to Francis Gilbert, University of Nottingham, for helpful comments and Suzanne Pollack, Cairo, for proofreading. Rosalina Nuñez washed and sorted shells with great care and dedication while managing our whole household with grace and efficiency. Without her assistance I could never have managed. Gratitude beyond measure I express to my husband John Michael Villaume for love, patience, financing, driving, and companionship.

Special thanks are due to Boutros (Paolo) Isaac of Cairo (www.dbprepress.com) and Rick Seaman of Portland, Oregon (Pro-Video Clinic) for their extraordinary knowledge of photography and cameras and light, and their ability to convey their expertise so clearly. I doubt either of them had ever encountered anyone with a more abysmal understanding of those subjects than I had in 2004. It is only through their patient and unstinting assistance that I was able to take the pictures. Any inadequacies in the results simply reflect my incomplete mastery of their subject. For additional photographic advice I am grateful to Alan Wood (formerly of the International Institute of Entomology, www.alanwood.net).

Sally Boylan gets eternal gratitude for her magnificent settings of the photographs. And abundant appreciation for patience and enthusiasm for the project.

And for years of quiet, patient, calm and consistent encouragement I am so grateful to my editor at the American University in Cairo Press, Neil Hewison.

The contributions of so many people made this book possible and provided unexpected evidence of tremendous generosity. That so many of them have also become real friends is a wonderful bonus. I can never repay the debt but hope they accept my gratitude. Of course I accept full responsibility for any errors.

Foreword

The Red Sea is a body of warm tropical water nearly 2000 km in length, bordered mainly by desert. These sandy and rocky borders have little visible life, in stark contrast to the wealth of marine life found below the water's surface. The most famous are the Red Sea's beautiful coral reefs, which give shelter to a wide variety of animal species. The empty shells of molluscs (one large group) are frequently washed up on the beaches. For many years the richness of marine life has attracted explorers and scientists, and in the last decades many tourists as well. The Red Sea forms the most northwestern part of the vast Indo-Pacific Ocean, its closest point to Europe. Almost 250 years ago European scientists were drawn to study the animals found here. In 1761–67 the Danish "Arabia Felix" expedition carried out the first biological survey of the Red Sea, and yielded numerous new species of animals and plants.

Many more explorations were to follow, all of which produced new insights and information. The Italian Arthuro Issel published a book with a summary of the knowledge so far gleaned on Red Sea shells in 1869. This was also the year that the Suez Canal, planned by the French engineer Ferdinand de Lesseps, was opened for ships to cross the stretch of land between the Red Sea and the Mediterranean Sea. The Suez Canal has played—and will continue to play—an important role for the migration of many species from the Red Sea into the Mediterranean Sea (Lessepsian migrants). Many originally Red Sea fish, molluscs, crustaceans and so on can now be found living in the Mediterranean.

The book *Red Sea Shells* by Doreen Sharabati (1984) was the first book to show photographs of many Red Sea shells, but is now out of print. The bivalves are treated by Graham Oliver in his large volume *Bivalved Seashells of the Red Sea* (1992). A compilation of all the known mollusc species was made by Dekker and Orlin in 2000, but contained no pictures. What has been missing is a book which is easy to access and read, and contains photographs of most of the shells found on the beach and through diving. Mary Lyn Rusmore-Villaume has searched the beaches of Egypt for fifteen years to establish which species can be found here. The results of this research have now been drawn together in this book. Many hours of studying, writing, and photographing shells have resulted in a comprehensive guide which will be useful to the tourist, the diver, the shell collector, and the scientist.

The growing awareness of the need to protect our natural heritage is especially important for the Red Sea. Being a rather isolated sea, it contains many species found only here (endemics). This makes it all the more important to maintain the coral reefs in a healthy state and the water unpolluted so that the marine life can flourish. The demands of tourism and industrial activity are putting pressure on the ecosystem. It is hoped that through the development of marine parks and by observing strict rules the environment and its remarkable biodiversity will be properly protected, so visitors can enjoy swimming in the natural aquarium known as the Red Sea forever.

Henk Dekker
Honorary Research Associate
Zoological Museum
Amsterdam, the Netherlands

Mediterranean Sea

Egypt

Sinai

Suez
Ayun Musa
Ein Sukhna
Ras Sudr
Taba
Zafarana
Gulf of Suez
Nuweiba
Gulf of Aqaba
Ras Gharib
Dahab
South
Sinai
Ras Mohamed
National Park
Hurghada
Safaga
Quseir
Red Sea
Marsa Alam
Wadi Gimaal National Park
Wadi Lahmi
Ras Banas
Shalatein

Introduction

This book is intended to serve as a guide to a wide selection of the shelled molluscs of the Egyptian Red Sea and includes all the commonly seen species. The high biodiversity of the Red Sea is indicated by the large number of species considered uncommon or rare. But the selection in this book is in no way exhaustive—it was unfortunately impossible to include everything. All the shells featured were found in Egypt as empty shells by the author or her friends, usually when walking along the beach (or creeping and crawling in the case of micro shells!) and a few were found while snorkeling or diving. All photographs were taken by the author, and many species are pictured here for the first time in a general reference work. A minimum of specialized terminology has been used, but every effort has been made to ensure scientific accuracy. The photographs facilitate visual recognition by amateurs and highlight the significant distinguishing characteristics of each species, making the book suitable for serious conchologists as well. Ecologists will find the distribution information useful as a baseline for future comparisons as climate change progresses.

A note about taxonomy—the naming and grouping of living things

All living organisms are classified and named under a system originated by the Swedish naturalist Linnaeus (1707–78) in 1758. Every creature has two names, the genus and the species, usually given in Latin or Greek. For instance, we are all human beings. Our scientific name is *Homo sapiens*. The genus *Homo* is Man and *sapiens*, the species name, means knowing or thinking. It is a convention that the genus name is capitalized and the species name is not, and both are italicized or underlined. The complete name of every species also includes the name of the person who first published a description of the creature and a name for it, and the date of the publication: for example, *Trochus maculatus* Linnaeus, 1758.

Every individual in a species is so much like every other individual in that species that no significant predictable differences can be determined. They can reproduce and the offspring will mature into the same kind of creature as the parents.

1

Numerous species can belong to the same genus, a grouping of creatures which are the same in many important and predictable ways. The plural of genus is genera. Similar genera are grouped by taxonomists into families, families into orders, orders into classes, and classes into phyla (singular phylum). This book deals only with the shelled creatures within the phylum Mollusca.

The word mollusc means 'soft bodied.' Thus all creatures called molluscs have soft bodies and no bones. They are invertebrates. The two largest groups (classes) of molluscs are gastropods (snails) and bivalves (clams and all other clam-like creatures having two shells). There are a number of other groups of molluscs. Whether they should be called classes, orders, subclasses, suborders, or just groups depends on which author you read. As this book makes no claim to furthering the knowledge or discussion of higher taxa, I have resorted just to calling them 'groups.'

The scientific names change fairly frequently due to advances in science. Originally all identifications and groupings of molluscs were made on the basis of the appearance of the shell. Gradually anatomical features of the animal became significant factors. Today DNA considerations are being added. Name changes can be annoying, but are made in the best interests of more complete knowledge.

In the first 150 to 200 years after Linneaus many people gave names to shells. Due to the lack of rapid communications at that time sometimes several people gave different names to exactly the same creature. When two or more names refer to the same shell they are called 'synonyms.' The opposite also took place—different people gave the same name to different shells. If the same name refers to a different shell it will be mentioned as 'non' (see page 254 *Loxoglypta clathrata*). According to Dekker and Orlin (2000) Deshayes published the name *clathrata* for this shell a few months earlier in 1835 than Gaimard published the name *rhomboides* for the same shell. So *clathrata* is the valid name (being the one first given) and *rhomboides* is a synonym. In 1791 Gmelin published the name *rhomboides* for a different shell, so this is not a synonym and is shown as 'non-Gmelin, 1791.'

The designation 'of some authors' *(auctorum* in Latin) means that one or more authors have referred to this creature by the name shown. However this is not the correct name of the species under discussion; it refers to a different species.

The rules of the International Commission on Zoological Nomenclature state that, unless specifically excepted, the oldest published species name is considered the valid one. This name cannot change. The only way a familiar shell can be called by a different species name is when a researcher discovers that similar shells (which were all called by one name) have turned out to belong to different species. A recent case in point is found in the genus *Anodontia* of the bivalve family Lucinidae. All the toothless, globose, plain white thin shells found in the Red Sea (and some other areas) have been long called *Anodontia edentula*. In 2005 two illustrious, and very industrious, specialists published the results of their long and painstaking study of all the *Anodontia* species of the world. They determined that at least three different species of *Anodontia* are found in the Red Sea, now known as *A. kora*, *A. ovulum*, and *A. ovum*.

The genus name, by contrast, might change rather often. One eminent scientist told me "Genus names are a matter of opinion—that's why they change so often." For example, when I first started working with the shells of the Egyptian Red Sea, all cowries were in the genus *Cypraea*. Since then specialists have divided them into many different genera. When the genus name is changed the name of the author of the species name and the date of publication will be placed in parentheses. So the species *Cypraea annulus* Linnaeus, 1758 is now correctly written as *Erosaria annulus* (Linnaeus, 1758).

In Latin both nouns and adjectives have gender and are declined according to their own systems. Specialists in Latin work to decide the correct genders and spellings of new names; for example, the small gastropod *Hipponix conicus*. When the genus changed to *Sabia*, a feminine word, the species name had to change to a feminine form to match it, in this case *conica*. Although this all seems complicated and difficult, it is much more efficient than using common names, which can vary from region to region, even when the people using them all speak the same language.

The names in this book are the most current available. In almost all cases they have been taken from the *Check-list of Red Sea Mollusca* by Henk Dekker and Zvi Orlin (2000). In the case of bivalves I have occasionally used names preferred by Graham Oliver. One set of names in the subfamily Macominae I researched with considerable help from many sources. I discovered and described (in 2005) a new species, also included in this book.

Where molluscs live

Molluscs—the animals inside the shells—live in every imaginable part of the marine world. So why don't we see them when we're snorkeling? Because they are hiding from predators—other creatures that eat them! They protect themselves by burrowing or creeping under the sand or mud, or excavating a burrow into stone or coral or wood, or hiding in cracks or living under mushroom corals, or even inside other animals. Others attach themselves to hard rocks or coral or other shells, or even manufactured surfaces such as metal. Some live only in deep water or shallow water, or in the area that is exposed as beach or rocks or wooden pilings when the tide is out. Many other organisms such as algae grow on them and camouflage them.

Some species live only in certain geographic areas. All the shells featured in this book are found in the Red Sea. If they are not found outside the Red Sea they are called 'endemic.' Only four species included in this book are endemic to the northern Red Sea: *Ethminolia hemprichi* (Issel, 1869), all areas; *Sigatica mienisi* (Kilburn, 1988), Gulf of Aqaba and South Sinai; *Gari sharabatiae*

M.L. Rusmore-Villaume, 2005, northern Gulf of Suez only, and *Pecten erythraeensis* Sowerby II, 1842, Gulf of Suez only. These are so indicated in the text.

Identifying parts of shells

It is very useful to learn the names of the different parts of the shell. When you know the standard names of the parts, you can understand the descriptions in this and most other books about shells. You are able to recognize and talk about the diagnostic features that distinguish families, genera, and species. You can also communicate accurately with amateurs and professionals interested in shells. Definitions of all terms used in this book are contained in the Glossary. If you want to learn even more terms, I encourage you to consult any of the excellent books mentioned in the Bibliography.

A few features and their names are common to both bivalves and gastropods. **Pericostracum** is the most common of these and refers to the outermost covering of the shell, a thin "skin" which protects the shell of the living animal. In some species it has hairs or bristles. It usually disappears shortly after the animal dies. It is only rarely useful in identifying a shell, and in those cases usually the hairs, bristles, or color are the important characteristics.

Parts of a gastropod shell

All the shells in this book have either one or two shells. Those with one shell are usually coiled and are in the class Gastropoda. The ordinary garden snail is a gastropod.

The shell is a tube that coils around an imaginary axis from the narrow **apex** at the top to the broader base. Each rotation of the tube of the shell around the axis is a **whorl**. The line where the whorls join each other is the **suture**. The final whorl is the **body whorl**. The opening in the body whorl is the **aperture**. The

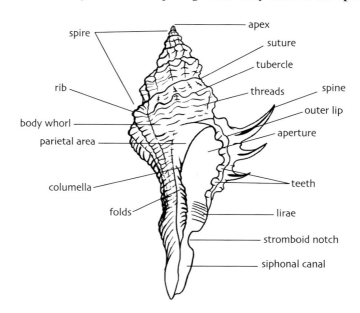

animal extends itself a little way out of the aperture in order to move about and to feed. The edge of the aperture is the lip. The edge farther from the axis is, logically enough, the **outer lip**; the one closer to it is the **inner lip** or **parietal wall**. A thick outer lip usually indicates the animal has reached maturity.

The structural element under the inner lip is the **columella**, a 'little column.' (Sometimes the words columella and inner lip are used interchangeably as in a plicate columella or plicate inner lip.) It is the part that winds most closely around the imaginary axis. This is often a very important feature in distinguishing species. It may be straight or curved, smooth or with 'teeth' (**dentate**) or 'folds' (**plicate**), colored or white. In a few species it grows to become a long tube which protects the inhalent or feeding tube of the animal. This is known as the **siphonal canal**. The most common shell here with such a canal is *Fusinus verrucosus* of the family Fasciolariidae. A posterior or **exhalent canal** is present in a few shells, mostly in the Bursidae. If the columella winds a measurable distance away from the axis there will be a resulting empty space, the **umbilicus**. Shells of the genus *Rubritrochus* have a large umbilicus. The presence or absence of the umbilicus and its size, texture, and depth are often determining features in otherwise very similar shells.

The external surface of gastropods may be smooth or rough. Usually they have very fine lines parallel to the outer lip called **axial growth lines**. A species may have strong or weak raised **axial ribs**. The **interstices** or interspaces are the spaces between the ribs. There may also be spiral sculpture that runs along the direction of growth. The heavier ones are called **cords**; the weaker ones **threads**. Spiral sculpture may be incised, as though cut into the shell. These lines are formally called **striae**, but are also known as **lines** or **grooves**. **Cancellate** or **decussate sculpture** occurs when both spiral and axial elements cross each other forming little squarish or diamond-shaped blocks respectively. **Nodules** or **tubercles** are protrusions from the shell.

Parts of a bivalve shell

Bivalvia is the second-largest class of molluscs after Gastropoda. Bivalved animals have two shells, known as valves. The animal opens its valves a little to take in water and food. It closes them tight if it senses danger. It uses adductor muscles to pull the valves shut, which leave marks on the inside of the shells called **adductor scars**. Most bivalves have two adductor muscle scars on each valve, but certain families have only one. The **pallial line** connects the two scars. The **pallial sinus** is an area inside a slightly shiny line, always beginning at the posterior end of the shell. The pallial sinus may merge for a long or short portion of its lower edge with the pallial line.

The two valves are held together by the **ligament**, which is always to the posterior of the **beaks**. The beaks are the embryonic valves, the very first shell parts to form. They are usually the highest, or right under the highest, point of the shell.

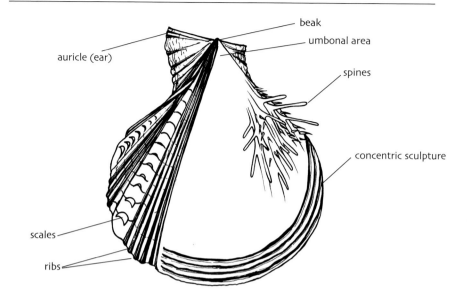

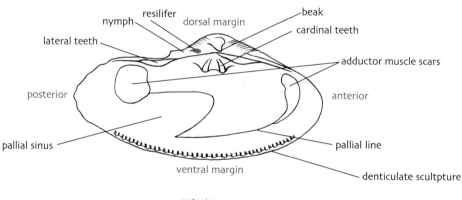

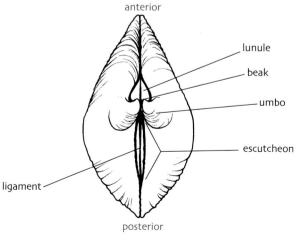

The area from the beaks to about one quarter to one third of the shell toward the ventral margin is the **umbo** (plural umbones). (Some authors use beak and umbo interchangeably.) Some species, such as the venerid *Circe rugifera*, have diagnostic sculpture in the umbonal area.

Most bivalves have shell structures called **teeth** near the ligament and the umbones. These help the two valves to remain tightly shut during storms and predators' attacks. The teeth under the beak or umbo are called the **cardinal teeth** and the longer ones to the sides are the **lateral teeth**. These are important features for grouping shells into families. The whole area below the umbones and extending to the distant ends of the lateral teeth is known as the **hinge**. The hinge is almost always on the **dorsal margin** of the shell. The opposite margin, the side that opens the widest, is the **ventral margin**.

If you hold a bivalve shell so that the dorsal margin is upward and the ligament is between you and the umbones:

- The **anterior** of the shell is the part farthest away from you.
- The **posterior** is toward you.
- The **right valve** is on the right.
- The **left valve** is on the left.

In this book RV is the abbreviation for the right valve and LV for the left valve. The only exception is the Chamidae, where LV stands for lower valve, the one attached to the rock or coral, and UV refers to the upper valve. BV always indicates both valves.

The exterior of bivalve shells also has useful identifying features. On the dorsal margin in front of (anterior to) the umbones is the **lunule**, usually a slightly sunken short, wide, or narrow area. Behind (posterior to) the umbones and related to the ligament is the **escutcheon**. (These two features may be strong, weak, differently colored or textured, outlined, or absent, depending on the species.) It is usually different from the rest of the shell; in many species it has little colored bars across it. It is easiest to see the lunule and the escutcheon on a shell with both valves present and closed.

The sculpture of bivalves is described using many of the same terms as for gastropods. The sculpture is arranged **radially**—growing out from the umbo to the ventral margin, or **concentrically** (comarginally)—parallel to the margins. In a few species it is **oblique** or **diagonal**. There can be raised **threads** or **cords**, or **incised lines**. Thin extended concentric growths are called **lamellae**; the sculpture lamellate. **Ribs** are long, narrow, raised structures beginning on or near the umbones and extending to the ventral margin. **Scales** are thin, usually small, protrusions of shell. **Spines** are like needles or thorns. Scales are generally more consistent within a species than spines and thus more useful for identification.

A word of caution about color

Shells come in many different colors, most of them beautiful and eye-catching. A few species can be recognized in ways related to color. For example the gastropod *Myurella affinis* never has an orange aperture, and the relatively similar *M. nebulosa* usually does. But color may vary from one individual to another within a species. For example, the bivalve *Asaphis violascens* always has dull rough external sculpture and a glossy brightly colored interior—which could be white, pink, yellow, orange, or purple. Color always fades in the sun, and is difficult to reproduce exactly in print. In most cases shell color is not as reliable as sculpture for identification purposes.

Using this book to identify shells

The shells are presented in groups of related shells, first the class Gastropoda, then the class Bivalvia. Within the class they are arranged by family, sequenced according to the generally accepted order at present. The species within the families are presented alphabetically by genus and then species.

To identify a shell, note if it is a bivalve or a gastropod. Then start looking at photographs within that class. The simplest way to identify a shell is to look at the pictures until you find one like the shell in your hand. Using the knowledge you have gained from the previous section about the parts of the shell, compare your shell with the most similar pictures. The one or two most diagnostic features of a species—those that allow you to say it is species A and not species B—are indicated in this book by an arrow →. If your shell looks like the photograph and has exactly the same important features, it is most probably that shell.

The more you use the book the more familiar the terms will be and the more proficient you will become at identification. The best way to become skilled at identifying shells is to go to the beach often and take this book with you—and use it. You can also look at the pictures at night before going to sleep—sometimes you will find that you recognize a certain shell the next morning. In most cases several different characteristics must be considered together in order to determine the species.

The relative abundance and frequency of occurrence of a species is indicated as follows:

- **Abundant:** You will always find a great number of specimens on the beach
- **Common:** At least ten specimens on any given day
- **Uncommon:** Not often and not many
- **Infrequent:** Fewer than ten specimens and not on every visit
- **Rare:** I have found fewer than six
- **Very rare:** I have found one specimen in fifteen years of looking.

Many factors influence the presence of shells on a beach, including tides and storms. It is possible that developmental stages of the shells, disease, and predator behavior may also have an effect. The presence of shells on any given day defies precise prediction. Thus you will find some species somewhat vaguely described as "locally and intermittently common, usually uncommon."

The distribution ranges indicate where I have found that particular species, usually based on many visits. All living things have certain requirements and thrive only in habitats that provide what they need. In addition to food and oxygen, molluscs must have the necessary kind of substrate. For example, sand-dwelling clams will not be found in areas without sand. Rock-clinging limpets cannot dwell in mudflats. Certain species need clean coral sand, others need a bit of mud, some require living coral, and so on. The range given for a particular species does not guarantee either that you will find it there or that you will *not* find it anywhere else. The map on page xii illustrates these geographical distribution ranges.

The size ranges indicated at the beginning of each species description are those of the specimens I actually examined, measured along their longest dimension. All specimens, unless otherwise noted, are figured at actual size; the size in millimeters of the largest one shown is indicated at the end of the description. Very small shells are enlarged as indicated (x2, x3, etc.) to better show their identifying features.

As this book deals only with shells from Egyptian waters, no attempt is made to distinguish these shells from similar ones in the Indian Ocean or the rest of the Indo-Pacific range.

As the print date for this book approached, there was a necessary cut-off point after which no more species could be included. It therefore contains only a fraction of all the currently known seashells of the Red Sea. However, it is as comprehensive as feasible and contains at least 80 percent of the species I have seen in the Egyptian Red Sea—and surely many more remain to be discovered! I hope you enjoy reading this book, looking at the photographs, and get as much pleasure from using it as I had in creating it.

Class Gastropoda—The Gastropods

This is the largest group of shelled marine molluscs. They have only one shell, usually coiled. The name implies that the stomach sits on top of the foot. The animals generally use the foot to help them move around in search of food. Carnivores, herbivores, and omnivores are all found among the gastropods. Most gastropods, including the opisthobranchs (page 148), have gills toward the front of their body and are referred to as prosobranchs.

The shells of the two following families, Nacellidae and Eoacmaeidae, are commonly called limpets. The animals live on rocks intertidally. They move about slowly at night grazing on algae and return every dawn to their home spot.

Family NACELLIDAE
Cellana rota (Gmelin, 1791)
10–50 mm. Subcircular outline. Large shell, conical or nearly flat, apex usually worn. Diverse appearances, some with radial rays. Interior glossy silvery white, apricot, beige, or yellow. Some with brown owl-shaped scar. (41 mm)
Distribution: Common, all regions.

Family EOACMAEIDAE
Eoacmaea sp.
Patelloida profunda (Deshayes, 1863) of authors
11–15 mm. Ovoid, conical with straight sides, numerous fine cream-colored radial ribs, inside pale orange with distinct muscle scar. (15 mm)
Distribution: Highly localized, uncommon, Hurghada–Safaga and South Sinai. Pictured specimens found by Henk Dekker and Pam Piombino.

Cellana rota

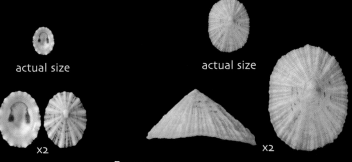

actual size

actual size

×2

×2

Eoacmaea sp.

Family HALIOTIDAE

Also known as the ear shells or abalones. These flat shells have a beautiful iridescent surface inside and are remarkable for the row of open holes along one side. They hold fast to rocks with their large foot and creep along eating algae.

Haliotis pustulata Reeve, 1846

9–50 mm. Ovoid. Iridescent interior. → Numerous small bumps on the surface, usually with spiral cords. Margins of ovoid holes only slighlty raised. (27 mm)
Distribution: Common, all areas.

Haliotis unilateralis Lamarck, 1822

Endemic
34 mm. Ovoid. Spiral cords weak, few to none. Holes round, large, elevated and widely spaced. → Parallel to the line of holes is a deeply impressed line followed by a bulging roll at the periphery of the shell. (34 mm)
Distribution: Very rare, Hurghada–Safaga region.
Notes: The surface of *H. unilateralis* is much less bumpy than that of the other two species.

Haliotis venusta A. Adams & Reeve, 1850

10–28 mm. → Subcircular shape, very bumpy surface, closed holes strongly raised. Dead shells found on the beach in the northern Gulf of Suez are often all white. Elsewhere mottled orange brown. (24 mm)
Distribution: Common in the northern Gulf of Suez. Very rare elsewhere.

Family FISSURELLIDAE

The animals of this family look and behave like limpets but are not related. All species of Fissurellidae have a fissure (opening) in the shell for the intake of water and expulsion of waste. This may be a slit in the anterior margin of the shell or a hole in the apex.

Diodora funiculata (Reeve, 1850)

18–25 mm. → Fine cancellate sculpture between larger radial ribs. Darker and lighter sections independent of sculpture.→ Outline straight sided, hole in apex. (25 mm)
Distribution: Uncommon, northern Gulf of Suez, Bitter Lakes.

Diodora ruppellii (Sowerby, 1834)

6–26 mm. → Alternating dark and light radial rays. Conical shell with coarse irregularly alternating high and low strong radial ribs with narrow concentric ridges between them. → Upper outline rounded, hole slightly lower than highest point of shell. (14 mm)
Distribution: Common in the Gulf of Suez and all the way to Shalatein. Uncommon in the Gulf of Aqaba.

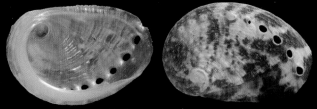

Haliotis pustulata

Haliotis unilateralis

Haliotis venusta

actual size

x2

Diodora funiculata

Diodora ruppellii

Emarginella cuvieri (Audouin, 1826)
10.5 mm. → Bruise-colored around apex. Area above slit with arched sculpture. Sculpture cancellate with radial stronger than concentric. (13 mm)
Distribution: Very rare, northern Gulf of Suez.

Hemitoma arabica (A. Adams, 1852)
9 mm. Low spire, ovoid with low radial ribs, → short slit. (9 mm)
Distribution: Rare, found in all regions.
Notes: The slit distinguishes it from the similar looking but unrelated *Siphonaria crenata*.

Hemitoma panhi (Quoy & Gaimard, 1834)
14–19 mm. → Keyhole outline, high conical shell, strong coarse radial and concentric ribs. Raised rib at the center of the narrower end of the shell shelters the canal. → Interior sometimes green. (18 mm)
Distribution: All areas but always uncommon.

Macroschisma compressa A. Adams, 1851
7.7–9 mm. Elliptical in outline. Exceptionally large slit (exactly what its genus name means) centrally. Red markings on the sides near the anterior, these visible both inside and out. (7.7 mm)
Distribution: Very rare, northern Gulf of Suez, Dahab.

Scutus rueppelli (Philippi, 1851)
12–34 mm. → Extremely flat, elongate shell. Tiny low-beaked spire, weak anterior indentation. Concentric growth lines follow the shape of the indentation. All white. (33.5 mm)
Distribution: Rare, Gulf of Suez to Safaga.

Zeidora nesta (Pilsbry, 1891)
Endemic
3–5.5 mm. Tiny, elongate-ovoid shell, peak extends beyond margin, anterior slit short. (5 mm)
Distribution: Uncommon, northern Gulf of Suez, south of Marsa Alam.

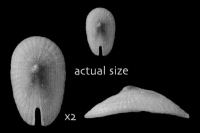

actual size

x2

Emarginella cuvieri

actual size

x3

Hemitoma arabica

x2

actual size

Hemitoma panhi

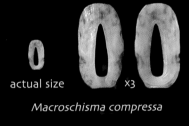

actual size

x3

Macroschisma compressa

actual size

x2

Scutus rueppelli

actual size

x4

Zeidora nesta

Family TROCHIDAE

Trochidae are often called top shells for their resemblance to toy tops children some-times use in games. Most species feed on algae, others are filter feeders. They live in shallow to deep water. The shell has a nacreous or pearly layer under the outer layer. People have long harvested certain species of Trochidae for use as mother-of-pearl.

Agagus agagus (Jousseaume, 1894)

4–10 mm. → Pyramidal shape, nearly equilateral. Stellate, basal periphery with numer-ous little spiky protrusions, apex sharply pointed. Umbilicus deeply cone shaped. Beige, pink, red, olive green, or charcoal. Sometimes with narrow rays of contrasting color. (9mm)
Distribution: Occasional in all areas, abundant in Wadi Lahmi.

Agagus sp.

Probably endemic
3–7 mm. Very similar to *Agagus agagus* above but with → a white raised rib on the body whorl extending out onto each stellate protrusion. Fewer stellate protrusions than *A. agagus.* (6 mm)
Distribution: Uncommon, northern Gulf of Suez, Dahab.

Calliotrochus marmoreus (Pease, 1861)

Marbled Top Shell
3–6 mm. Tiny, glossy, translucent shell with cloudy opaque areas, white, red, or other colors. No spiral cords, axial growth lines only. Umbilicus a pinpoint or chink.
Distribution: Rare, all areas. Intermittently common in South Sinai. (4.5 mm)
Notes: The general shape of *Ethalia bellardii* (see page 18) is similar, but that species has spiral threads on its upper surface. The patterns and colors of both species are quite variable.

Clanculus pharaonius (Linnaeus, 1758)

Strawberry Top Shell
5–25 mm. → Bright red! Completely covered by tiny red and black and white beads arranged in tight spiral rows. Pattern remarkably consistent from one individual to the next. Aperture lirate → two rough teeth opposite each other. Umbilicus deep, 'toothy.'
Distribution: Moderately common in all regions. (18 mm)
Notes: Juveniles have the same exterior pattern as the adult but the teeth in the aperture and umbilicus are not yet developed, thus the base looks totally different.

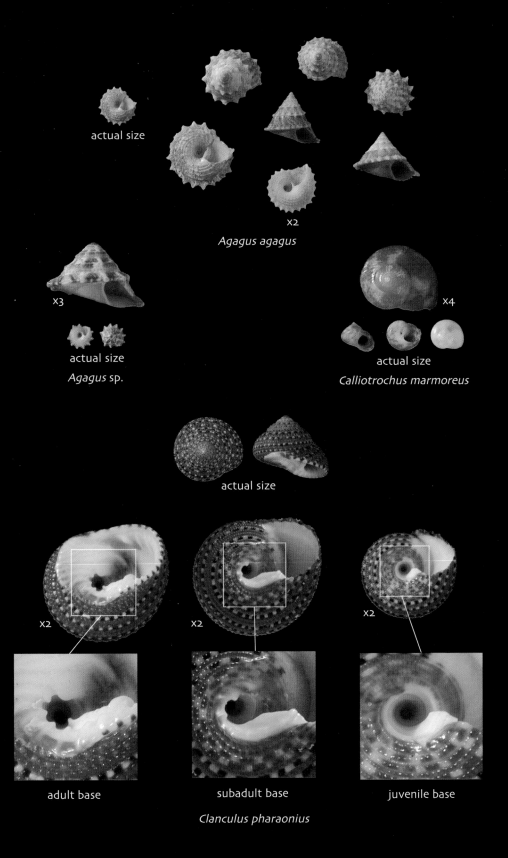

actual size

x2

Agagus agagus

x3

actual size

Agagus sp.

x4

actual size

Calliotrochus marmoreus

actual size

x2

x2

x2

adult base

subadult base

juvenile base

Clanculus pharaonius

Clanculus tonnerrei (G. & H. Nevill, 1874)

Synonyms *Clanculus gennesi* H. Fischer, 1901; *Euchelus erythraeensis* Sturany, 1903
3–8 mm. → Beaded cord sculpture, particularly noticeable at rounded periphery and base. Columella smooth, straight, plunging into the deep narrow umbilicus. Aperture round, lirate, and iridescent. Shell color and pattern variable. (6 mm)
Distribution: Locally and occasionally common in the Gulfs of Aqaba and Suez and between Hurghada and Safaga.
Notes: Trochus erithreus is more evenly pyramidal in shape. Specimens of the latter small enough to be confused with *C. tonnerrei* (because of similarity in color) are easily distinguished by their very pointed apex and sharp keel at the periphery.

Ethalia bellardii (Issel, 1869)

Synonym *Vitrinella meneghinii* Caramagna, 1888
Bellardi's Tiny Top Shell
5–8 mm. Low spire, → numerous very fine tightly spaced smooth spiral threadlets. Columella thick, white, slightly obscuring tiny round umbilicus. Colors and patterns many and various. (6 mm)
Distribution: Uncommon, found in shell grit in Gulfs of Aqaba and Suez.

Ethminolia hemprichii (Issel, 1869)

Endemic to the northern Red Sea
1–4 mm. Rounded all over, smooth surface, spire varying in height, but never acute or flat. Umbilicus is round, tiny, and deep. Aperture nearly round but columella straight. Light beige, often pinkish, with small regular darker markings with clearly defined edges. (4.5 mm)
Distribution: Locally and intermittently abundant in the Gulf of Suez. Occasional in all other regions.

Monodonta nebulosa (Forsskål in Niebuhr, 1775)

Synonym *Monodonta dama* (Philippi, 1848)
Cloudy Top Shell
Endemic
8–23 mm. → Single tooth (for which the genus is named) at base of white columella, then a squarish notch. Pattern of slightly blurry (nebulous or cloudy) dark and light bits arranged in spiral rows around the shell. Colors might include dull pink, green, brown, black, and beige. Most shells have only two colors, but some have more. They live on rocks near the edge of the sea. (16 mm)
Distribution: Very common in the Gulf of Aqaba, common on rocks or concrete in the Gulf of Suez, occasional Hurghada to Shalatein.
Notes: The smoothly rounded shape of *Monodonta nebulosa* distinguishes it from all other Red Sea species with a toothed or notched columella.

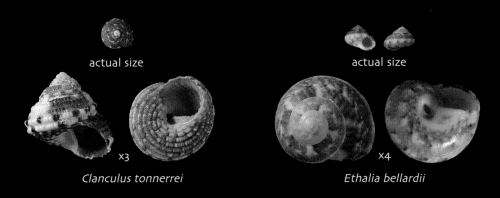

actual size

actual size

x3

x4

Clanculus tonnerrei

Ethalia bellardii

x3

actual size

Ethminolia hemprichii

x2

actual size

x5

Monodonta nebulosa

Perrinia stellata (A. Adams, 1864)

6–13 mm. → Pagoda-shaped small white shell, five or more whorls. A peripheral cord extends out above the succeeding whorl and its edge is bordered with triangular points giving it a star-like appearance, thus the name *stellata*. (12 mm)
Distribution: All regions. Rare in the Gulf of Aqaba, moderately common in Wadi Lahmi.

Priotrochus obscurus (Wood, 1828)

4.5–12 mm. → Usually pinkish or beige in color, with one narrow spiral row of alternating dark and light dots in the middle of the base and continuing into the aperture. Low nodules below the suture on the body whorl. Very low tooth (more like a wiggle) on the short curved columella. Aperture lirate. Umbilicus deep, but very narrow and partially obscured by the columella. (9 mm)
Distribution: Moderately common, northern Gulf of Aqaba, Dahab.

Pseudominolia gradata (Sowerby III, 1895)

4–9 mm. → Stepped whorls with sharp spiral ridges. Base with even closely spaced threads. Umbilicus small, round, deep, not obstructed. Color pale with darker pink, red, or brown axial markings. (9 mm)
Distribution: Uncommon, northern Gulf of Aqaba.

Rubritrochus declivis (Forsskål in Niebuhr, 1775)

6–27 mm. → Strong axial ribs, one tooth at base of columella, deep open umbilicus. Spire tall or short, color and pattern variable, usually beige or reddish with flecks of darker color on narrow spiral cords. (24 mm)
Distribution: Common in both the Gulf of Aqaba and the Gulf of Suez. Rare from Hurghada to Shalatein.

Tectus dentatus (Forsskål in Niebuhr, 1775)

Toothed Top Shell

15–110 mm. → The only pyramidal species in the Red Sea with big knobs. Usually with green spiral band in the center of the base. (100 mm)
Distribution: All regions, moderately common.
Notes: On juveniles (smallest shell figured) the knobs are more like strong protruding scales, but are more widely spaced than those of *Trochus virgatus*, page 23. Specimens from the northern Gulf of Suez are smaller and lack the green band. *T. dentatus*, like *Lambis truncata sebae* and *Tridacna maxima*, is a source of protein for the traditional shore-dwelling people.

actual size

x2

Perrinia stellata

actual size

x2

Priotrochus obscurus

actual size

x2

Pseudominolia gradata

Rubritrochus declivis

juvenile

Tectus dentatus

Trochus erithreus Brocchi, 1821
Red Sea Top Shell

3–43 mm. → Pyramidal with numerous small knobs arranged in spiral rows of varying strength. Columella without notch or teeth. Aperture nacreous, iridescent, → never lirate. Smooth open cone-shaped umbilicus. Shell usually mottled pink and white; may be red and white or rarely black and white. (25 mm)

Distribution: All regions. Abundant in the Gulf of Suez. Common from Safaga south. Occasional in the Gulf of Aqaba.

Notes: Juveniles (far right-hand shell) are more brightly colored and more sharply pointed than adults.

Trochus maculatus (Linnaeus, 1758)
Red Spotted Top Shell

29–65 mm. Pyramidal shape covered with coarse bumpy spiral cords. Adults with red and white axial flame-like patterns. Juveniles more solidly red. → Umbilicus open, columella with multiple strong teeth, aperture lirate. (46 mm)

Distribution: Occasional in the Gulf of Aqaba and south of Marsa Alam. Not found in the Gulf of Suez.

Notes: Juveniles of *T. maculatus* do not have the little peripheral scales of *T. virgatus*. The basic appearance of these two species is very similar, but the difference in the columella makes them easy to distinguish: *T. virgatus* has a completely smooth columella and aperture.

Trochus submorum (Abrard, 1942)
Endemic

17–23 mm. Beaded red shell with a few black beaded spiral cords. Columella long and straight descending directly into the bottom of the wide smooth umbilicus. Aperture lirate, iridescent. (21 mm)

Distribution: Very rare, northern Gulf of Aqaba, Hurghada–Safaga.

Notes: The differences in the columella and aperture eliminate any confusion with adults of *Clanculus pharaonius*, above, which also has many more black spiral rows.

Trochus virgatus Gmelin, 1791
Smooth Mouthed Top Shell

30–65 mm. Pyramidal shell with sharp edges and apex, may be blunted by wear. Columella smooth with one sharp tooth at base. Aperture mildly iridescent, → never lirate. (60 mm)

Distribution: Occasional in all regions and habitats. Rare in the Gulf of Suez.

Notes: Juveniles (far right, lower shell) have protruding scales at periphery, reminiscent of those of *T. dentatus*, but much finer. See also *T. maculatus* above.

juvenile

Trochus erithreus

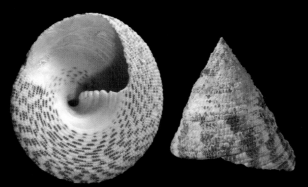

Trochus maculatus

Trochus submorum

x2

actual size

juvenile

Trochus virgatus

Family STOMATELLIDAE

These shells have very few whorls. The low spire is close to one end of the shell rather than near the middle. The aperture is very large.

Stomatella modesta (H. & A. Adams, 1864)

6–7 mm. → Somewhat compressed ovate form, slightly nacreous interior with a green hue. Never patterned. (7 mm)
Distribution: Rare, Hurghada to Shalatein.

Stomatella varia (A. Adams, 1853)

6–18 mm. → Low, elongate, multicolored, fragile, thin. Aperture nearly the whole length of the shell. Interior shiny, sometimes iridescent. (18 mm)
Distribution: Abundant locally in rocky areas from Ras Ghaliib south, occasional in the Gulf of Aqaba and between Hurghada and Safaga. Uncommon in the Gulf of Suez.

Stomatia duplicata Sowerby, 1831

6–13 mm. → Elevated off-center spire, two spiral cords, one at the periphery and one above it. Aperture very large, lirate, and sometimes iridescent light green or yellowish. (12 mm)
Distribution: Uncommon, Gulf of Aqaba.

Stomatia phymotis Helbling, 1779

14–36 mm. → Elongate oval shape, irregularly wrinkled and corded surface, color red, pink, beige, or a mix. The tightly curled spire may be high or low. Aperture white or silvery nacrous. (35 mm)
Distribution: Frequent in the Gulf of Suez. Occasional south of Marsa Alam.
Notes: Given the range of apex heights and diversity of sculptural elements found on the specimens from Egyptian waters, it seems that there is only one quite variable species here.

Family TURBINIDAE

These are commonly called Turban Shells because of the way the whorls resemble a turban. They eat algae and range in size from tiny to reasonably large.

Turbo petholatus Linnaeus, 1758

Tapestry Turban Shell
25–56 mm. → Wonderfully patterned, beautiful chocolate brown shell with darker bands around it and lighter almost pinkish patches. A very shiny shell, catches your eye immediately. Usually seen on the bottom of the sea near a reef. Please be considerate of others who also love the beauties of nature—leave it in its place. (45 mm)
Distribution: Uncommon, Gulf of Aqaba and the reefs in the Straits of Tiran and Gubal, and mid-south offshore reefs.

Stomatella modesta

Stomatella duplicata

Stomatella varia

Stomatella phymotis

x2 *Turbo pethalatus* actual size

Turbo radiatus Gmelin, 1791

9–93 mm. Globose but straight-sided shell, nearly smooth or with very well-developed tubercles. Beige to brown, plain, or with a mottled pattern. Operculum frequently found separately, called tiger's eye or cat's eye (two upper left images). (55 mm)
Distribution: Common in all regions.
Notes: Specimens smaller than 8 mm may have two keels per whorl. Individuals in our waters usually develop the adult rounded shape and begin to produce spines at around 12–15 mm. The length and strength of the spines vary depending on environmental circumstances.

Family COLLONIIDAE

Bothropoma isseli Thiele, 1924

Endemic

3–5 mm. Globose, few whorls, very short spire. Spiral cords, not beaded, cover the body whorl with a stronger one, occasionally patterned, at periphery. → Aperture completely round, lip usually thickened and white. Shell may be almost any color, including red, black, white, or brown, plain, or patterned. (5 mm)
Distribution: Uncommon, but intermittently locally common. South Sinai, Gulfs of Aqaba and Suez. Usually found in shell grit.

Collonista arsinoensis (Issel, 1869)

Endemic

2.5–4 mm. Tiny, globose shell. → White with red spots, flat or depressed spire. Numerous spiral cords, those on upper whorl distinctly beaded. Umbilicus round and deep with beads at the opening. Aperture round. (4 mm)
Distribution: Uncommon, northern Gulf of Suez.
Notes: The rounded spire and aperture plus the absence of black beads separate this species from juveniles of *Clanculus pharaonius* which are white with red and black beads, with a sharply pointed apex and a straight columella.

Homalopoma pustulata (Brocchi, 1821)

Endemic

10–15 mm. → Covered with small low bumps (pustules) arranged in spiral rows. Aperture round, no umbilicus. (10 mm)
Distribution: Rare, Gulf of Suez, Safaga, and South Sinai.
Notes: Possibly extinct in Egyptian waters; the shells seen here are subfossils.

Turbo radiatus

x4   actual size

Bothropoma isseli

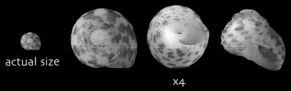

actual size

x4

Collonista arsinoensis

actual size

x2

Homalopoma pustulata

Family PHASIANELLIDAE
Phasianella solida (Born, 1778)

3–21 mm. → Shell completely smooth and glossy, with detailed patterns of very fine lines in shades of white, beige, brown, and occasionally orange. Columella smoothly curved, white. Lip thin. (14 mm)

Distribution: All regions, locally and intermittently common. Other times scarce or absent.

Notes: Another shell, *Littoraria intermedia*, is of similar size and shape, but it has numerous finely incised spiral lines, whereas *P. solida* is always smooth.

Family VITRINELLIDAE
Circulus modesta (Gould, 1861)

5–9 mm. Few whorls, several strong cords on each, one well beaded. All white. (7 mm)

Distribution: Rare, Hurghada–Safaga area.

Family NERITOPSIDAE
Neritopsis cf. *radula* (Linnaeus, 1758)

23 mm. Spire more extended than the Neritidae. No shelf or teeth. Large gap centrally in columella. Strong regularly spaced lightly nodulose spiral cords cover the shell. Small tightly spaced wiggly axial ribs fill the interspaces between the cords. Aperture noticeably larger than body whorl opposite it. Inner part of the aperture slightly thickened, milky white. (20 mm)

Distribution: Very rare, 18 meters depth, coral sand substrate, South Sinai and Gulf of Aqaba only.

Notes: Conchologists may note that this shell is of the same species as that pictured by Sharabati (1984) Pl. 2, figs. 17, 17a.

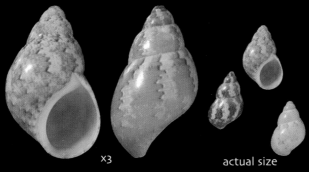

x3   actual size

Phasianella solida

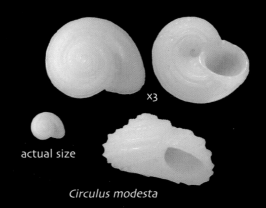

x3

actual size

Circulus modesta

x2

actual size

Neritopsis cf. *radula*

Family NERITIDAE
Also known as slipper winkles, most species have a 'shelf' next to the aperture. Neritids are commonly seen on intertidal rocks. They eat algae, and during low tides can be above water for several hours.

Nerita orbignyana Récluz, 1842
5–23 mm. → Smooth and shiny, many different colors and color combinations, including pink, gray, black, brown, and orange. (20 mm)
Distribution: Moderately common in the Gulf of Aqaba, uncommon elsewhere.
Notes: At first it is a little difficult to tell *N. orbignyana* and *N. sanguinolenta* apart. *N. orbignyana* is always shiny. It never has raised cords on its body whorl, but it might have fine incised spiral lines. *N. sanguinolenta* never has a shiny surface, and has only two color patterns: orange or black and white (see below).

Nerita quadricolor Gmelin, 1791
21–31 mm. → Strong spiral cords, strong teeth. (27 mm)
Distribution: On rocky coasts from Safaga south. Frequent in the right habitat, but never abundant.
Notes: Lives near the top of the high-tide zone attached to limestone cliffs. If you see live ones, do not touch them or try to remove them from the rocks. Remember, the seashore is their home. We humans are the intruders.

Nerita sanguinolenta Menke, 1829
Endemic
8–34 mm. Two different color patterns: black and white, and bright orange or red, sometimes with white or beige markings. The species gets its name from the red ones: *sanguine* means bloody in Latin. Low spiral cords, becoming obsolete on older individuals. Aperture white or yellow. → Matte texture, never glossy. (25 mm)
Distribution: Common in all regions.
Notes: These three species of *Nerita* never live where they would be submerged under water for a long time. An interesting point about *N. sanguinolenta* and *N. orbignyana* is that sometimes their color is the same as the rocks on which they live. Particularly in the northern part of the Gulf of Aqaba you will find red ones on red granite rocks, black and white ones on black and white rocks, and greenish ones on greenish rocks! Perhaps their predators are color-sensitive and pick off the ones that stand out against the rock. These little animals cling tight to the rocks. Do not try to remove them because they take a long time to stick on again and in the meantime could be washed away by a wave.

Nerita orbignyana

Nerita quadricolor

Nerita sanguinolenta

Smaragdia rangiana (Récluz, 1842)

3–9 mm. → Green with delicate black and white markings. Often blown by the wind into clusters caught in dry seaweed. The only truly green shell in the Red Sea. (8.5 mm)
Distribution: All regions. Locally and intermittently common.
Notes: Occurs rarely in other colors too, even reddish. The spire is always slightly lower and the shelf more calcareous than on *S. souverbiana* (see below).

Smaragdia souverbiana (Montrouzier, 1863)

2–3.5 mm. Translucent or milky white with unreasonably intricate fine black designs. It is worth bringing a small magnifying glass to the beach just to appreciate these patterns! (4 mm)
Distribution: All regions. Locally and intermittently common. Usually found in the same accumulations of shell grit as *S. rangiana.*
Notes: The 'pulled'-looking spire is characteristic and consistent, regardless of color or pattern.

Family PHENACOLEPADIDAE

The shells in this family look like fragile white translucent limpets. But due to the anatomy of the animals, they belong in a large group known as Neritimorpha; in other words, animals similar to or shaped like the neritids. Their blood is red and contains hemoglobin (as does human blood). This enables them to survive in oxygen-poor water.

Plesiothyreus arabica (Thiele, 1909)

2.5–10 mm. → Broad, elliptical, subcircular shape, no scales, surface smooth, → fine radial riblets, curving slightly as they approach the anterior margin. Posterior-facing peak even with edge of margin but slightly off to one side. (7 mm)
Distribution: Infrequent, but locally common. Safaga area and south.

Plesiothyreus osculans (C.B. Adams, 1852)

4.5–5 mm. → Nearly flat, narrow elliptical shell, no scales. → Concentric ridges and radial threadlets, giving cancellate effect. Peak tips toward posterior, even with edge of margin, sometimes extending beyond. (5 mm)
Distribution: Very rare, Safaga to Wadi Lahmi.

Plesiothyreus pararabica (Christiaens, 1988)

11–20 mm. Outline of a regular ellipse. Sculpture of narrow scaly rays, radiating from the peak to the margins. → Very rough to the touch. (20 mm)
Distribution: Uncommon, Marsa Alam to Shalatein.
Notes: The largest Red Sea species of the family.

actual size

x5

Smaragdia rangiana

actual size

x6

Smaragdia souverbiana

x5   actual size

Plesiothyreus arabica

x6   actual size

Plesiothyreus osculans

x3   actual size

Plesiothyreus pararabica

Family CERITHIIDAE

More than twenty-five different species of ceriths are known from the Red Sea. The shells are usually long with many whorls and ornamented with axial ribs, spiral cords, and tubercles. Most of them are rather drab in color. Almost all of them live intertidally, and all are vegetarians. Different species prefer different substrates such as mud, sand, rocks, clean coral sand, or algae beds.

Correct identification of ceriths is difficult because individuals of the same species, even from the same location, may show many differences. In addition, the shape and appearance of the shell may change a great deal during its growth from juvenile to immature to fully mature adult.

Cerithium adansonii Bruguière, 1792
Synonym *Cerithium erythraeonense* Lamarck, 1822
20–68 mm. Large, with large regular knobs, almost glossy, brown and white. Aperture may be all white or have some fulvous markings at the lip. → In some specimens the base of the apertural lip extends across the anterior siphonal canal. (65 mm)
Distribution: Common in the Gulf of Suez and all the way south to Shalatein. Uncommon in the Gulf of Aqaba.

Cerithium caeruleum Sowerby, 1855
13–37 mm. → Heavy shell, apex usually dull, eroded. Nodules arranged spirally. Mottled reddish brown or black. Aperture white, may have dark lines inside. It lives in very shallow water in areas of fine sand or sand and silt. (39 mm)
Distribution: Common, all regions.
Notes: The only shell likely to be confused with *C. caeruleum* is *Rhinoclavis sinensis* (see pages 40, 41), especially the juveniles, because the apex of both is usually still intact. Look closely at the spiral row of large nodules. If it is at or immediately below the suture it is *R. sinensis*. On *C. caeruleum* the row of large nodules is set well below the suture.

Cerithium columna Sowerby, 1834
7.5–34 mm. Two morphs (shapes). → One relatively smooth, usually plain white or beige with charcoal gray whorls at the apex. →The second with rough texture, sharp tubercles, and numerous fine spiral threads. These are often brown between the axial ribs and tubercles, apex same color as the body. Immature and subadult individuals of each form look very much like their respective adult forms. Occasionally intermediate forms are found. (30 mm)
Distribution: Very common in the Gulf of Aqaba. Occasional from Hurghada to Shalatein. In the south the spiky ones more common than the smooth ones. Neither is found in the Gulf of Suez.

Cerithium adansonii

juvenile

Cerithium caeruleum

Cerithium columna

Cerithium echinatum Lamarck, 1822

20–48 mm. → Tubercles on the penultimate whorl, the one just above the body whorl, are the largest, often pointing upward. Body whorl with about five to seven spiral rows of equally sized tubercles, lowest ones pointing downward. Ventral side often smooth, as though the animal preferred not to have sharp tubercles slowing it down as it creeps over the reef.
Distribution: Uncommon, offshore reefs, all regions. (45 mm)
Notes: This shell is sometimes mistaken for *C. adansonii*, but *C. echinatum* is proportionately shorter and spikier.

Cerithium egenum Gould, 1849

3–10 mm. → Relatively smooth surface, numerous very fine spiral striae. May have very small nodules arranged in a few spiral rows, but never strong sharp ones. Outer lip is thickened, white, and smooth. Color ivory. Different specimens may have delicate to strong patterns in caramel, milk chocolate, or coffee colors. (10 mm)
Distribution: Locally and intermittently common in the northern Gulf of Aqaba, occasional between Hurghada and Safaga.

Cerithium interstriatum Sowerby, 1855

6.5–12 mm. → Fine spiral rows of densely spaced tiny tubercles. Characteristically with a smooth spiral threadlet in between. Some lack this. Yellow beige with large weak darker spots. (12 mm)
Distribution: Intermittently common around Hurghada.

Cerithium nesioticum Pilbry & Vanatta, 1906

8–22 mm. → Small subtle low spiral threads with tiny pustules evenly cover the whole shell. May have one spiral row of very small widely spaced brown dots just below the suture on some or all of the whorls. (16 mm)
Distribution: Intermittently common in the Gulf of Aqaba, occasional or rare from Hurghada south.

Cerithium rostratum Sowerby, 1855

6.5–21 mm. → Fragile, body whorl rarely intact. Whorls rounded. Numerous fine spiral threads. Axial ribs formed of raised dashes. One varix opposite the aperture that flows gracefully into the siphonal canal. White, beige, may be brown between the ribs. (18 mm)
Distribution: Common in sandy and silty lagoons from Hurghada south.
Notes: Specimens from Wadi Lahmi have one white varix per whorl rather than only on the body whorl. There is usually a darker brown area next to these varices.

actual size

x2

Cerithium egenum

actual size

x2

Cerithium echinatum

actual size

x5

Cerithium interstriatum

actual size

x2

Cerithium nesioticum

x2

actual size

Cerithium rostratum

Cerithium rueppelli Philippi, 1848

10–42 mm. → Very spiky appearance. Basally two rows of tubercles point downward. One main spiral cord per whorl carrying strong pointed tubercles. Excellent specimens with somewhat long, slightly recurved siphonal canal. White or brownish, with or without brown markings. (40 mm)
Distribution: Locally and intermittently common in northern Gulf of Aqaba, occasional in the far south, not found in the Gulf of Suez.

Cerithium scabridum Philippi, 1848

8–24 mm. Variable. Rough or coarse looking. Generally with relatively strong axial ribs crossed by two or three spiral cords producing strong or weak tubercles on each rib. The body whorl does not have axial ribs and usually has five spiral cords with tubercles. Most specimens have shiny caramel or dark brown dashes on the spiral cords. (20 mm)
Distribution: Abundant in the Gulf of Suez. Occasional elsewhere.
Notes: → Specimens with axial ribs and shiny colored dashes are definitely *C. scabridum.* *Rhinoclavis kochi* normally has three spiral cords on the upper whorls rather than two and never has shiny dashes. Undeveloped juveniles may have to be lumped together as unidentifiable.

Clypeomorus bifasciata (Sowerby, 1855)

7.5–22 mm. Variable, but always with spiral rows of raised dots or dashes of brown or white or black. The base color can be white or brown. The name means that it has two stripes but that color pattern is rare. (19 mm)
Distribution: Locally common in the Gulfs of Aqaba and Suez and the Hurghada–Safaga area. Only occasionally found between Marsa Alam and Shalatein.

Clypeomorus petrosa isseli (Pagenstecher, 1877)

8–28 mm. → Relatively broader base than in most species of ceriths. White with spiral rows of raised black dashes or dots. An occasional juvenile will be a surprising clear light pink with black and white dashes. A few adults keep this pink color on their spire. (22 mm)
Distribution: Abundant in the northern Gulf of Aqaba, rarely found in the Gulf of Suez. Moderately common from Hurghada to Marsa Alam, particularly in areas with rocks.
Notes: Only a few Egyptian specimens of *C. petrosa isseli* have a varix. In those, it is always directly opposite the outer lip of the aperture. In *C. bifasciata* the varix, if present, is closer to the columella.

Colina pinguis (A. Adams, 1855)

9–16 mm. → Outline indents between body whorl and spire, body whorl smaller than preceeding one. Very odd looking. Unlike the adults, juveniles have a flat base. (16 mm)
Distribution: Rare, Hurghada–Safaga area.

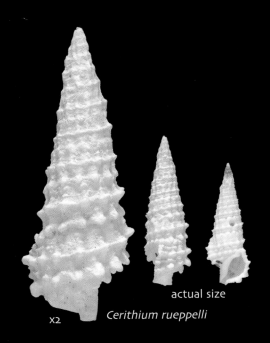

actual size

x2   *Cerithium rueppelli*

actual size

x2   *Cerithium scabridum*

x2   actual size

Clypeomorus bifasciata

x2

juvenile   actual size   x2

Clypeomorus petrosa isseli

actual size   x2   juvenile

actual size

Colina pinguis

Dahlakia proteum (Jousseaume, 1930)
4–9 mm. Apex and ribs white, body toffee color. Whorls slightly rounded. Axial ribs with weak knobs on each rib. An easily overlooked shell. (9 mm)
Distribution: Locally and intermittently common in the Safaga area.
Notes: Potamides conicus could be confused with *D. proteum.* The latter is slightly less elongate and its whorls more distinct and rounded.

Rhinoclavis aspera (Linnaeus, 1758)
10–41 mm. → Long, highly recurved siphonal canal. Nine or ten spiral rows of neatly arranged small nodules on the body whorl. Parietal lip raised, with knob. Columella with one strong fold centrally and a weaker one above it. Varix very weak or absent. (41 mm)
Distribution: Common in clean coral sand, South Sinai to far south.

Rhinoclavis fasciata (Bruguière, 1792)
25–68 mm. → Unusually glossy for a cerith. Smooth surface, no tubercles, ribs weak or absent. Long recurved siphonal canal, folds in the columella, parietal lip well developed. White with seven to ten narrow brown spiral lines on the body whorl, five or six on earlier whorls. Sometimes with brown blotches. (68 mm)
Distribution: Never common, Gulf of Aqaba, quiet reefs from Hurghada south.
Notes: Terebra cerithina never has a long recurved siphonal canal, but is otherwise similar in shape.

Rhinoclavis kochi (Philippi, 1848)
10–43 mm. Nodulose spiral cords with threadlets between them. Columella smooth, no folds. Aperture with incised lines. → Adults always have a varix opposite the outer lip on the body whorl. Varices may remain on earlier whorls. Sculpture variable. (43 mm)
Distribution: Moderately common in the Gulf of Suez. Uncommon elsewhere.
Notes: R. kochi prefers a habitat with a bit of mud or silt and sea grass. May have one or more spiral rows of brown dots but → never has raised shiny dashes. Specimens with extremely fine light brown spiral lines are always this species, but not every specimen has them.

Rhinoclavis sinensis (Gmelin, 1791)
19–41 mm. → Tidy appearance with one spiral row of large tubercles immediately below the suture. Two or three spiral cords with small nodules on them on each of the earlier whorls and between eight and ten on the body whorl. Siphonal canal sharply recurved close to base. Parietal lip well developed basally. (36 mm)
Distribution: Locally and intermittently common in the northern Gulf of Aqaba and Wadi Gimaal, occasional to rare elsewhere. I have found the presence of *R. sinensis* to be very unpredictable, and increasingly rare.

actual size

×4

Dahlakia proteum

Rhinoclavis aspera

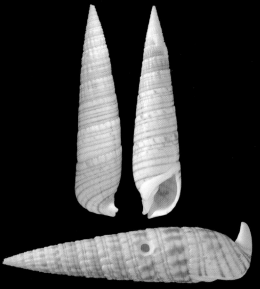

Rhinoclavis fasciata

Rhinoclavis kochi

Rhinoclavis sinensis

Royella sinon (Bayle, 1880)

9–16 mm. → Two raised rows of tiny tubercles per whorl with a deeply recessed space between whorls. All white. (11 mm)

Distribution: Uncommon, northern Gulf of Aqaba, Hurghada–Safaga area.

Family THIARIDAE

Melanoides tuberculatus (Müller, 1774)

8–31 mm. → Translucent brown with darker brown wavy axial flames composed of colored dashes on the spiral cords. Columella smoothly curving, white. (15.5 mm)

Distribution: Locally common, northern Gulf of Suez.

Notes: The animal lives in warm fresh water, especially in the hot spring of Ein Sukhna.

Family TURRITELLIDAE

Archimediella maculata (Reeve, 1849)

31–82 mm. Elongate, lightweight, and somewhat fragile shell, bumpily rounded whorls with two or three raised spiral cords each. → Aperture nearly round, with the columella forming part of the circle. White, beige, or brown with irregular brown spots and axial lines. (56 mm)

Distribution: Gulf of Aqaba, South Sinai, Hurghada to Safaga and nearby reefs.

Notes: You can tell this is not a *Terebra* species by its round aperture and curved columella.

Family PLANAXIDAE

Hinea punctostriata (E.A. Smith, 1872)

Endemic

3.5–7 mm. → Brown spiral lines on a translucent beige field. Note the characteristic planaxid notch at the base of the columella. (7 mm)

Distribution: Locally and intermittently common, otherwise rare. Known from the northern Gulf of Aqaba and the Hurghada–Safaga area.

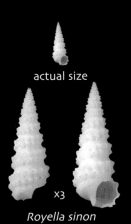

actual size

x3

Royella sinon

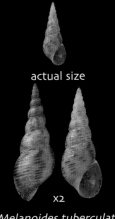

actual size

x2

Melanoides tuberculatus

Archimediella maculata

actual size

x4

Hinea punctostriata

Planaxis savignyi Deshayes, 1844
Synonym *Planaxis griseus* (Brocchi, 1821)
Cluster Whelks
8–23 mm. → Incised spiral lines, columella white, with small notch at its base. Aperture lirate. Many possible patterns, usually brown or black and white, some obscuring the definitive sculpture. (22 mm)
Distribution: Common in all regions.
Notes: These animals live on low intertidal rocks. There may be more than one hundred of them clustered closely together. If you find such a group of live animals, please do not disturb them or try to pick them up. Just look closely at them. You may notice a variety of colors and patterns among them.

Fossarus trochlearis (A. Adams, 1855)
2.5–6 mm. → Three extremely strong keels on body whorl. Aperture very large. Outer lip not thickened, keels appear there as three deep open protrusions. (6 mm)
Distribution: Rare. Known from the northern Gulf of Aqaba, South Sinai, and the Safaga area.

Family POTAMIDIDAE
Potamides conicus (Blainville, 1826)
4–15 mm. Elongate, conical, strong and heavy for the size, covered with small rounded nodules. → Spiral bands of varying shades of brown, beige, yellow ocher, and white, rather dull. (15 mm)
Distribution: Abundant in all regions.
Notes: Thrives in hypersaline conditions; sometimes literally millions are found in drying lagoons. Juveniles of *P. conicus* are dull dark brown and completely lacking in ribs or beads.

Family MODULIDAE
Modulus tectum (Gmelin, 1791)
10–30 mm. → Spire of two flat whorls, body whorl globose. Shell with or without strong oblique axial ribs at the shoulder and weak spiral cords. Aperture white, very large, → columella with sharp tooth basally. Shell usually covered with chalky encrustation. Clean shell off-white with brown spots on spire and/or dashes along spiral cord medially on body whorl. (20 mm)
Distribution: Occasional, Gulf of Aqaba, Hurghada to Wadi Gimaal.
Notes: Spire height varies considerably.

x2

actual size

Planaxis savignyi

actual size

x4

Fossarus trochlearis

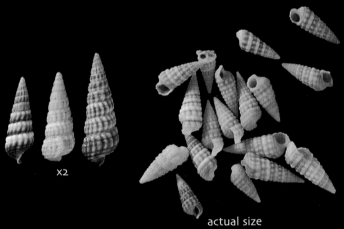

x2

actual size

Potamides conicus

x2

actual size

Modulus tectum

Family PLESIOTROCHIDAE
Plesiotrochus unicinctus (A. Adams, 1853)
Synonym *Plesiotrochus souverbiana* (P. Fischer, 1878)
3.5–10 mm. Pagodiform, all whorls straight sided, lowest whorls with numerous short rounded axial ribs. Aperture angular at its outside edge with a → single spiral cord. Beige or white, with or without very small light brown dots or dashes or axial flames. (3.5 mm)
Distribution: Locally and intermittently common in the Gulf of Suez. Rare to occasional in the Gulf of Suez and south to Safaga.

Plesiotrochus sp.
6–8 mm. As above but with two spiral cords at periphery and → lower whorls rounded with a few long axial ribs or varices. Aperture with → two spiral cords. (8 mm)
Distribution: Rare. Gulfs of Aqaba and Suez.

Family LITTORINIDAE
These animals, sometimes called periwinkles, live on intertidal rocks at the shore and eat algae. The Latin word *'littorin'* means shore dwellers.

Echinolittorina marisrubri Reid, 2007
Echinolittorina cf. *arabica* (El Assal, 1990) of some authors
4–13 mm. → Pink protoconch, stubby sharply conical shell, slightly stepped spire and three strong spiral rows of (usually white) → round nodules on the body whorl. Spiral threadlets between the rows of nodules. Top of lip attaches exactly on top of the lower row of nodules on the preceding whorl. (12 mm)
Distribution: Locally common in rocky areas in the Gulf of Aqaba, rare elsewhere.
Notes: The nodules are more closely spaced in their rows than in *E. subnodosa.*

Echinolittorina millegrana (Phillipi, 1848)
5–12 mm. → Somewhat globose in shape, rounded whorls. → Shiny black protoconch, body whorl lighter in color than preceding whorls. May be smooth with almost no sculpture or granulose—covered with tiny grains or nodes. (*Millegrana* means thousands of grains.) Aperture orange-brown to black. (12 mm)
Distribution: Locally common in the Gulf of Aqaba, occasional in other rocky areas.
Notes: Smooth specimens are more common here than granulose ones.

Echinolittorina subnodosa (Phillipi, 1847)
9.5–12 mm.→ Pointed conical shape with straight sides down to the periphery of the body whorl with three relatively widely spaced spiral rows of nodules on the body whorl. → Nodules like triangular plates (not round) extending out from the shell. Lip extends upward and attaches between upper and middle rows of nodules on preceding whorl. (12 mm)
Distribution: Uncommon, more likely to be found in southern areas.
Notes: E. subnodosa and *E. marisrubri* can be confused. *E. subnodosa* lacks spiral threadlets and as the name implies, has altogether fewer nodules.

x5   actual size

Plesiotrochus unicinctus

actual size

x4

Plesiotrochus sp.

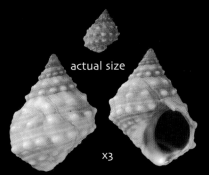

actual size

x3

Echinolittorina marisrubri

x3

x5

actual size

Echinolittorina millegrana

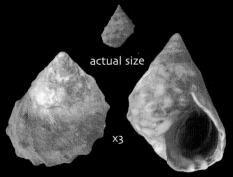

actual size

x3

Echinolittorina subnodosa

Littoraria intermedia (Philippi, 1846)
8.5–20 mm. Light shell, in both color and weight, → fine incised spiral lines. (20 mm)
Distribution: Nabq, Ras Mohamed, and south. Common in areas with mangroves.
Notes: Please also see *Phasianella solida*, pages 28–29, and *Planaxis savignyi*, pages 44–45.

Peasiella isseli (Issel, 1869)
2–5 mm. → Tiny, squat shell with black apex. Usually orange, but may be brown or
black. → Spiral micro threads on whorls. Outline dome-like, resembling an old style
beehive. About three whorls, each with small thin whitish keel, plain or spotted, usually
adhering to the shoulder of the next whorl, flaring on base. (4 mm)
Distribution: Common in all areas.
Notes: Another member of this genus, *P. infracostata* (Issel, 1869), is also found. Always
yellow-orange with a dark brown apex, but → no spiral threadlets on the whorls. Smooth
surface with thin brown axial lines. It is smaller, squatter, with squarish shoulders, and
very rare. Most likely in northern Gulf of Suez. Not illustrated.

Family RISSOIDAE
These are quite small conical to elongate shells. The surface is smooth or sculptured but
never spiny. Beached shells are usually white and may resemble grains of rice. The animals eat algae. Often several different species will be found together at the high tideline
in shell grit. Only a few of the many species are included here.

Rissoina bertholleti Issel 1869
4.5–7 mm. Strong, smooth axial ribs, interstices of the same width. Often with small
siphonal canal or glazed extended area. (5.5 mm)
Distribution: Common in the Gulf of Suez to Hurghada, frequent in the Gulf of Aqaba.
The most commonly found *Rissoina* in the Gulf of Suez.

Rissoina dorbignyi A. Adams, 1851
6–15 mm. → Wonderful sculpture: upper whorls stepped with strong oblique axial ribs.
Lower whorls smoothly rounded, no sculpture. (12 mm)
Distribution: Uncommon but found in all regions.

Zebina tridenta (Michaud, 1830)
6–10 mm→ Three teeth on lower inside of lip. Strong glossy white pyramidal shell, sharp
apex, relatively broad base. (7 mm)
Distribution: Rare.
Notes: In many specimens the teeth may be weak and difficult to see. Can be mistaken
for a species of Eulimidae, but those never have teeth and are rarely as broad basally.

x3

actual size

Littoraria intermedia

actual size

x5

Peasiella isseli

actual size

x5

Rissoina bertholleti

actual size

x4

Rissoina dorbignyi

actual size

x5

Zebina tridenta

Family STROMBIDAE

The shells in this family are commonly known as conches. Many strombids have extravagant shapes and lovely colors. Typically they have a notch in the shell next to the siphonal canal, the stromboid notch (see *Gibberulus gibberulus albus* page 55 for a good example). When the animal is looking about, its eye stalk extends out through this notch. They are vegetarians. They have a peculiar way of moving about: they extend the sharp end of the operculum—the 'door' that closes the aperture— and stick it into the fine sediment of the seabed. Then they suddenly jerk themselves forward, in sharp contrast to the slow gliding motion of most gastropods. Conches are an important traditional source of protein for the indigenous shore-dwelling human population.

These beautiful, over-exploited shells are protected by law; never touch a live specimen or buy shells. Many species live in very shallow water near the shore, and habitat destruction due to resort development is drastically threatening their existence.

Canarium erythrinum (Dillwyn, 1817)

18–45 mm. → Numerous strong axial ribs on each whorl, tall spire, sloping shoulders. Ventral area may be smooth or ribbed. Dark brown exterior lip interrupted by three or four narrow white stripes. Both sides of the aperture are lirate. Mid-columella may be smooth. Most specimens have a dark brown ring all around the inside of the aperture, but some are yellow. Further in, the aperture is white or beige, never pink or orange. (41 mm) *Distribution:* Common in the Gulf of Aqaba and from Hurghada to Shalatein. Occasional in the Gulf of Suez.

Canarium fusiformis (Sowerby, 1842)

26–33 mm. → Outer lip sweeps up to the top of the penultimate whorl. This long graceful line distinguishes it from all other species. (31 mm) *Distribution:* Rare, Gulf of Aqaba, Safaga.

Canarium mutabilis (Swainson, 1821)

15–32.5 mm. Strongly and variously patterned in many shades of white, beige, caramel, brown, and, rarely, black. (Its name means changeable.) Aperture usually pastel pink or apricot or more rarely white. (30 mm) *Distribution:* Abundant in Gulf of Aqaba, common from Hurghada to Shalatein. *Notes: C. mutabilis* never has simple spiral lines like *Conomurex fasciatus* or a dark ring around aperture like *Canarium erythrinum*. Some suspect the specimens figured in the lower row may be a different, as yet unnamed species, as their pattern is consistently composed of a spiral series of markings rather than a loose, interrupted spiral band. Shells with this pattern are less frequently found.

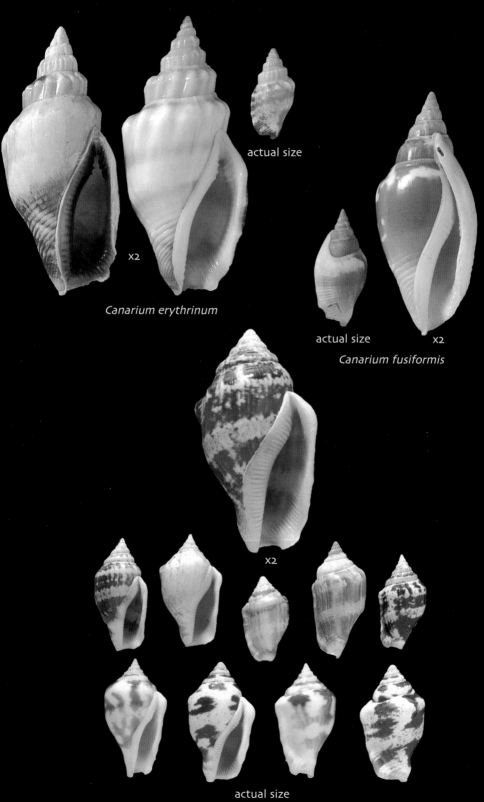

actual size

x2

Canarium erythrinum

actual size   x2

Canarium fusiformis

x2

actual size

Canarium mutabilis

Conomurex fasciatus (Born, 1778)
Lineated Conch
Endemic
15–65 mm. The name comes from the → light to dark brown to black spiral lines going around the light-colored shell. Aperture → usually intensely coral orange, columella white, may have light color blush. (53 mm)
Distribution: Gulf of Suez and mainland south to Shalatein. Locally abundant in the south. Rare in the Gulf of Aqaba.
Notes: It has been reported that the empty shell is often found outside the caves of octopi. It may be one of that creature's favorite foods.

Dolomena plicata plicata (Röding, 1798)
35–57 mm. Plicata means 'wrinkled' or 'pleated.' Many axial ribs on the spire and the inside of the flaring outer lip highly wrinkled, columella with numerous folds on its entire length with or without dark color. Ventrum either wrinkled or smooth. (57 mm)
Distribution: Abundant in the Gulf of Suez, occasional to rare elsewhere. Kristen Potter found the shell pictured in the two images on the far right.

Euprotomus aurora Kronenberg, 2002
Strombus bulla (Röding, 1798) of some authors
59 mm. → Single extension of the lip rising like a finger pointing in the same direction as the apex, spiral ribs extending from the dorsum up this projection. Numerous broad knobs on the dorsum, all more or less the same size. Many spiral cords. (59 mm)
Distribution: Rare, far south only. Northern shells are subfossil.
Notes: Until 2002 this shell was considered to be *Strombus bulla* (Röding, 1798), but it was then discovered that it is a different species. The only possible confusion could be with *Tricornis tricornis*, but that has a smooth surface, completely lacking in spiral cords.

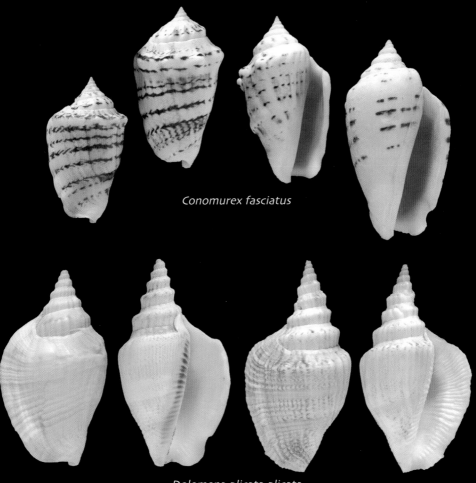

Conomurex fasciatus

Dolomena plicata plicata

Euprotomus aurora

Gibberulus gibberulus albus (Mörch, 1850)
Endemic to the Red Sea

20–57 mm. Spire whorls with one or more thickened white varices. Some with short axial ribs or nodules on the spire, others smooth. Exterior smooth, white or light brown with fine white spiral lines. → Aperture light to intense carmine pink. → ventrum flat. (37 mm)
Distribution: Common, Gulf of Aqaba and Hurghada to Shalatein.

Gibberulus terebellatus (Sowerby, 1842)
28–37.5 mm. → Body whorl wraps itself around the previous whorl at a downward sloping angle. The shoulder of the body whorl attaches at a relatively low point on the preceding whorl. Notch broad and flat. No nodules or ribs, but there may be a line of brown spots just below the suture on the body whorl. Smooth glossy surface. (36 mm)
Distribution: Rare. Found in all areas except the Gulf of Suez.

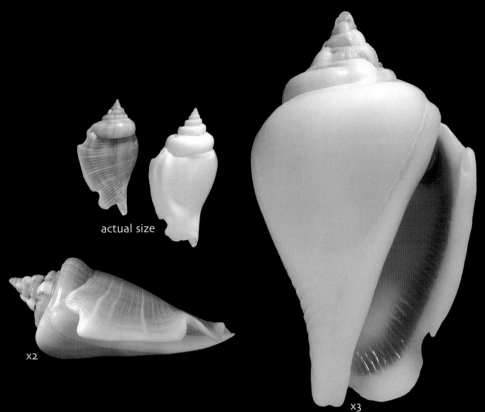

actual size

x2

x3

Gibberulus gibberulus albus

x3

x2

actual size

Gibberulus terebellatus

Lambis truncata sebae (Kiener, 1843)

Seven-fingered Conch

19–280 mm. → Large. Mature specimens with seven long protrusions, like fingers (dig-itations) extending off the lip. Females may have broader and shorter digitations. If the 'fingers' are not fully developed the shell is not fully mature. The juveniles and adoles-cents look very different from the adults (see the small figures, upper right, facing page. 30 mm). The color inside the shell ranges from light pink to dark coral. You can 'hear the sea' when you hold it to your ear. (200 mm)

Distribution: Occasional in Gulf of Aqaba and from Hurghada south. Not found in the Gulf of Suez.

Notes: As with *Charonia tritonis* humans are the main predator of this species. From approximately 1850 to 1950 this shell was much sought after by collectors. Thanks to increasing worldwide environmental awareness the decimation of the population for sale to collectors has virtually ceased. It is illegal to buy or sell seashells in Egypt; if you see one in a shop DO NOT BUY IT. The local Bedouin people have traditionally collected *L. truncata sebae* for food. If the Bedouin are allowed sufficient access to the reefs where these animals live, they are careful not to take too many. But as hotels limit access the people need to harvest more from the few areas they have left in order to provide enough food for their families. You may see piles of these beautiful shells on the beach with holes broken in the backs of the shells. These have been harvested for food. Over-development of the shoreline in many countries has caused the serious decline of many marine species. We hope this will not be the fate of *L. truncata sebae*.

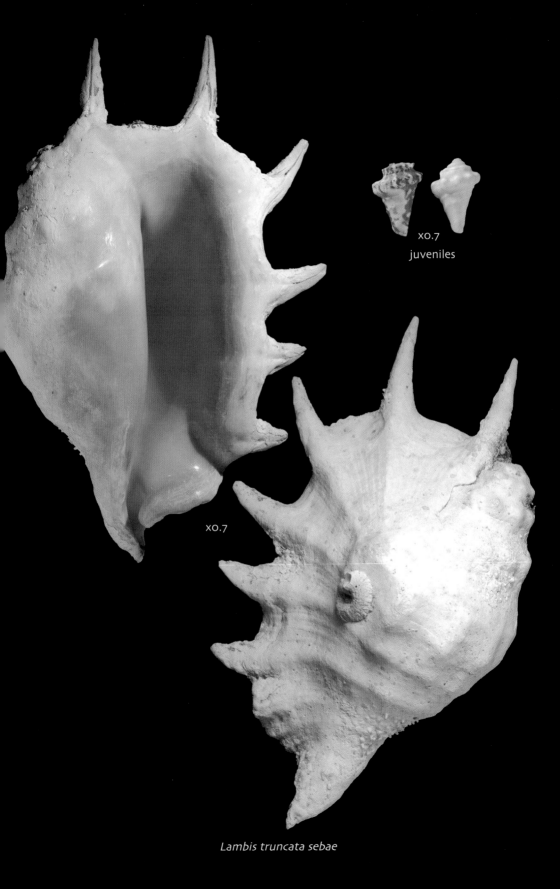

x0.7
juveniles

x0.7

Lambis truncata sebae

Tricornis tricornis (Lightfoot, 1786)
Three-horned or Three-knobbed Conch
Endemic to the Red Sea
80–165 mm. → Single extension of the outer lip, may be long or short, thick or thin. (155 mm). Juvenile specimens (small figures, upper right, 49 mm) lack the protrusion and resemble a fragile cone shell in shape.
Distribution: All regions, common.
Notes: Some small specimens (80–90 mm) called 'dwarf' by some authors, (lower left figure, 80 mm) have a very thick outer lip, usually an adult characteristic. On these individuals the protrusion is not very long. Longer (up to 165 mm), lighter, and thinner specimens appear in the south. These specimens have a much longer protrusion and may be fulvous red inside. Specimens from the Gulf of Suez are variably thick or thin. According to current scientific knowledge, all these are variations of the same one species.

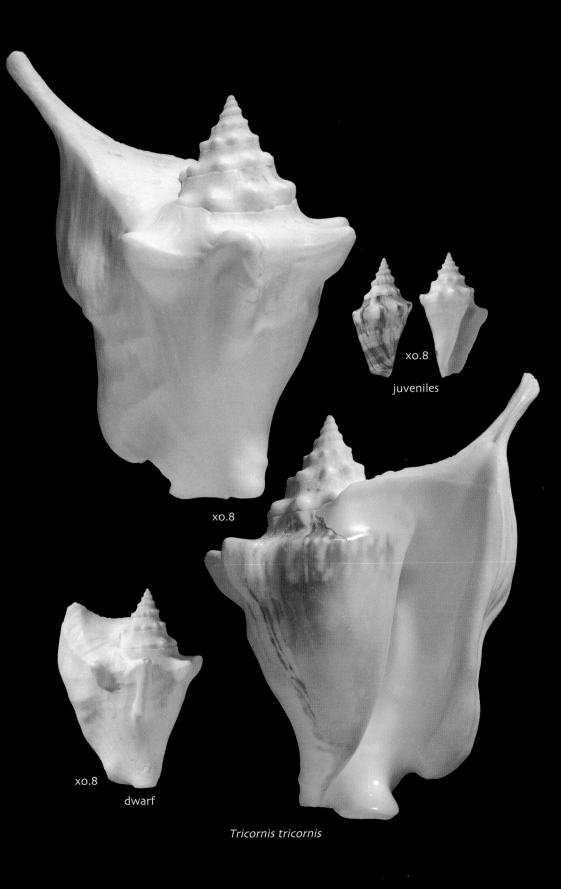

xo.8

juveniles

xo.8

xo.8

dwarf

Tricornis tricornis

Family SERAPHSIDAE

Terebellum terebellum (Linnaeus, 1758)
22–41 mm. → Fragile, glossy, bullet-shaped shell, variously patterned. (37 mm)
Distribution: Infrequent in northern Gulf of Aqaba. Rare in the Safaga area.

Family HIPPONICIDAE

The animals in this family attach themselves to solid surfaces such as rocks and other shells. The shape of the base, and sometimes the whole shell, is influenced by this habit. Although the shells can resemble limpets in shape, the animals can live completely and perpetually underwater and are a separate family.

Cheilea cicatricosa (Reeve, 1858)
12–40 mm. Irregularly conical shell with a wrinkled appearance. Radial and concentric microsculpture. Apex towards the posterior. Odd looking growth on the inside. (39 mm)
Distribution: Occasional from Hurghada to Marsa Alam. Rare elsewhere.

Sabia conica (Schumacher, 1817)
7–16 mm. → Radial sculpture. Never with concentric sculpture. Shape variable, circular to elliptical. Profile varies from nearly flat to steeply conical like a volcano. Apex near posterior margin, peak curls even farther in that direction. Shell exterior dull. Interior glossy white, brown, orange, yellow, or pink. (12 mm)
Distribution: Common in the Gulf of Aqaba and the Hurghada–Safaga area.

Family VANIKORIDAE

This family lives in clean sand near coral, but very little else is known about the habits of these small creatures. Research suggests that an individual may change its gender from male to female and alter its sculpture as well. The deep umbilicus and very large aperture distinguish them from other globose tiny white gastropods.

Vanikoro plicata (Récluz, 1844)
2–8 mm. → Very strong ribs for the size of the shell. Spiral threadlets in the interstices, right from the very first whorl. (7 mm)
Distribution: Moderately common, Gulf of Aqaba to Ras Banas.

Vanikoro acuta (Récluz, 1844)
3–8 mm. Axial ribs predominate on earliest whorl, becoming obsolete by the body whorl. Umbilicus tiny, round, extending all the way up the spire. (8 mm)
Distribution: Rare, Gulf of Aqaba and Hurghada to south of Marsa Alam.

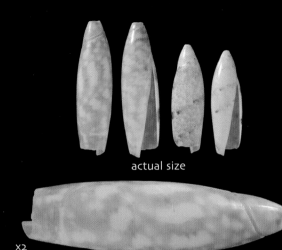

actual size

x2

Terebellum terebellum

Cheilea cicatricosa

actual size

x2

Sabia conica

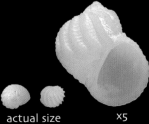

actual size

x5

Vanikoro plicata

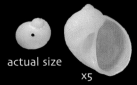

actual size

x5

Vanikoro acuta

Family CYPRAEIDAE

Most cowries live in shallow water on the reefs and hide during the daytime. They are carnivorous and come out at night to eat the animal parts of corals and sponges. In life a patterned mantle of living tissue camouflages the shell. The mantle also protects the shell from scratches by rocks or coral, which is why living cowries have such beautiful shiny surfaces. But the surface is relatively soft, and without the mantle quickly becomes scratched and dull. Juveniles look different from adults: thin shelled, visible spire, large aperture with thin lip and no teeth. The adult patterns and colors are not developed in juveniles and thus identification is very difficult.

Buying cowrie shells or any other Red Sea shell in Egypt is illegal and contributes to the destruction of species.

Bistolida erythraeensis (Sowerby, 1837)
Red Sea Cowrie
15–16 mm. Mature shell with beige dorsum, one or two large light brown spiral patches. Both sets of teeth extend to margin. (15 mm)
Distribution: Rare, Hurghada to Ras Banas.

Cribrarula cribraria (Linnaeus, 1758)
Sieve Cowrie
22–26 mm. Unmistakable pattern of clear white spots on plain brown. (26 mm)
Distribution: Rare, Marsa Alam to Ras Banas.

Erosaria annulus (Linnaeus, 1758)
Ringed Cowrie
18–27.5 mm.→ Gold ring around dorsum, margins only slightly calloused. (25 mm)
Distribution: Infrequent, Safaga to Ras Banas.

Erosaria macandrewi (Sowerby, 1870)
MacAndrew's Cowrie
13–17 mm. Few small distinct darker spots on paler dorsum and at outer edges of base. Labial teeth with orange line. Terminal canals never colored. (17 mm)
Distribution: Rare, Hurghada–Safaga area.
Notes: This species is named after Robert MacAndrew who made an important shell-collecting expedition in the Gulf of Suez in 1869.

Erosaria nebrites nebrites (Melvill, 1888)
17–42 mm. Brown lines on the base, large dark spot in the center of each side of the shell, just above the callus. Even very worn specimens retain dark spots on the sides. (30 mm)
Distribution: Common in the Gulf of Aqaba and south to Ras Banas. Rare in the Gulf of Suez.

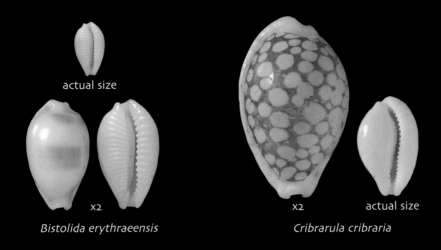

actual size

x2

Bistolida erythraeensis

x2

actual size

Cribrarula cribraria

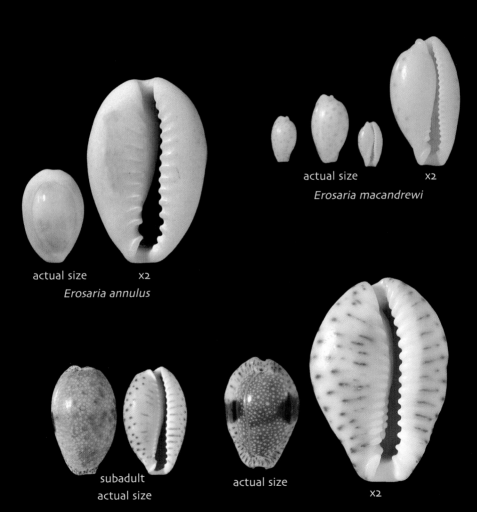

actual size

x2

Erosaria annulus

actual size

x2

Erosaria macandrewi

subadult
actual size

actual size

x2

Erosaria nebrites nebrites

Erosaria turdus (Lamarck, 1810)
Lark Cowrie
25–48 mm.→ Small blurry brown spots on light blue-gray field, larger ones on whitish margins. Teeth relatively large, few, and coarse. Base white. (47 mm)
Distribution: Common in the Gulf of Suez, especially near Ras Sudr, moderately common in the Gulf of Aqaba, and not found elsewhere.
Notes: In the Ras Sudr area many specimens have a milky white background.

Erronea caurica quinquefasciata (Röding, 1798)
24–50 mm. → Wide aperture, orange spaces between the strong outer teeth which extend to the margin. Columellar teeth small, weak. Strong dark spots or blotches on callus. Dorsum with very tiny brown spots densely sprinkled all over it. (50 mm)
Distribution: Common from the Safaga area all the way south to Ras Banas.

Luria isabella (Gray, 1824)
Isabella Cowrie
10–33 mm. → Mushroom dorsum with dark vertical lines, tips orange, exceedingly fine teeth. (31 mm)
Distribution: Moderately common in the Gulf of Aqaba and between Hurghada and Ras Banas.
Notes: Specimens south of Marsa Alam tend to be larger and proportionally broader than northern specimens. Some lack the dark lines.

Luria pulchra (Gray, 1824)
62 mm. → Two large dark brown spots at each extremity and dark brown teeth. (62 mm)
Distribution: Very rare, Gulf of Aqaba.

Lyncina camelopardalis (Perry, 1811)
Camel Cowrie
Endemic
22–72 mm. Very large. Camel colored, with or without white spots. → Spaces between teeth stained black or dark purple. (70 mm)
Distribution: Rare, known from all areas.

Erosaria turdus

subadult

Erronea caurica quinquefasciata

Luria isabella

Luria pulchra

Lyncina camelopardalis

Lyncina carneola (Linnaeus, 1758)
Carnelian Cowrie
23–45 mm. → Alternating stripes, slightly darker and lighter orange-ish or tan, soft purple band just above the margin. Columella violet, pink in faded specimens. (41 mm)
Distribution: Moderately common from Ras Mohamed south to Shalatein. Rare in the Gulfs of Aqaba and Suez.

Lyncina lynx (Linnaeus, 1758)
Lynx Cowrie
31–46 mm. Large and small blurry brown spots on beige or whitish shell. A few much darker and larger spots stand out. → Intense orange color between the teeth which never extend to the margin. Margins without callus. (46 mm)
Distribution: South only, from Marsa Alam to Shalatein.
Notes: This is the opposite pattern of *Mauritia grayana* (below) which has white spots. *Erronea caurica quinquefasciata* has larger more widely spaced teeth extending to the margin, very small dots, and a band of dark brown spots on the callus which remain strong even on very faded shells.

Mauritia grayana (F.A. Schilder, 1930)
33–60 mm. → Dark axial lines interrupted by small white or beige spots encircled by dark brown. Teeth orange to dark brown (not the spaces between). (50 mm)
Distribution: Gulf of Aqaba south to Wadi Gimaal. More common in the south. Not found in the Gulf of Suez.
Notes: The pattern is somewhat variable. Cowrie specialists have special names for each variation.

Purpuradusta gracilis notata (Gill, 1858)
13–22 mm. → Small, widely spaced brown dots on base of the shell, → none on dorsum. Axial blotch on dorsum. Two purple stains on each end, both inside and outside. (22 mm)
Distribution: Infrequent, all areas.

Purpuradusta microdon (Gray, 1828)
8.5–10 mm. → Tiny brown dots on caramel dorsum, → none on base. Very small teeth. Never with axial marks on dorsum. Purple stains on tips. (10 mm)
Distribution: Rare, Gulf of Aqaba, Marsa Alam.

Cypraea sp.
Juvenile and subadult cowries look so different from adults it can be hard to believe they are even in the same family until you see several specimens in a growth progression. (34 mm)

Lyncina carneola

Lyncina lynx

Mauritia grayana

Purpuradusta gracilis notata

actual size   x2

Purpuradusta microdon

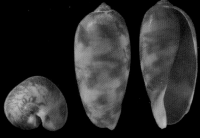

*Cypraea sp.
subadult*

Pustularia cicercula (Linnaeus, 1758)
Chickpea Cowrie
8–17 mm. Rounded shell, subterminal area becoming elongated, both ends protruding.
→ Sunken brown dot at one end. Base, teeth, and spaces between all the same color.
→ Teeth all the same thickness, may be shorter centrally. Dorsum smooth or granulated,
may have some very small chestnut dots. (17 mm)
Distribution: Rare, Gulf of Aqaba, Hurghada area to far south.

Pustularia globulus brevirostris (F.A. & M. Schilder, 1938)
11–15 mm. Highly globose, both ends protruding. Never with single sunken brown dot
at end. → Teeth brownish-orange on mushroom base, may be absent medially. Dorsum
always smooth, may have some small chestnut dots. (14 mm)
Distribution: Rare, Hurghada south.

Staphylaea nucleus madagascariensis (Gmelin, 1791)
13–23 mm. → Numerous small orange-beige pustules on dorsum. Protuberances orange
but tips white. Teeth sharply defined, extend across entire base and up onto dorsum.
Teeth same color as base. A very fine dark orange line borders both sides of each tooth
and extends up the dorsum as very narrow orange threads and around the pustules,
some reaching the sulcus. (23 mm)
Distribution: Rare from Hurghada to Marsa Alam, locally common farther south.

Family OVULIDAE
The shells in this family can be pear shaped, somewhat resembling cowries, or very elongate. The outer lip has tiny teeth. Most of them live on corals in deeper water. All are rare.

Procalpurnus lacteus (Lamarck, 1810)
9–11 mm. All white, slightly pear shaped, smooth surface. Inner edge of lip with numerous tiny teeth. Margins and base pure milk white; hence the name (from the Latin for
milk). (11 mm)
Distribution: Rare, South Sinai, Marsa Alam.

Prosimnia semperi (Weinkauff, 1881)
Crenovolva cf. renovata (Iredale, 1930) of authors
6.5 mm. Very slim pink shell with elongated extremities. Spiral (usually called transverse
in describing this genus) striations. → Lip entirely toothed or knobby. (6.5 mm)
Distribution: Very rare, Hurghada–Safaga area.

Pseudocypraea adamsonii (Sowerby II, 1832)
8–9 mm. → Very fine cancellate sculpture, light brown blotches on cream shell. (8 mm)
Distribution: Rare, Hurghada, Safaga, Marsa Alam.

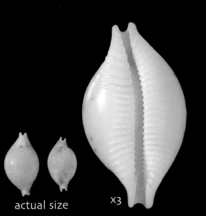

actual size   x3

Pustularia cicercula

actual size   x3

Pustularia globulus brevirostris

actual size   x3

Staphylaea nucleus madagascariensis

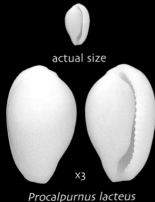

actual size

x3

Procalpurnus lacteus

actual size

x3

Prosimnia semperi

actual size

x3

Pseudocypraea adamsonii

Family TRIVIIDAE

The shells in this family are closely related to cowries, but the teeth on the base extend all the way up to the sulcus in the middle of the dorsum. You could say that the teeth become ribs. The shells in Egypt are all very small.

Trivirostra sp.

6–8.6 mm. Description as for the family. Shells all white. (7.5 mm)

Distribution: Moderately common, Gulf of Aqaba and from Hurghada south. Not found in the Gulf of Suez.

Notes: Until recently all the white specimens of Triviidae in the Red Sea were considered to be one species, *Trivirostra oryza* (Lamarck, 1811). These have recently been separated into several different species but I have not yet learned how to distinguish one from the other, so I have grouped them all together under the genus *Trivirostra*.

Austrotrivia rubramaculosa (Fehse & Greco, 2002)

Endemic

4–6 mm. → Tiny white shell with red spots, exactly as its name says. (6 mm)

Distribution: Uncommon, all areas except the Gulf of Suez.

Family ERATOIDAE

Eratoena sulcifera (Sowerby II, 1832)

4–6 mm. → Sulcus line or groove running the length of the dorsum. Surface pocked or pustulose. Anterior much narrower than posterior and has a small purple or orange blotch at the tip. About 20 tiny denticles along the completely straight apertural lip. Beige. (5.5 mm)

Distribution: Rare, northern Gulf of Aqaba, the Hurghada–Safaga area, and Wadi Lahmi.

Family NATICIDAE

The common name for this family is moon snails. Most of the naticids found in the northern Red Sea are globose. The spire may be quite even with the upper whorls or slightly raised. The outer lip is never thickened. The shells usually have a visible umbilicus but it may be partly or fully blocked by a protrusion called the funicle. The animals are carnivorous, and drill a tiny round hole in the shell of their prey. Look for these sharp-edged holes in other shells, particularly the lucine clams (Lucinidae).

Naticids lay eggs in gelatinous ribbons that incorporate sand and form rosettes on the shallow sandy sea floor. These are easily seen by the observant snorkeler.

Eunaticina papilla (Gmelin, 1791)

6–29 mm. → Spiral grooves. No funicle. Thin parietal callus only slightly obscures the open umbilicus. Entirely white. The enlarged image shows a shell with partial pericostracum. (22 mm)

Distribution: Uncommon, found in all regions.

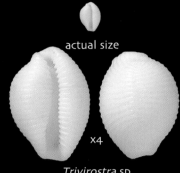

actual size

x4

Trivirostra sp.

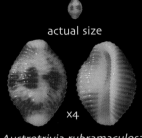

actual size

x4

Austrotrivia rubramaculosa

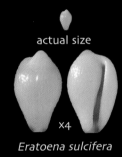

actual size

x4

Eratoena sulcifera

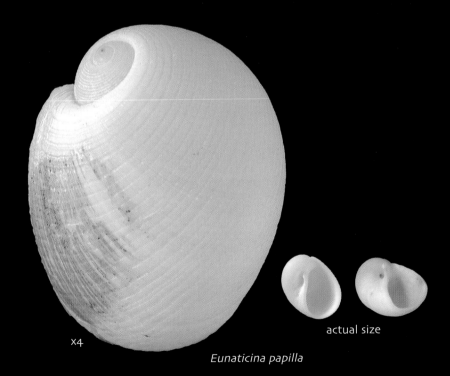

x4

actual size

Eunaticina papilla

Mammilla melanostoma (Gmelin, 1791)
Black Mouthed Moon Snail

10–44 mm. → Broad bands with slightly blurry edges of different shades of grayish-brown and white. Even if the exterior is faded to completely white you can identify this shell by the very dark brown parietal callus. (30 mm)

Distribution: Abundant in Gulf of Aqaba and from Safaga south. Not found in the Gulf of Suez.

Notes: The absence of this species from the Gulf of Suez is interesting given its abundance everywhere else.

Mammilla simiae (Deshayes in Deshayes & Milne Edwards, 1838)

10–37 mm. → Crisp brown bands with darker edges to the broad medial band. Brown columella usually with a white patch in the middle. (21 mm)

Distribution: Common in the Gulf of Aqaba. Rare elsewhere.

Notes: M. melanostoma (above) never with white on its columella. Its patterns are less sharp than *M. simiae*.

Naticarius onca (Röding, 1798)

8–25 mm. → Clear separate brown markings on white shell. Umbilicus large. (25 mm)

Distribution: Rare, Gulf of Suez.

Notocochlis gualtieriana (Récluz, 1843)

5–23 mm. → Smooth, round shape and olive green to brownish-gray color. No dark brown mark on or next to the columella. Funicle nearly fills umbilicus. (19 mm)

Distribution: Common in the Gulf of Aqaba and from Safaga to Sudan.

Notes: Small juveniles have tiny lines in a spiral row at the suture on the upper whorls.

Polinices mammilla (Linnaeus, 1758)
Milky Moon Snail

8–42 mm. → Always pure white with a lovely silky feel when you hold it in your hand. Callus very large completely covering the area between the aperture and the base of the last whorl, thus obscuring the umbilicus. (34 mm)

Distribution: Moderately common in the Gulf of Aqaba and from Safaga south. Not found in the Gulf of Suez.

Notes: This shell is a favorite home for the hermit crabs *Coenobita scaveola* (Forsskål in Niebuhr, 1775) that live in the sand just above the waterline. These crabs are very active at night and you can see their tracks near the high tideline, especially very early in the morning. If you pick up one of these shells you may see the hermit crab's big claw filling the entire aperture and protecting itself against predators. If you are very quiet and still the crab may start to emerge. Resist the temptation to touch or tease it, and put it carefully back where you found it.

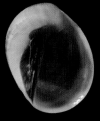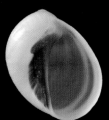

Mammilla melanostoma

Naticarius onca

Mammilla simiae

actual size   ×3

juvenile

Notocochlis gualtieriana

Polinices mammilla

Polinices peselephanti (Link, 1807)
Elephant's Foot Moon Snail
30–50 mm. → Large shell, unusually large open umbilicus. White, sometimes with an orange tinge. (38 mm)
Distribution: Rare, limited to the Ras Sudr area in the Gulf of Suez.

Sigatica mienisi (Kilburn, 1988)
Endemic to the Gulf of Aqaba and South Sinai
11 mm. → Deep open umbilicus with a 'tooth' protruding into it from the outside of the columella. Shell white with three brown interrupted spiral bands on body whorl. (11 mm)
Distribution: Rare, N. Gulf of Aqaba, South Sinai.

Family BURSIDAE
The family Bursidae is distinctive for its heavy coarse shells and a strong posterior canal at the upper corner of the aperture. Most species live near coral. Sometimes they are called Frog Shells.

Bursa granularis Röding, 1798
Granular Frog Shell
9–52 mm. Two varices per whorl. Two strong spiral rows of well-defined nodules and up to five rows of small ones. → Aperture white or beige. (43 mm)
Distribution: Common in the Gulf of Aqaba and from Hurghada to Wadi Gimaal. Not found in the Gulf of Suez.
Notes: B. granularis is by far the most common species of Bursidae in the Egyptian Red Sea.

Bursa lamarckii (Deshayes, 1853)
Lamarck's Frog Shell
60 mm. → Posterior sinuses line up. Black lines between numerous folds on columella.
Distribution: Very rare, possibly extinct in Egypt. Gulf of Aqaba only.

Tutufa bufo (Röding, 1798)
96–105 mm. Large, knobby shell, → large orange aperture, about ten lirate teeth, columella smooth, a few very weak folds at lower end, not wrinkled. Very dark orange or red band encircling aperture behind teeth. (105 mm)
Distribution: Rare, Gulf of Aqaba only.

Polinices peselephanti

actual size

x3

Sigatica mienisi

Bursa granularis

Bursa lamarckii

Tutufa bufo

Family CASSIDAE

These attractive shells are nourished by the animals' carnivorous diet of sea urchins and other invertebrates. They usually prefer to live in a sandy habitat.

Casmaria erinaceus Linnaeus, 1758

30–55 mm. → Relatively slender, a few sharp denticles only on the lower portion of the lip, never with dark brown markings below the suture. Shoulder may be nodulose or smooth. (34 mm)
Distribution: Rare, Gulf of Aqaba and the southern regions, never in the Gulf of Suez.

Casmaria ponderosa unicolor (Dautzenberg in Pallary, 1929)

14–55 mm. → Globose, glossy shell with sparse row of dark brown squares or rectangles just below the suture of the body. Sometimes with small nodules below the dark spots. Very sharp pointed teeth line the entire length of the lip. (48 mm)
Distribution: Common in the Gulf of Aqaba, occasional from Safaga south to Wadi Gimaal.
Notes: As visitor levels to the beaches have increased, the number of these shells seen lying there has decreased. Please remember that it is a courtesy to other visitors to admire shells in their place and leave them there for others to enjoy.

Semicassis faurotis (Jousseaume, 1888)

46–66 mm. → Globose shell, dark purple apex, unique and complicated structure at its base, involving the columella, the umbilicus, and the siphonal canal. Distinct darker squares neatly arranged over entire shell. (61 mm)
Distribution: Uncommon, most likely to be seen in the Gulf of Suez.

Family PERSONIDAE

Shells in this family always have irregular and distorted whorls. This characteristic makes them a bit strange-looking but also very easy to recognize.

Distorsio anus (Linnaeus, 1758)

28–51 mm. → Lumpy, irregular shape with a very delicate flange, usually chipped, extending outward on the ventrum of the shell from the columella. (45 mm)
Distribution: Common in the Gulf of Aqaba and the south. Rare in the Gulf of Suez.

Casmaria erinaceus

juvenile

Casmaria ponderosa unicolor

Semicassis faurotis

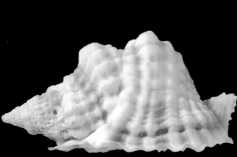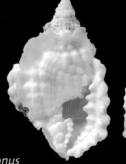

Distorsio anus

Family RANELLIDAE

Most species of this family have coarse knobby sculpture and a short or moderate siphonal canal. The outstanding exception is *Charonia tritonis* which is smooth and beautifully patterned. They all live near coral and sand.

Charonia tritonis (Linnaeus, 1758)
Triton's Trumpet
60–300 mm. This is one of the most famous shells in the world and one of the largest in the Red Sea. It is instantly recognizable for its dramatic shape and beautiful and intricate pattern, a delight to study. More significant than its beauty (and perhaps less well known) is its importance to the health of the coral reefs. *C. tritonis* is one of the few natural predators of the Crown of Thorns Starfish, one of the most serious predators of coral, and considered by some as a hazard to the health of the entire reef community. When *C. tritonis* and the Crown of Thorns remain in the correct balance, the starfish eats some coral and the Triton eats some starfish, and it balances out. Unfortunately, human beings are the most dangerous predator of *C. tritonis*. If the population of Tritons gets too small the Crown of Thorns can multiply rapidly and eat too much coral. If you ever see a live *C. tritonis*, stay far away and leave it in peace. Never buy the shell because that encourages collectors to kill more of them. *C. tritonis* was hunted extensively for shell collections during the last 150 years, and now it is unusual to find one in our area longer than 220 mm. The figured specimen is immature. Like all the shells in this book, it was found after the animal had died and disappeared. (101 mm)
Distribution: Rare, Gulf of Aqaba and around reefs from South Sinai to Shalatein.

Cymatium aquatile (Reeve, 1844)
19–70 mm. → Aperture and columella orange, teeth and columnar lirae white. Shell orange-brown and white. Body whorl with a strong varix, white with two dark bars. (50 mm)
Distribution: Common in the south, rare in the Gulf of Suez, found in all areas.

Cymatium exile (Reeve, 1844)
31–36 mm. → Siphonal canal very long, nearly straight. Two prominent tubercles on the dorsum. (33 mm)
Distribution: Rare, Gulf of Aqaba and Safaga only.
Notes: Strongest protuberances on *C. trilineatum* are at the shoulder; on *C. exile*, medially on the body whorl. Dorsal protuberance encompasses two spiral cords on *C. exile*, only one on *C. trilineatum* (see page 80).

Cymatium marerubrum Garcia Talavera, 1985
Endemic
15–38 mm. → Red or orange in color. Columella orange or red with white lirae. Sculpture of regular beaded spiral cords. (38 mm)
Distribution: Occasional in all regions except Gulf of Suez.

Cymatium aquatile

Charonia tritonis

Cymatium exile

actual size

x2

Cymatium marerubrum

Cymatium trilineatum (Reeve, 1844)

45–77 mm. Siphonal canal long curved, long strong teeth inside crenulate outer lip, one prominent tubercle on the dorsum. Shell with alternating brown and white spiral color bands. (77 mm)

Distribution: Rare, all areas.

Notes: Teeth distinctly larger, fewer, and more widely spaced than in *Cymatium aquatile*. See also *Cymatium exile* on page 78.

Gyrineum concinnum (Dunker, 1862)

15–20 mm. Varices line up neatly on both sides of the shell. Siphonal canal short, straight. Caramel color with one white spiral line on the body whorl. (15 mm)

Distribution: Rare, generally considered to be more common in areas south of Egypt; also known from Safaga.

Notes: Rarely found in good condition, most specimens are subfossils.

Family TONNIDAE

The shells of the Tonnidae family—tun shells—are thin and globose. The name is derived from the Latin word for barrel. Some of them are among the largest shells in the Egyptian Red Sea. Most of the animals live offshore and eat sea cucumbers. The recent over-harvesting of sea cucumbers for export has seriously depleted the food supply for the tun shells, and as a result the animals may become endangered. Normally the shells are rarely found on beaches because of their fragility and preference for deeper water.

Malea pomum (Linnaeus, 1758)

Grinning Tun Shell

20–46 mm. Thick outer lip with numerous sharp teeth. Sculpture of rounded spiral cords separated by channels. Fresh shells mottled with orange-brown and white patches. The color fades quickly in the sun, but its sculpture and toothy grin make it easy to identify. (41 mm)

Distribution: Occasional in the Gulf of Aqaba and from the Straits of Gubal to Wadi Lahmi.

Tonna perdix (Linnaeus, 1758)

Partridge Tun Shell

19–93 mm. Lip thin, no teeth. Tan and white color pattern calls to mind the feathers of a partridge. Protoconch pink. Shoulders sloping directly from suture. (19.5 mm)

Distribution: Occasional from Hurghada south, rare in the Gulf of Aqaba, never in the Gulf of Suez.

Notes: The most common *Tonna* in the Egyptian Red Sea and the only one with this pattern of large dashes. Both the body color and the pattern color can vary from very light to very dark.

juvenile

Cymatium trilineatum

x2   actual size

Gyrineum concinnum

Malea pomum

juvenile

Tonna perdix

Family TRIPHORIDAE

These shells are small, elongate, and feed on sponges. The surface is highly sculptured, many with beaded spiral cords. Most species coil in the opposite direction from the vast majority of other gastropods—the aperture is to the left of the columella. The term for this is sinestral. More than 50 named species are reported to be found in the Red Sea. Most of them are very difficult to identify.

Viriola corrugata (Hinds, 1843)
6–14 mm. Elongate, straight sided, complex spiral and cancellate sculpture. Variegated brown. (14 mm)
Distribution: Uncommon. Hurghada to far south.

Family EPITONIIDAE

The common English name of these fascinating delicate shells is Dutch: wentletrap, meaning staircase, after the narrow spiral stairs in old Dutch houses. The animals are parasitic, eating live anemones and corals. They all begin life as males and when mature become female. The small size and fragility of these beautiful shells makes them disproportionately rarely found. The surface of the shell may be smooth or have spiral sculpture between the ribs. Most species have axial ribs, called costae. The outline of the costae may be smoothly rounded, peaked, or angular. Some are simple and extend straight out from the shell; others curl back, opposite to the direction of growth. Costae may be continuous from one whorl to the next, or discontinuous.

The characteristics of the shell surface and the costae are important for identifying the shell. The characteristics of the protoconch are also important, but in beached shells it is usually missing.

Cycloscala hyalina (Sowerby, 1844)
10 mm. Exquisitely constructed shell: → none of the whorls connect to each other. Costae peaked. (10 mm)
Distribution: Rare, Safaga only.

Epitonium agitabilis (Jousseaume, 1912)
8 mm. Stubby shape, smoothly rounded whorls. Rounded continuous costae. → Costae fuse with apertural lip at base. No umbilicus. (8 mm)
Distribution: Rare, Gulf of Aqaba.
Notes: High magnification reveals fine spiral striae; these not visible on beach-worn shells.

Epitonium amicum (Jousseaume, 1894)
3.5–9 mm. Moderately elongate shell, rounded whorls, deeply indented sutures. Numerous fine closely spaced low axial ribs, slightly oblique. Minute spiral striae between costae. No umbilicus. Aperture obliquely oval, almost pointed at posterior end, slightly extended and open at anterior, as if smoothed out by the siphon. All white. (6 mm)
Distribution: Moderately common, all areas.
Notes: The most common member of its family in Egypt.

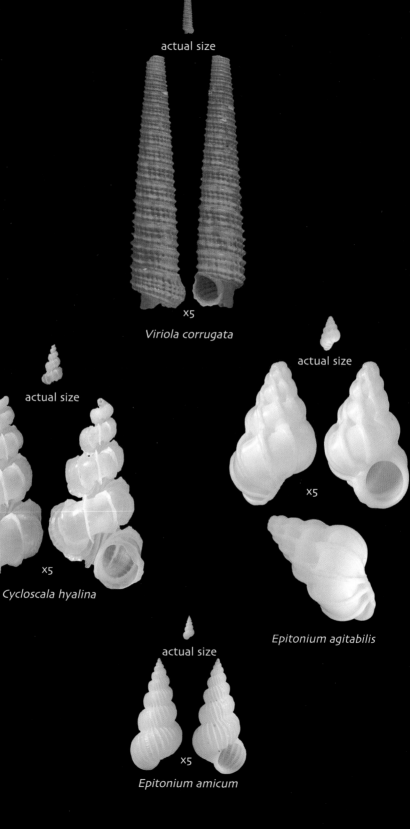

actual size

×5

Viriola corrugata

actual size

×5

Cycloscala hyalina

actual size

×5

Epitonium agitabilis

actual size

×5

Epitonium amicum

Epitonium fucatum (Pease, 1861)

6–9 mm. → Widely spaced continuous ribs with vertical peaks, whorls lightly connected, numerous (20–30) micro spiral threads and even finer axial ones between costae. (6 mm)
Distribution: Very rare, South Sinai, Gulf of Aqaba. Pictured specimen found by Pamela Piombino.

Epitonium jomardi (Audouin, 1826)

5–10 mm. → Very rounded whorls, intented sutures, numerous very fine densely spaced somewhat ragged, retroflected costae. → No spiral sculpture visible between costae without high magnification. → Umbilicus appears slit-like, mostly obscured by columella. Light beige, with darker beige spiral band, may fade to all white. (10 mm)
Distribution: Relatively common, all regions except the Gulf of Suez.
Notes: Variability exists among individuals regarding the shape of the shell (elongate or stout) and the number of costae on the body whorl. If the obscuring flange of the columella/aperture is broken away, one can see up the umbilicus almost to the apex.

Epitonium lyra (Sowerby, 1844)

6–11.5 mm. Stubby shape, thin, weak, low costae. → Fine spiral striae visible between them. Umbilicus very small. White with two brown spiral bands on the body whorl, may fade to all white. (8 mm)
Distribution: Rare, northern Gulf of Aqaba, Hurghada–Safaga area.
Notes: In distinguishing between *E. jomardi* and *E. lyra* the relative strength of the spiral sculpture between the costae is the most important feature as shape, size, number of costae, and even the exact appearance of the umbilicus may vary. In terms of occurrence, *E. jomardi* is considerably more common.

Epitonium marmoratum (Sowerby, 1844)

12–22 mm. Protoconch on this dramatic shell has two light brown glassy whorls. Next two whorls shiny brown with white costae. Remaining whorls white with → brown honeycomb markings. Costae with small projection just below the shoulder, not strongly pronounced. Whorls separate from each other, connected only by the costae. (22 mm)
Distribution: Rare, all areas except the Gulf of Suez.

Epitonium pyramidale (Sowerby II, 1844)

4–25 mm. → Whorls joined only by the widely spaced strong oblique costae, these with triangular peak at outside edge. Whorls smooth, may have brown patches. (19 mm)
Distribution: Moderately common, all areas except the Gulf of Suez.
Notes: The space between the whorls is large enough that one can see between them into the empty space of the umbilicus.

actual size

x4

Epitonium fucatum

actual size

x4

Epitonium jomardi

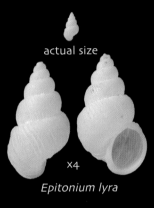

actual size

x4

Epitonium lyra

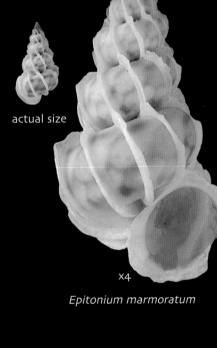

actual size

x4

Epitonium marmoratum

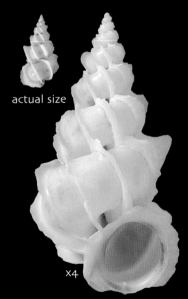

actual size

x4

Epitonium pyramidale

Epitonium sandwichense (Nyst, 1871)
7 mm. → Very elongate, upper spire glossy brown. Lower part white. Costae smooth, continuous. Whorls smoothly rounded but not globose. Micro spiral threads (and even smaller axial ones) between costae. (7 mm)
Distribution: Very rare, Gulf of Aqaba.

Epitonium savignyi (Jousseaume, 1912)
11.5 mm. Somewhat stubby shape. Whorls slightly separated, no striae. Costae large, continuous, with vertical peak close to body. Flange around ovoid aperture large. (11.5 mm)
Distribution: Very rare, South Sinai.

Gyroscala lamellosa (Lamarck, 1822)
14 mm. → Narrow spiral cord running beneath the ribs on shell base. Costae continuous, rounded, widely spaced. Shell brown or white, usually with dark brown spiral band below the sutures. (14 mm)
Distribution: Rare, South Sinai, Far South.
Notes: Figured specimen is broken, apex missing.

Family JANTHINIDAE
The animals in this family have the unusual habit of floating on the surface of the sea. The shells are purple and extremely fragile.

Janthina umbilicata (Orbigny, 1840)
3–7 mm. → Protruding protoconch, umbilicus small but visible. Fine sculpture, clear triangular ribs like a broad > symbol. (7 mm)
Distribution: Rare, usually found on beaches facing northeast, toward the prevailing wind. Very rarely found intact.

Family EULIMIDAE
The animals are parasitic on various echinoderms. The shells are usually solid, elongate, and glossy white. The spire is usually acute. The aperture is ovoid, not round, and somewhat pointed at the upper end. A great number of species are reported from the Red Sea; only two are presented here as examples.

Hemiliostraca metcalfei (A. Adams in Sowerby, 1854)
5.5–7 mm. Typically with the apex missing. Transparent white with brown markings. (7 mm)
Distribution: Uncommon, Hurghada–Safaga.

Hypermastus cf. *epiphanes* (Melvill, 1897)
4.5–14 mm. Elongate, glossy white shell with sharply pointed apex and straight sides. Aperture a narrow teardrop shape. (14 mm)
Distribution: Occasional, the Gulf of Suez.

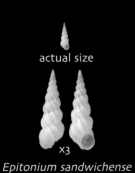

actual size

x3

Epitonium sandwichense

actual size

x3

Epitonium savignyi

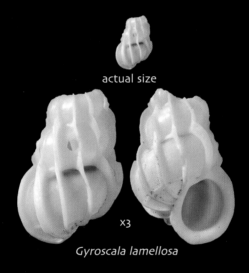

actual size

x3

Gyroscala lamellosa

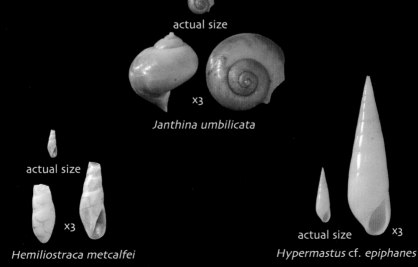

actual size

x3

Janthina umbilicata

actual size

x3

Hemiliostraca metcalfei

actual size

x3

Hypermastus cf. *epiphanes*

Family MURICIDAE
Chicoreus corrugatus corrugatus (Sowerby, 1841)
29–42 mm. Two broad ribs between the varices, → no strong spine at shoulder, short siphonal canal. In profile the pentultimate whorl extends below the ventral line. Umbilicus open. (42 mm)
Distribution: Very rare, Gulf of Suez.

Chicoreus erythraeus (Fischer, 1870)
Chicoreus virgineus (Röding, 1798) of authors
15–130 mm. → Long siphonal canal. Varices may be fluted but the ornamentation never branches. Aperture somewhat teardrop shaped, occasionally with a pink band around the inside. → Top shoulder spine very strong, extended, curling backward, opposite the direction of growth. (56 mm)
Distribution: Common in the Gulf of Suez.
Notes: A dwarf form is common in the northern Gulf of Suez. It appears to reach maturity at around 30 mm. Even the smallest specimes, about 10 mm, have a small sharp dominant spine on the shoulder. It is uniformly pinkish-beige with less developed ornamentation.

Chicoreus ramosus (Linnaeus, 1758)
Ramose Murex
75–95 mm. Mature specimens have a well-defined notch at the top of the aperture for the posterior canal, fine dark brown spiral threads on the whorls. Always with an enlarged protruding tooth in lower third of outer lip. The animal uses this to pry open the shells of its bivalve prey. The prominent shoulder spine is only slightly retroflected. Aperture large and nearly round, may have a pink band inside. (79 mm)
Distribution: Rare, all areas.
Notes: Well-developed freshly unoccupied specimens from quiet waters are unmistakable for their elongated and elaborated sculpture. The sculpture of those from rougher waters is stubby and indistinct making discrimination from *C. erythraeus* difficult.

Chicoreus corrugatus corrugatus

Chicoreus erythraeus

Chicoreus ramosus

Drupa lischkei (Hidalgo, 1904)
Synonym *Drupa hadari* Emerson & Cernohorsky, 1973
Endemic
15–35 mm. Sharp spines evenly distributed over the body whorl. Exterior usually covered with white encrustation. Aperture glossy white, some with a few dark brown squarish dots at the upper columellar surface. Adults with teeth on the inside of the outer lip and columella. (31 mm)
Distribution: Common, all areas except Gulf of Suez.
Notes: Juveniles do not have teeth or spines but are covered with regular dark brown dots. Immature and subadult specimens seem to develop teeth and spines at rates not governed strictly by size. Some immature specimens have teeth but no spines, whereas others have spines but no teeth.

Drupa lobata (Blainville, 1832)
18–30 mm. Extraordinary digitations and scaly underside. Aperture with very dark band, interior orange or yellow. Figured adult shell found by Kaki Rusmore. (30 mm)
Distribution: Rare, offshore reefs.

Drupa morum Röding, 1798
20–45 mm. Strong, blunt, brown tubercles, white shell, aperture pink or purple. Strong teeth on the apertural lip, three folds on the columella. (37 mm)
Distribution: Common in the Gulf of Aqaba and from Marsa Alam south. Prefers rocky habitats.
Notes: D. *morum* is normally heavier and has a thicker lip than *D. lischkei.* The tooth structure and apparently unpredictable growth patterns of both species are very similar.

Drupella cornus Röding, 1798
Horned Drupella
13–35 mm. Somewhat elongate white encrusted shell with spiral rows of pointed tubercles. Brown spiral threads, usually hidden under the encrustation. Aperture white, dentate, may be orange inside. (32 mm)
Distribution: Occasional in all regions.
Notes: This species eats living coral.

juvenile

Drupa lischkei

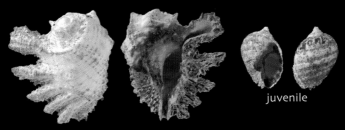

juvenile

Drupa lobata

Drupa morum

juvenile

Drupella cornus

subadult

Ergalatax contracta (Reeve, 1846)

24–30 mm. Tall spire, strong neat rather widely spaced axial ribs on all whorls, crossed by numerous tightly spaced but well-defined spiral cords. Small light-colored tubercle on the shoulder. Shell lightly mottled beige, caramel, and white. Aperture may be dentate or not. Columella and inner lip white, siphonal canal and deeper in the aperture may be caramel. (29 mm)
Distribution: Uncommon, Gulf of Suez. Very rare in the Gulf of Aqaba.
Notes: While some specimens may appear as intergrades between *E. obscura* and *E. contracta*, this latter never has dark paired dashes or dark tubercles on the axial ribs.

Ergalatax obscura (Houart, 1996)

8–24 mm. Strong broad axial ribs crossed by spiral cords and threads, dark brown as they cross the ribs. Sometimes entire cord dark brown. Umbilicus closed, with just a little slit showing between final basal cord and outer edge of siphonal canal. Fully mature specimens with thickened lip and five or more small denticles. Aperture the same whitish color as the body of the shell. (22 mm)
Distribution: Uncommon, Hurghada–Safaga, Gulf of Suez, rare in Gulf of Aqaba, not found south of Safaga.

Maculotriton serriale (Deshayes in Laborde, 1834)

9–14.5 mm. → Elongate beige or white shell with brown or dark brown dots in spiral rows. Lip thick, numerous very small denticles just inside. (14 mm)
Distribution: Locally common, northern Gulf of Aqaba and Hurghada–Safaga area.

Morula anaxeres (Kiener, 1835)

5–13 mm. → Remarkable for the disproportionately large white beads in a spiral row around the center of the dark shell. (10 mm)
Distribution: Locally uncommon in the northern Gulf of Aqaba, rare elsewhere.
Notes: The specimens from the Wadi Gimaal area are twice as large as those from the north.

Morula aspera (Lamarck, 1816)

9–19 mm. Delicate prickly appearance. → White spiral cords run over the tops of the black or dark brown nodules. The dark bits are made up of dark dashes on three tightly spaced spiral cords. Aperture violet, usually five teeth on the inner lip. (17 mm)
Distribution: Usually uncommon, found in all regions.

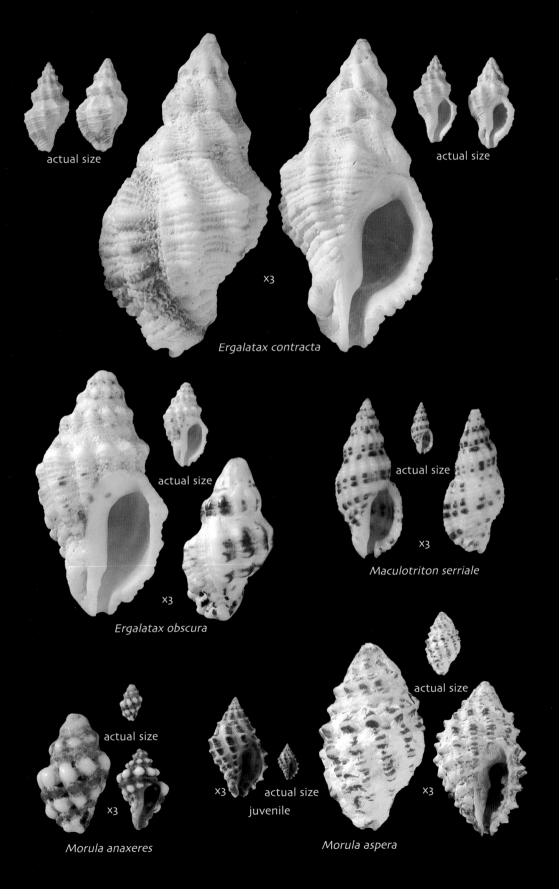

actual size

actual size

×3

Ergalatax contracta

actual size

×3

Ergalatax obscura

actual size

×3

Maculotriton serriale

actual size

actual size

×3

Morula anaxeres

×3   actual size

juvenile

actual size

×3

Morula aspera

Morula chrysostoma (Deshayes, 1844)
Golden Mouthed Morula

7.5–24 mm. Variable in shape, always at least a little spiny with two lighter spiral bands against the darker shell color. Often encrusted. All this combines to make it difficult to identify. (24 mm)

Distribution: Rare, Gulf of Aqaba, South Sinai and associated reefs, Hurghada.

Notes: M. chrysostoma is named for the golden yellow to orange aperture it displays in more southern waters. In our northern waters these colors are less noticeable.

Morula granulata (Duclos, 1832)
Granulated Morula

10–20 mm. The pattern of this shell looks like a black and white tile floor. But the squarish black or brown 'tiles' are rounded, not flat. They are never extended into spines or tubercles. Aperture denticulate. (17 mm)

Distribution: Common in rocky areas of the Gulf of Aqaba, occasional in the south. Not found in the Gulf of Suez.

Notes: The larger size and extended tubercles of *Thais savignyi* should be sufficient to distinguish these two species. In addition, a juvenile of *T. savignyi* small enough (under 20 mm) to be confused with *M. granulata* will have a very thin lip. The sunken white areas and lack of spines on *M. granulata* distinguish it from *M. aspera* (see previous page).

Murex forskoehlii Röding, 1798
Forsskål's Murex

13–115 mm. → Long spines, very long siphonal canal. Juveniles miniatures of adults.

Distribution: Moderately common in the Gulf of Suez and down the mainland coast to Shalatein. Rare to never in the Gulf of Aqaba. (104 mm)

Notes: Most of the year the animals live offshore in sand or muddy sand but in the early spring come into quiet, sandy, silty lagoons to breed. By late spring the shells cover the bottoms and shores of these lagoons.

actual size
x2
actual size
juvenile

Morula chrysostoma

x2

actual size

Morula granulata

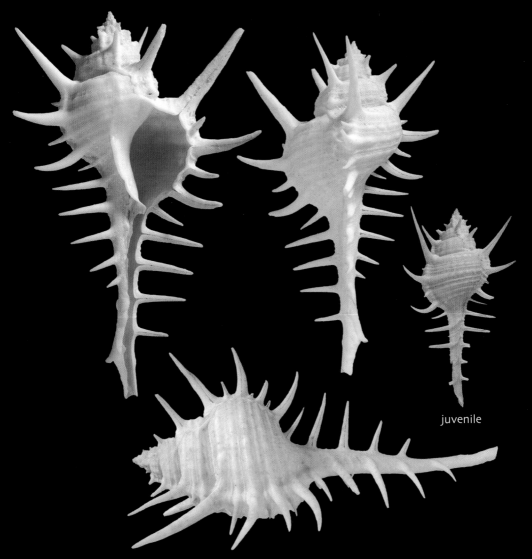

juvenile

Murex forskoehlii

Muricodrupa funiculus (Wood, 1828)

9–32 mm. Stepped conical spire, body whorl with strong axial ribs crossed by strong spiral cords, leaving sunken rectangles between them. Aperture denticulate, lavender in fresh specimens, fading to pale pink or gray. Often completely encrusted or very worn. (29 mm)

Distribution: Moderately common, Gulf of Aqaba and area around Wadi Gimaal. Also found, but rarely, near offshore reefs near Hurghada and in the Gulf of Suez. These latter tend to be in very poor condition.

Nassa situla (Reeve, 1846)

Synonym *Pusio kossmannii* Pagenstecher, 1877

15–58 mm. → Thin, smooth-surfaced shell, usually with a few white spiral lines, but no real pattern. (27 mm)

Distribution: Common in the Gulf of Aqaba, occasional from Hurghada south. Not found in the Gulf of Suez.

Notes: Nassa situla might be confused with *Pisania ignea*. Note that the aperture of *N. situla* is more than twice the length of the spire. The aperture and the spire of *P. ignea* are about equal in length. *N. situla* never has a pattern of axial flames.

Rapana rapiformis (Born, 1778)

29–77 mm. → Very globose, unusually large aperture, umbilicus very deep. Varying shades of beige; sometimes with a coral blush in the aperture. (60 mm)

Distribution: Uncommon, the Gulf of Suez.

Thais savignyi (Deshayes in Deshayes & Milne Edwards, 1844)

24–50 mm. → Four spiral rows of distinct, well-separated, pointed, gray-brown tubercles on lighter shell. Inner edge of lip with large dark chocolate brown patches, denticles within. Aperture, columella white, sometimes with a bit of pink, often with a small bend in the middle and a brown base. Always associated with rocks. (48 mm)

Distribution: Occasional on rocky beaches in all regions.

Muricodrupa funiculus

immature

Nassa situla

Rapana rapiformis

Thais savignyi

Family CORALLIOPHILIDAE
All of these inhabit living coral. The name means 'lovers of coral.'

Coralliophila costularis (Lamarck, 1816)
16–17 mm. → Lower part of excellent specimens densely covered with relatively long narrow tubular spines. Shape variable, elongate or stubby. (16 mm)
Distribution: Rare, Hurghada south.

Coralliophila erosa (Röding, 1798)
19–21.5 mm. → Globose centrally but with sharply conical spire and base. Large wide aperture and a short pointed spire whose base is much narrower than the body whorl from which it rises. Umbilicus visible. (22 mm)
Distribution: Rare, Gulf of Aqaba, far south.

Coralliophila neritoidea (Lamarck, 1816)
13–25 mm. Large, globose body whorl. → Aperture lirate. The aperture is completely violet. Because the columella and a narrow parietal shield are also completely violet, the mouth of the shell looks much larger than it really is. (22 mm)
Distribution: Rare, near offshore coral.
Notes: Unlike *C. madreporara*, the body whorl to the left of the columella of *C. neritoidea* is considerably larger than the aperture.

Quoyula madreporara (Sowerby, 1832)
6.5–26.5 mm. → Aperture almost twice as large as the solid part of the shell next to the columella. External sculpture of very fine threads. Columella violet, aperture white with violet stain basally, never lirate. (26.5 mm)
Distribution: Locally common in the northern Gulf of Aqaba, rare elsewhere.
Notes: This shell and *C. neritoidea* can be confused at first (see above).

actual size

actual size

x2

x2

Coralliophila costularis

Coralliophila erosa

actual size

x2

Coralliophila neritoidea

actual size

x2

Quoyula madreporara

Family BUCCINIDAE

Antillophos roseatus (Hinds, 1844)

18–26.5 mm. → Tall shell with around seven rounded whorls and clear sculptural detail. Many strong axial ribs and occasional varices, all crossed by fine spiral threads. Aperture wide, short, strongly lirate inside. Color varies from white to brown, usually with a rose tint. Aperture white to lavender. (18 mm)

Distribution: Usually uncommon, but locally and intermittently common in the northern Gulf of Aqaba. Very rare, Hurghada–Safaga.

Clivipollia incarnata (Deshayes in Laborde, 1834)

Endemic

14–24 mm. Sculpture of slightly oblique rounded axial ribs crossed by sharp brown spiral cords. Five to seven denticles on the inside of the lip. Two small folds on columella. → Aperture bright pink. (23.5 mm)

Distribution: Occasional in Gulf of Aqaba, locally and occasionally common between Hurghada–Safaga. Rare elsewhere.

Engina mendicaria (Linnaeus, 1758)

9–16 mm. → Dramatic stripes. Usually black and white or brown and white, sometimes black and yellow. (14 mm)

Distribution: Common in the Gulf of Aqaba, occasional elsewhere.

Notes: May be seen living in shallow tidepools. If you see live ones, please do not pick them up; just quietly enjoy watching them going about their business of eating algae.

Pisania ignea (Gmelin 1791)

22–27 mm. → Axial 'flames' pattern, smooth surface. Top part of spire usually missing. Inner edge of the outer lip is lightly scalloped, but not dentate. (25 mm)

Distribution: Rare in the Gulf of Aqaba, very uncommon from Hurghada south, and never in the Gulf of Suez.

Notes: Shape very similar to the muricid *Nassa situla*, but that species never has any axial pattern.

actual size   x2

Antillophos roseatus

actual size   x2

Clivipollia incarnata

actual size   x2

Engina mendicaria

actual size

x2

Pisania ignea

Family COLUBRARIIDAE

The common name—vampire shells—comes from the unusual way of feeding. The animals in this family insert their unusually long proboscis into a vulnerable area of a sleeping fish, such as the mouth, and feed by sucking blood. Their most common victims are parrotfish (Scaridae) who oblige them by sleeping soundly most of the night, wrapped in their own self-made mucus sleeping bags.

Colubraria muricata (Lightfoot, 1786)

44–56 mm. Relatively large, heavy shell with a high spire. Cancellate sculpture on the entire shell, two varices per whorl. Siphonal canal short and recurved. Lip thickened, dentate within. Thick glossy parietal shield extends beyond the shell off the siphonal canal, its outer edge ruffled. Color light brown with darker brown and chestnut spiral bands. Interior creamy white flushed with light apricot. (56 mm)
Distribution: Rare, offshore reefs. Known from all areas except the Gulf of Suez.

Family COLUMBELLIDAE

Euplica festiva (Deshayes in Laborde, 1834)

8.5–11 mm. Solid and strong for its small size, white or beige, patterned with brown or black, appearance quite variable. Surface smooth, some with coronations and/or tubercles at shoulder. About five tiny teeth inside the thickened outer lip. → One or two folds on the columella. (10 mm)
Distribution: Locally and occasionally abundant in the Gulf of Aqaba, infrequent elsewhere. Rare south of Safaga.

Mitrella albina (Kiener, 1841)

12–19 mm. Slightly elongate, glossy, light colored, variously patterned in shades of brown, some with purple-brown markings at the base. About five slightly elongate denticles on the inside of the outer lip, these sometimes surrounded by lavender. Columella weakly lirate, but without folds. (16 mm)
Distribution: Locally and occasionally common in the Safaga area and northern Gulf of Aqaba. Not found in the Gulf of Suez or south of Safaga.
Notes: Always more elongate than *Euplica festiva.*

Mitrella loyaltyensis (Hervier, 1899)

7–9.5 mm. Elongate, glossy shell. Straight-sided spire at least twice as long as aperture. Edge of lip thickened. Patterns variable, usually with fine chestnut markings. (9mm)
Distribution: Rare, northern Gulf of Aqaba. Uncommon, Hurghada–Safaga area.

x3

actual size

Euplica festiva

actual size

actual size

Mitrella albina

x3

x3

Colubraria muricata

x3

actual size

Mitrella loyaltyensis

Pyrene flava (Bruguière, 1789)
15–18 mm. Apex sharply pointed, spire stepped. Shell broadest midway between base and apex. → Body whorl with spiral threads. Immature specimens have a thin toothless lip. Adult lip thick with about five very small teeth. Yellowish to very dark caramel or chestnut color with irregular white markings. Pam Piombino found the two shells shown enlarged. (18 mm)
Distribution: Rare, northern Gulf of Suez and South Sinai.

Zafra savignyi (Moazzo, 1939)
Endemic
3–4.5 mm. Smoothly biconical, low white axial ribs on all whorls. Body whorl with fine wavery axial chestnut lines. Lip and columella smooth. Color caramel, beige, or white. (3.7 mm)
Distribution: Locally abundant in the northern Gulf of Suez.

Family NASSARIIDAE

The common name for shells in this family is mud snails. The shells are usually compact and have strongly sculptured surfaces. The animals are usually carnivorous; most of them live in shallow water in places with some silt or mud. It is possible, especially just before sundown, to see them creeping along the muddy bottom at the edge of the water, looking like a common garden snail.

Cyclope neritea (Linnaeus, 1758)
10–11 mm. → Unusually flat, ovoid, and smooth. Columella curved, two small teeth, one at the top and one at the bottom. No umbilicus. Thin shiny callus on base. Brown or beige. (11 mm)
Distribution: A Mediterranean species common in Lake Timsah. Not found in the Gulf of Suez.

Nassarius castus (Gould, 1850)
22–30 mm. → Rounded axial ribs cut by a deeply incised line below the suture. This produces a little knob at the top of each rib. Several more strong incised spiral lines on the lower part of the body whorl. Brown, orange, or pink, with a white line a little below the knobs. (24 mm)
Distribution: Uncommon, but found in all areas.
Notes: The body whorl is never cancellate.

Nassarius conoidalis labordei Mari, 1925
25–30 mm. → Strong, heavy shell covered with distinct square or oblong blocks, clear interspaces. (28 mm)
Distribution: Uncommon, the Gulf of Suez, Hurghada–Safaga area, Dahab.

actual size

x2

subadult

x2

Pyrene flava

x5

actual size

Zafra savignyi

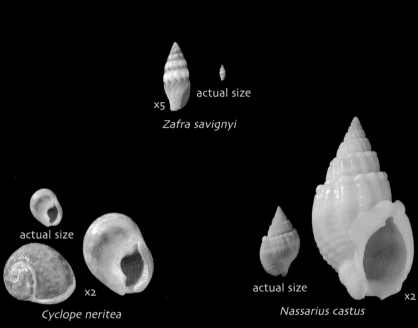

actual size

x2

Cyclope neritea

actual size

x2

Nassarius castus

actual size

x2

Nassarius conoidalis labordei

Nassarius coronatus (Bruguière, 1789)

21–27 mm. → Body whorl smooth, crown of nodules just below the suture. Striae at base of body whorl only. (27 mm)
Distribution: Uncommon, Dahab, Hurghada, and silty areas in the far south. Not found in the Gulf of Suez.

Nassarius dekkeri Kool, 2001

6–10 mm. → Glossy white shell, strong axial ribs. Some specimens have a pointed nodule at the top of each rib of the body whorl. Some with weak spiral striae but not cancellate. May or may not have irregular or spiral brown markings. (10 mm)
Distribution: Northern Gulf of Aqaba, occasionally locally abundant, otherwise rare.
Notes: Named after the Dutch conchologist Henk Dekker.

Nassarius erythraeus (Issel, 1869)

6–8 mm. Regular rounded axial ribs with about seven tiny spiral threads. Nodulose, slightly prickly appearance. Light creamy caramel color, some specimens banded. → Aperture never lirate. Lip thickened, dentate. (7.5 mm)
Distribution: Uncommon, northern Gulf of Aqaba and Hurghada–Safaga area.
Notes: See *N. neoproductus.*

Nassarius fenistratus (Marrat, 1877)

Nassarius albescens gemmuliferus of some authors
6–27 mm. → Fine, tight, irregular subcancellate sculpture. → Very small nodules all over the shell, more regular on the upper whorls. First row of nodules below the suture may be slightly stronger. Pattern variable, mostly white with irregular brown markings. Fully mature shells have a small parietal shield. (16 mm)
Distribution: Abundant in the Gulf of Aqaba, common in the south.

Nassarius obvelatus (Deshayes in Laborde, 1834)

Nassarius arcularia plicatus of some authors
14–27 mm. → Giant white callus. Sharp oblique ribs, incised spiral lines. (23 mm)
Distribution: Occasional in the Gulf of Aqaba, common from Safaga to Shalatein.

Nassarius neoproductus Kool & Dekker, 2007

9–12 mm. Moderately elongate shell. Numerous rounded axial ribs crossed by minute spiral threadlets. Strong chestnut brown band on the lower half of the dorsum of the body whorl, some with one or two additional spiral lines of dots on the upper whorls. → Aperture lirate, lip thickened, appears dentate. (12 mm)
Distribution: Moderately common in the northern Gulf of Aqaba, occasional in the northern Gulf of Suez and the Hurghada–Safaga area.
Notes: *N. erythraeus* has very similar shape and sculpture, but is usually light caramel yellow all over or may have darker spiral bands on the upper half of each whorl. It never grows larger than 8 mm. Its denticles never extend back into the aperture.

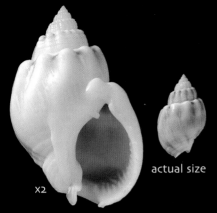

x2

actual size

Nassarius coronatus

x2

actual size

Nassarius dekkeri

actual size

x2

x2

juvenile
actual size

Nassarius fenistratus

actual size

x2

subadult
Nassarius obvelatus

x2

actual size

Nassarius erythraeus5

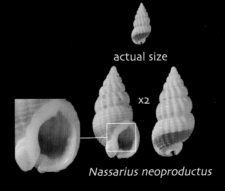

actual size

x2

Nassarius neoproductus

Family MELONGENIDAE
Volema paradisiaca nodosa (Lamarck, 1822)
14–55 mm. Smooth surface, ring of nodules at shoulder, → light and dark spiral stripes on body whorl which show in the aperture. Juveniles orange-caramel in color with white tubercles and fine spiral striae. (38 mm)
Distribution: Common in the Gulf of Suez and all the way south to Shalatein.

Family FASCIOLARIIDAE
All members of this family are predatory carnivores. Those in the genera *Fusinus* and *Pleuroploca* have a long anterior canal. These are sometimes called Spindle Shells on account of their shape.

Fusinus verrucosus (Gmelin, 1791)
Endemic
6–110 mm. Spindle shaped, but extremely variable in length, width, whorl shape, and relative length of spindle to entire shell. Numerous spiral cords on the exterior. → Columella smooth, no folds. Shell variably beige, sometimes with yellowish or ivory areas, small brown or chestnut dots or dashes. Aperture lirate, color ranging from white to brown to intense purple. (110 mm)
Distribution: Common in all areas.
Notes: The great variability in shape has caused taxonomists to attempt to name different shapes. I studied a large number of specimens from the Egyptian Red Sea and found no consistent structural break between various shapes, and so I consider them all one species. In parts of the Gulf of Suez purple-mouthed specimens predominate.

actual size

x2

actual size

juvenile

Volema paradisiaca nodosa

Fusinus verrucosus

Latirus polygonus (Gmelin, 1791)

65–99 mm. Heavy shell, → weak folds in the aperture on the columella, these barely visible because they are mostly inside the opening. Outline of whorls never rounded. Exterior appearance similar to the angular specimens of *Fusinus verrucosus* (above). (99 mm)

Distribution: Rare, all areas.

Notes: Because the folds are so hard to see it is easy to mistake this shell for *Fusinus verrucosus*.

Turrilatirus turritus (Gmelin, 1791)

12–33 mm. Stubby fusiform, never slim or elongate, short siphonal canal. Dark brown slightly raised spiral cords covering the entire caramel-colored shell. (28 mm)

Distribution: Common in the Gulf of Aqaba and across South Sinai. Occasional from Hurghada to Quseir.

Notes: The shell is often covered with white encrustation, even while alive. In totally encrusted shells look for broad rounded ribs on the body whorl. Sometimes the brown spiral lines show through the aperture.

Pleuroploca trapezium (Linnaeus, 1758)

90–120 mm. Large shell, smooth surface. Single spiral row of blunt tubercles at the widest point on each whorl. Columella with folds. (90 mm)

Distribution: Rare, Gulf of Aqaba, Hurghada, Wadi Lahmi area.

Latirus polygonus

Turrilatirus turritus

Pleuroploca trapezium

Family TURBINELLIDAE
Vasum turbinellus (Linnaeus, 1758)
32–70 mm. Heavy, conical in shape (like the vase, 'vasum,' in its name), long dramatic spines at shoulder may be straight or curved. → About four folds on the columella. Aperture white, yellow, or orange. (57 mm)
Distribution: Increasingly rare, occasional in Gulf of Aqaba, South Sinai, Hurghada Reefs and Wadi Lahmi.
Notes: V. turbinellus requires a habitat containing both sand and rocks. It preys on sea worms found in this specialized environment. It sometimes creeps around on the sand in very shallow water during the day. If you see one give it plenty of room to go about its business. Very short-spined or worn specimens bear some resemblance to the murid *Thais savignyi*, but that species never has folds on the columella.

Family OLIVIDAE
Olive shells have a smooth, shiny surface. The animal is both carnivorous and a scavenger. Sometimes you can see it on mud or sandflats at low tide, even at midday, pushing its way through the sand. The mantle covers most of the shell and keeps it from getting scratched.

Do not touch it or poke it; just enjoy watching it quietly looking for something to eat among the sand grains.

Ancilla eburnea (Deshayes, 1830)
Endemic to the Gulf of Suez
6–19 mm. → Slightly stubby, spire glazed over. Large specimens with slightly enlarged posterior canal, often stained burnt orange. Shell caramel or white. (19 mm)
Distribution: Common in the Gulf of Suez. Never elsewhere.
Notes: See *A. lineolata* below.

Ancilla lineolata (A. Adams, 1853)
8–12.5 mm. → Relatively elongate, spire glazed, usually with axial lines on the body whorl. These may be in varying shades of beige, butterscotch, caramel, and white. It may also be all white. (12 mm)
Distribution: Moderately common, all regions.
Notes: The large stubby somewhat heavy *A. eburnea* is found only in the Gulf of Suez and immediately south of it. *A. lineolata* in our area never reaches the large size of *A. eburnea*. Specimens of the two species under 12 mm may be indistinguishable. Both white and caramel specimens are found throughout the Egyptian Red Sea. The large Suez form may result from environmental factors rather than a separate species. Further research is needed.

Oliva bulbosa (Röding, 1798)
Bulbous Olive Shell
24–38 mm. As its name implies, *O. bulbosa* is bulbous and shaped like an olive. Lovely patterns of many lines forming stripes and zigzags. (35 mm)
Distribution: Locally common in the south, rare elsewhere.

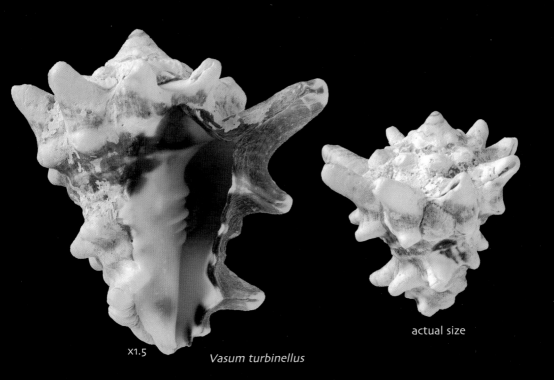

x1.5   *Vasum turbinellus*

actual size

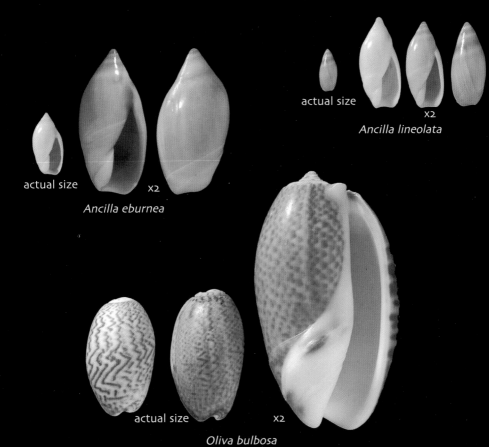

actual size   x2

Ancilla eburnea

actual size   x2

Ancilla lineolata

actual size   x2

Oliva bulbosa

Family HARPIDAE
Harpa amouretta (Röding, 1798)
8.5–42 mm. Unmistakable pattern and sculpture. The only *Harpa* in the Egyptian Red Sea. The spire is covered with small sharp points, like a many-layered crown. Despite the delicacy of its appearance, it is carnivorous, its favorite food being small crabs. When it finds a crab it covers it with a sticky mucous which nearly paralyzes the crab, then eats it at its leisure. *H. amouretta* prefers clean coral sand to hide under. It never lives in shallow water and sometimes lives on the sand in very deep water, up to 200 m. Because of this and its relative heaviness it is not commonly carried up onto the shore. (34 mm)
Distribution: Gulf of Aqaba, South Sinai, and south to Wadi Lahmi. Not found in the Gulf of Suez.

Family CYSTISCIDAE
These are all very small shells similar to those in the family Marginellidae, from which they have been recently separated.

Gibberula savignyi (Issel, 1869)
3–6.5 mm. This tiny, glossy white shell is cone shaped, has a low spire, and about four folds on the columella. (6.5 mm)
Distribution: Abundant throughout the Gulf of Suez.
Notes: G. sueziensis (Issel, 1869) is much smaller, never larger than 2.5 mm. Common in the northern Gulf of Suez. Not illustrated.

Family MITRIDAE
The miter shells are elongate and often beautifully colored. They live in sand.

Domiporta carnicolor (Reeve, 1844)
15–25 mm. Perfect specimens have a glassy dark pink protoconch. Fine spiral cords with tiny light chestnut squarish spots on a white or light cream background. → Aperture white with two pink bands corresponding to the exterior chestnut patches. (25 mm)
Distribution: Uncommon, white coral sand near reefs from Hurghada across to the Straits of Tiran.

Domiporta filaris (Linnaeus, 1771)
14–18 mm. → Raised spiral chestnut threads or filaments. The name *filaris* has the same Latin root as the English word 'filament.' (18 mm)
Distribution: Rare, around reefs in the Safaga area.

Domiporta granatina (Lamarck, 1811)
30–49 mm. → Broken or dashed chestnut markings along narrow raised spiral threads. (48 mm)
Distribution: Rare, South Sinai to Quseir.
Notes: The largest *Domiporta* in the Egyptian Red Sea.

actual size

juvenile

x2

x2

actual size

Harpa amouretta

actual size

actual size   x3

Gibberula savignyi

actual size

x2

Domiporta carnicolor

actual size

Domiporta filaris

x2

x2

actual size

Domiporta granatina

Mitra aurora floridula Sowerby, 1874

10–33 mm. Moderately elongate shell with tightly spaced flat spiral cords, punctuate grooves between. Chestnut to dark brown small white patches. (32 mm)
Distribution: Uncommon, Gulf of Aqaba and Hurghada–Safaga area, coral sand.

Mitra bovei Kiener, 1838

29–38 mm. → Intricate pattern and, in some specimens, small protrusions at the top of the later whorls. Medium brown and light bluish-gray and white. Faded specimens may appear orange-ish. Subfossil specimens are also found. (36 mm)
Distribution: Infrequent, all regions.
Notes: One of the few miters found in the Gulf of Suez. Considered rare in its western Indian Ocean range, but in Egypt it is more common than most other Mitridae.

Mitra cucumerina Lamarck, 1811

9–20 mm. → Broader in the middle than many other miters. Strong spiral cords. Dramatic bright red-orange color with an imprecise white spiral band on the body whorl. Apex may also be white. (9 mm)
Distribution: Infrequent, Hurghada–Safaga area, Gulf of Aqaba.
Notes: Specimen pictured is subadult. Adults are broader across and have a larger white area. Unfortunately no suitable adult specimen was available to photograph.

Mitra fasciolaris Deshayes in Laborde, 1834

22–25 mm.→ Smooth and glossy. Inside of lip finely crenulate. Light tan above, chestnut below. (22 mm)
Distribution: Very rare, Hurghada–Safaga area.

Mitra ferruginea Lamarck, 1811

16–19.5 mm. → Dark brown axial pattern broken by a broad clear white spiral band. Spiral cords are angular, not flat on top. Broad grooves between cords. Requires clean coral sand and deeper water. (19.5 mm)
Distribution: Rare, Gulf of Aqaba, Hurghada reefs.

Mitra litterata Lamarck, 1811

10–20 mm. → Smooth surface, stubby shape. White with brown or black irregular markings loosely arranged in spiral bands. Lip thickened centrally. (18 mm)
Distribution: Moderately common, Gulf of Aqaba, South Sinai, and from Hurghada all the way south.
Notes: The pericostracum is yellow which gives a newly dead shell a surprising golden sheen.

Mitra rueppellii Reeve, 1844

27–32 mm. → Strong, wide, rounded spiral cords with a narrow space between. Dark caramel, white apex. (31 mm)
Distribution: Gulf of Aqaba, Hurghada–Safaga area.

x2 actual size

Mitra aurora floridula

x2 actual size

Mitra bovei

x2 actual size

Mitra cucumerina

x2 actual size

Mitra fasciolaris

x2 actual size

Mitra ferruginea

x2 actual size

Mitra litterata

actual size

x2

Mitra rueppellii

Mitra typha Reeve, 1845
8–12 mm.→ Elongate, smooth small shell. Glossy white, ivory or caramel. Very faint spiral striae, stronger basally, about two weak folds on columella. (11 mm)
Distribution: Uncommon, very intermittent, Hurghada–Safaga area.
Notes: This is the smallest species of *Mitra* in the Red Sea.

Pterygia crenulata (Gmelin, 1791)
19.5–21.5 mm. Cylindrical shell covered with fine evenly spaced incised lines. Aperture runs about four-fifths of the length of the shell. Around eight sharp folds on the columella. Micro crenulations on lip. Glossy caramel color with white markings. (21.5 mm)
Distribution: Rare, Gulf of Aqaba, Quseir.

Scabricola fissurata (Lamarck, 1811)
30–50 mm. Elongate, glossy pinkish-beige shell with netted (reticulate) white pattern. (50 mm)
Distribution: Rare, Gulf of Aqaba.

Scabricola potensis (Montrouzier, 1858)
18 mm. Outline oval with pointed ends. Smoothly conical spire. Spire comprises about one-third of the total length. Spiral threads, regularly punctuate spiral grooves. About six folds on the columella. Beige or brown and white. (18 mm)
Distribution: Very rare, near offshore reefs, Hurghada–Safaga area.

Family COSTELLARIIDAE
Vexillum alauda (Sowerby, 1874)
16–22 mm. → Gracefully elongate, caramel- to toffee-colored spots on the raised axial ribs. (21 mm)
Distribution: Moderately common from Hurghada south.

Vexillum amabile (Reeve, 1845)
7–10.5 mm. Small, glossy shell, small axial ribs, light and dark spiral bands, always multicolored. (10.5 mm)
Distribution: Abundant in the northern Gulf of Aqaba. Occasional in the far south. Rare elsewhere.

Vexillum angustissimum (E.A. Smith, 1903)
9–13 mm. The species name of this elongate shell means 'the most narrow' and it describes it well. Very narrow, closely spaced raised axial ribs, spiral threadlets in the interspaces. Color highly variable. (9.5 mm)
Distribution: Rare, northern Gulf of Aqaba.

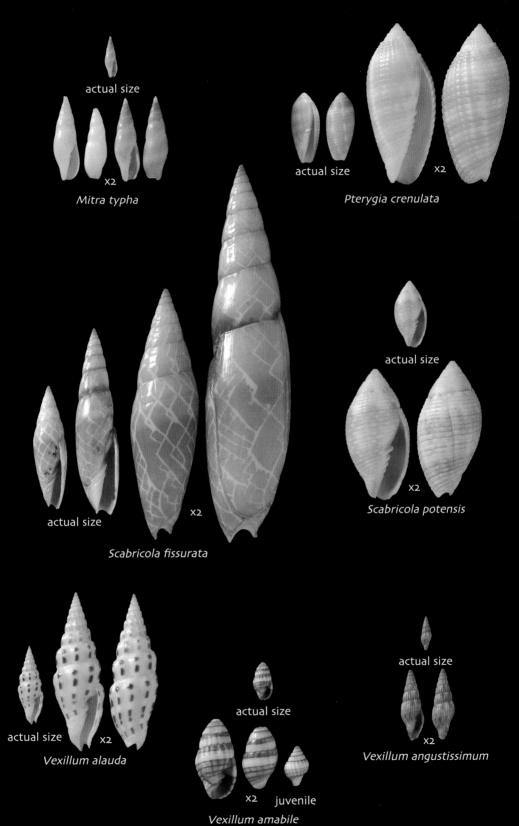

actual size

Mitra typha

x2

actual size

Pterygia crenulata

x2

actual size

Scabricola fissurata

x2

actual size

Scabricola potensis

x2

actual size

Vexillum alauda

x2

actual size

Vexillum amabile

x2

juvenile

actual size

Vexillum angustissimum

x2

Vexillum aureolatum (Reeve, 1845)

12–23 mm. → Golden color, one jagged white spiral line. Sunken spaces between raised cancellate sculpture. (22 mm)
Distribution: Rare, Hurghada and South Sinai.

Vexillum blandulum Turner, 1997

14–19 mm. Graceful elongate form and pleasing sculpture with slightly sinuous axial ribs. No coronations or color markings. Five folds on the columella, lowest very weak. (17 mm)
Distribution: Rare, Gulf of Aqaba, South Sinai, and Hurghada–Safaga area.

Vexillum consanguineum (Reeve, 1845)

Vexillum pardalis (Küster, 1840) of some authors.
8–18 mm. → Notably broad in the middle relative to its height. Upper whorls with weak axial ribs, but otherwise smooth. Base plain caramel or brown. The upper area usually predominately white with axial bars of the base color. Medial area with irregular patterns of both colors. (16 mm)
Distribution: Rare, Gulf of Aqaba and Safaga.
Notes: A last-minute personal communication from Henk Dekker indicates that he and Hans Turner believe that the valid name for this species is *Vexillum pardalis* (Küster, 1840) and that *Mitra consanguinea* Reeve, 1845 is a synonym.

Vexillum depexum (Deshayes in Laborde, 1834)

Endemic
11–17 mm. Numerous closely spaced, low, rounded axial ribs on upper whorls becoming obsolete on the body whorl. Upper two-thirds of the shell glossy white with small random irregular patches of medium to dark chestnut. Basal third chestnut, usually with three spiral rows of tiny white dots, may also have small white patches. No incised spiral striae. (13.5 mm)
Distribution: Occasional to rare in the Gulf of Aqaba and from Hurghada south.

Vexillum echinatum (A. Adams, 1853)

Vexillum concentricum (Reeve, 1844) of some authors
16–31.5 mm. → Short little spikes poking out from the axial ribs at the shoulders of the lower whorls. (30 mm)
Distribution: Relatively common in the Gulf of Aqaba, South Sinai, and the Hurghada–Safaga area. Known from Quseir, but not farther south.

Vexillum intermedium (Kiener, 1838)

39–55 mm. Largest, most dramatically colored *Vexillum* in the Egyptian Red Sea. Colors vary. (46 mm)
Distribution: Rare, south of Marsa Alam only.

actual size

x2

Vexillum aureolatum

actual size

x2

Vexillum blandulum

actual size

x2

Vexillum consanguineum

x2

actual size

Vexillum depexum

actual size

x2

Vexillum echinatum

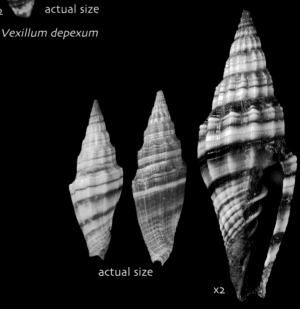

actual size

x2

Vexillum intermedium

Vexillum infaustum (Reeve, 1845)

10 mm. Small shell, covered with tightly spaced rounded axial ribs. Body whorl with medial spiral band of orange-brown, shows also at sutures. (10 mm)
Distribution: Rare, known from Gulf of Aqaba to Safaga.

Vexillum leucozonias (Deshayes in Laborde, 1834)

9–15 mm. White spiral band on caramel, brown, or black shell. Moderately spaced axial ribs cut by grooves between tightly spaced spiral threads. (15 mm)
Distribution: Rare, Northern Gulf of Aqaba, Hurghada–Safaga area.

Vexillum lucidum (Reeve, 1845)

21 mm. → Very strong, almost sharp, tightly spaced spiral cords over strong axial ribs. Upper two-thirds ivory, lower third dark brown. (21 mm)
Distribution: Rare, Marsa Alam south only.

Vexillum osiridis (Issel, 1869)

19–23 mm. → Coronations on every whorl. Dark brown to dark gray spiral on body whorl, light gray above. Spiral cords on lower third, none above dark spiral band. (22 mm)
Distribution: Rare, Gulf of Aqaba, Marsa Alam area.

Vexillum puerile (Cooke, 1885)

4.5–7 mm. → Tiny, light blue-gray or beige shell. Body whorl sometimes with darker band. (7 mm)
Distribution: Common in the northern Gulf of Aqaba.
Notes: There are many Turridae of this size, but they have sharper and more detailed sculpture. *V. puerile* of course does not have a turrid notch at the top of the outer lip.

Vexillum revelatum (Melvill, 1899)

Vexillum pacificum (Reeve, 1848) of some authors
11–19 mm. Smooth-feeling surface, may have nodules at shoulder, but no strong axial ribs on body whorl. May be all white or with broad light brown flecked or mottled band around the body whorl. Pink protoconch. (15.5 mm)
Distribution: Moderately common in all areas except the Gulf of Suez.

Vexillum tusum (Reeve, 1845)

6–10 mm. Smooth outline, nearly biconical. → Upper whorls with many tightly spaced axial ribs. Ribs weaker on the body whorl, all cut by fine incised spiral lines. Upper whorls white and brown or caramel. Lower portion darker color. (9.5 mm)
Distribution: Moderately common, found in all areas except the Gulf of Suez.
Notes: The incised spiral striae are important for distinguishing this shell from *V. depexum* (page 120) which has spiral rows of raised dots instead.

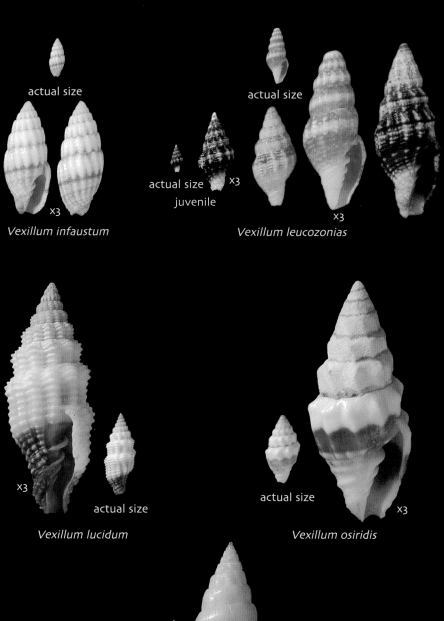

actual size

actual size

actual size
juvenile

x3

x3

Vexillum infaustum

Vexillum leucozonias

x3

actual size

Vexillum lucidum

actual size

x3

Vexillum osiridis

actual size

actual size

x3

Vexillum revelatum

actual size

x3

Vexillum puerile

x3

Vexillum tusum

Family CONIDAE

As the name suggests, cone shells are cone shaped. The aperture is almost always long and narrow. Many have beautiful colors and patterns.

Cones possess a harpoon-like appendage which is equipped with poisonous barbs. The toxin kills the prey and can cause intense pain and serious illness in humans. Deaths have been reported. Be smart: look but do not touch.

Conus arenatus aequipunctatus Dautzenberg, 1937
Sand Cone
15–63 mm. → Speckled with tiny brown dots, coronations on spire. (42 mm)
Distribution: Rare in Gulf of Suez, common in all other areas.

Conus aulicus Linnaeus, 1758
46 mm. Smoothly curved outline, → shoulders not broader than middle. Fine weak spiral sculpture on entire shell. (46 mm)
Distribution: Very rare, south only.
Notes: Variable tent or mountain pattern similar to *C. quasimagnificus*, but shoulder never as broad. DANGEROUS.

Conus emaciatus Reeve, 1849
50 mm. → Fine spiral ridges cover the entire surface. Shoulder slightly rounded, ridges continue on spire. White or very pale beige, with or without lighter band medially.
Distribution: Rare, south of Marsa Alam only. (50 mm)

Conus flavidus Lamarck, 1810
17–58 mm. → Spire always eroded. Light orange-tan, subtle axial streaks of darker and lighter tones with two somewhat blurry white spiral bands, one at the shoulder and one medially. Tip of base dark purple. (60 mm)
Distribution: Not found in the Gulf of Suez, common in all other areas.
Notes: This species is unusual in that it often has some of the rough brown protective covering (pericostracum) still attached (see the shell on the far right).

Conus generalis maldivus Hwass in Bruguière, 1792
35–67 mm. → Spire high, stepped or smooth, outline concave. Shell slim, caramel and white with brown spiral lines. (48 mm)
Distribution: Moderately common, Dahab, Hurghada Reefs, Hurghada–Safaga area.
Notes: See *C. namocanus* on pages 126–27.

Conus arenatus aequipunctatus

Conus aulicus

Conus emaciatus

Conus flavidus

Conus generalis maldivus

Conus geographus Linnaeus, 1758
22–86 mm. → Aperture unusually wide for a cone, shell fragile. (86 mm)
Distribution: Uncommon, Gulf of Aqaba, Straits of Gubal south to Ras Banas.
Notes: VERY DANGEROUS—DEATHS HAVE BEEN REPORTED. You should never touch any living shell; don't go anywhere near this one. Fossil specimens of this species are abundant in the desolate raised coral flats near Ras Ghaliib.

Conus miliaris Hwass in Bruguière, 1792
13–23 mm. → Exceptional pattern of zigzags, chevrons. Spire with coronations. Color white to orange to toffee. (18 mm)
Distribution: Infrequent, Gulf of Aqaba, South Sinai, and Hurghada south to the Marsa Alam area.

Conus namocanus Hwass in Bruguière, 1792
25–67 mm. → Spire dome shaped, eroded. Shoulder slightly rounded. Pattern shown is typical for the Egyptian Red Sea. (67 mm)
Distribution: Rare, Hurghada to Wadi Lahmi.
Notes: Color patterns of *C. namocanus* and *C. generalis maldivus* in Egypt are often similar. Spire outline of latter concave, *C. namocanus* never with concave spire.

Conus nigropunctatus Sowerby II, 1857
14–45 mm. → Fine spiral lines with brown or very dark brown dashes, alternating with white ones. Large irregular dark and light patches, and sometimes little white cloudy patches. Never with coronations. (33 mm)
Distribution: Common around Marsa Alam, and in the Gulf of Aqaba. Not found in the Gulf of Suez.
Notes: C. taeniatus has spiral dashes but not the dark and light patches.

Conus nussatella Linnaeus, 1758
22–47 mm. → Slender body, pattern of tiny brown or caramel dots arranged in spiral rows. (45 mm)
Distribution: Not found in the Gulf of Suez, infrequent in all other regions.

Conus parvatus sharmiensis Wils, 1986
6–18.5 mm. → Orange-brown spots, variously arranged, base dark purple. Other features variable. Shoulder smooth or slightly coronated. Aperture purple, white, or both. (17 mm)
Distribution: Common in all areas except the Gulf of Suez.
Notes: Spire never high as in *C. tessulatus*. See below.

Conus miliaris

Conus geographus

Conus nigropunctatus

Conus namocanus

Conus nussatella

Conus parvatus sharmiensis

Conus quasimagnificus Da Motta, 1982
Conus pennaceus Born, 1778 of some authors
Tent Cone
22–55 mm. → White flags, pennants, mountains, or tents on dark background. Broad shoulders. (53 mm)
Distribution: Common in the Gulf of Aqaba, rare elsewhere.
Notes: Very dangerous toxin (see also *C. textile neovicarius*, page 130). DANGEROUS! If you see one, do NOT attempt to touch it; take a photograph instead.

Conus quercinus Lightfoot, 1786
Synonym *Conus akabensis* Sowerby, 1887
28–62 mm. → Large heavy cone, white, cream, or beige, with virtually no pattern, some with fine brown spiral lines. Pericostracum dark brown or black. Base same color as body. (62 mm)
Distribution: Rare, Gulf of Aqaba and far south.

Conus rattus Hwass in Bruguière, 1792
17–39 mm. → Aperture violet, shell glossy brown to violet with light bluish cloudy patterns at the shoulder and a faint light spiral band submedially. Spire often worn or encrusted. (26 mm)
Distribution: Locally common in the far south, rare elsewhere.

Conus sanguinolentus Quoy & Gaimard, 1834
14–38 mm. → Plain medium chestnut shell with white coronations on the spire. Spiral rows of beads on the lower half. Aperture purple or white. (25 mm)
Distribution: Common in all areas except the Gulf of Suez.

Conus striatellus Link, 1807
31–49 mm. Spire whorls canalized, pattern similar to *C. striatus* (below), but → shoulders straight. (32 mm)
Distribution: Rare, Hurghada south.
Notes: Probably lives in deeper water.

Conus striatus Linnaeus, 1758
31–87 mm. Big heavy shell. Spire whorls canalized. → Shoulders slant inward. Whitish with patches and zigzags of darker color composed of very fine spiral lines of alternating dark and light (probably what gives it its name: 'striatus' in Latin means striped or striated). Aperture wider at base. (66 mm)
Distribution: Occasional in the Gulf of Aqaba and Straits of Tiran. Locally common from Marsa Alam south.
Notes: VERY DANGEROUS.

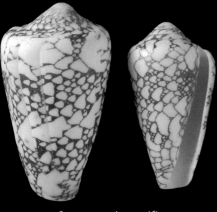

Conus quasimagnificus

Conus quercinus

Conus rattus

Conus sanguinolentus

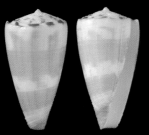

Conus striatellus

Conus striatus

Conus taeniatus Hwass in Bruguière, 1792

12–34 mm. → Spiral bands of strong alternating dark and light dashes on white or gray. Never with coronations. (33 mm)

Distribution: Common. Northern Gulf of Aqaba all the way to Shalatein. Very rare in the Gulf of Suez.

Notes: A smaller cone with a similar but finer, weaker pattern and coronations might be *Conus coronatus* Gmelin, 1791. Not illustrated. Rare. South of Marsa Alam only.

Conus tessulatus Born, 1778

Orange Spotted Cone

19–72 mm. The common name tells it all → shiny white with orange spots. Basal tip purple. Largest shell shown still has its pericostracum. (51 mm)

Distribution: Common northern Gulf of Aqaba south to Wadi Gimaal. Not found in the Gulf of Suez.

Notes: While diving you might see pure white shells in excellent condition of exactly the same shape and sculpture, as shown in the two all white shells below the orange-spotted ones. Are they albino variations of *C. tessulatus* or a different species? I wish I knew!

Conus textile neovicarius Da Motta, 1982

Subspecies endemic to the Red Sea

Textile Cone

15–75 mm. → Four colors: white tents, outlines in brown, gold-colored patches with dark brown wiggly lines running vertically through them. (73 mm)

Distribution: Occasional in the Gulf of Aqaba across South Sinai and south to Marsa Alam. Common from Marsa Alam to Wadi Lahmi. Not found in the Gulf of Suez.

Notes: Never touch this shell, even on the beach. It kills fish with its harpoon, and the sting can cause terrible pain and even death in humans. The 'harpoon' is long and can reach behind the broad end of the shell, so there is no safe place for touching or holding it. EXTREMELY DANGEROUS! You are unlikely to see a live *C. textile* during the day because they hide under coral rubble and come out at night to hunt. You should never lift up stones or coral blocks in the water as large numbers of creatures live under them. Most cannot hurt you, but there is no reason to destroy their home.

Conus vexillum sumatrensis Hwass in Bruguière, 1792

25–83 mm. Very large and heavy. Shoulder and medial band white, two very broad caramel bands, → strong wobbly dark brown axial markings. (80 mm)

Distribution: Occasional in the Gulf of Aqaba and from Marsa Alam south.

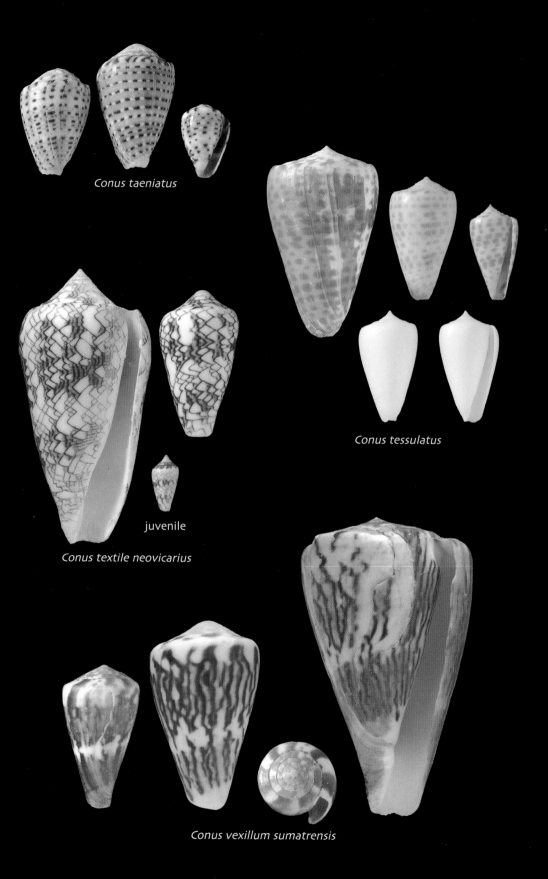

Conus taeniatus

Conus tessulatus

Conus textile neovicarius

juvenile

Conus vexillum sumatrensis

Family TURRIDAE

Turrids are related to the Terebridae and the Conidae. All three families are carnivores and have the ability to inject poison into their prey. Turridae are unique in having an empty slot near the top of their outer lip. This is called the 'turrid notch,' and when the animal is alive the posterior or exhalent siphon extends through it. The lip is fragile in many species, so this whole area may be damaged.

   Although many species are reported to live in the Red Sea, most are never seen on the beach because they live in very deep water. Those on beaches are very small and likely to be overlooked. These tend to have intricate sculpture, so looking for them is rewarding if you are patient and have a good magnifying glass or hand lens.

Eucithara coronata (Hinds, 1843)

7–14.5 mm. → Upper ends of axial ribs rise above the suture line, forming coronations. Usually all white, sometimes with a brown line or patch below the suture. (14.5 mm)
Distribution: Common in all areas, occasionally abundant.
Notes: There are many members of the genus *Eucithara*, most of them small, white, and difficult to separate. Only *E. coronata* has the coronations for which it is named.

Gemmula monilifera (Pease, 1861)

Synonym *Gemmula amabilis* (Weinkauff, 1875)
17–22 mm. Strongly beaded or nodulose spiral cord at the broadest point in each whorl terminates in the turrid notch. Apex darker brown than shell. (22 mm)
Distribution: Rare, quiet sandy areas of South Sinai.

Inquisitor sp.

45 mm. Elongate, many rounded whorls with undulating axial ribs. Aperture and notch large, lip thin. Fine spiral cords cover shell. (45 mm)
Distribution: Very rare, far south only, muddy habitat.

Lienardia rubicunda (A.A. Gould, 1860)

4–6 mm. → Dusty pink with one or two white spiral lines. (6 mm)
Distribution: Locally common, instantly recognizable, Hurghada and Wadi Lahmi.

Lophiotoma acuta (Perry, 1811)

29–39 mm. → Brown dots on the spiral cord set in the sunken area between the strongest, most protruding cords. (39 mm)
Distribution: Rare, Gulf of Aqaba and Wadi Gimaal.

Lophiotoma brevicaudata (Reeve, 1843)

18–28 mm. → Many fine raised threads, darker than the beige shell itself. Siphonal canal is usually a very dark brown. (28 mm)
Distribution: Generally rare, but occasionally a concentration may be seen. Coral sand bays, far south only.

actual size

x3

Eucithara coronata

x2   actual size

Gemmula monilifera

actual size

x3

Lienardia rubicunda

actual size

x2

Inquisitor sp.

x2   actual size

Lophiotoma acuta

x2   actual size

Lophiotoma brevicaudata

Lophiotoma cingulifera erythraea (Weinkauff, 1875)
Endemic
12–44 mm. → A 'belt' of fine paired brown dashes. (29 mm)
Distribution: Common in the Hurghada–Safaga area. Occasional in South Sinai and quiet sandy areas in the south.
Notes: This subspecies is endemic and is the most commonly found turrid in the Egyptian Red Sea.

Lophiotoma indica (Röding, 1798)
80 mm. → Very large shell, long spindle, and angular upper whorls.
Distribution: Very rare, Ras Sudr, Gulf of Suez only.
Notes: Possibly subfossil.

Tritonoturris cumingi (Powys, 1835)
32 mm. → Very lightweight, thin, and fragile. Neat-looking vertical narrow ribs with wide interspaces crossed by very fine widely spaced spiral threads. Spindle with obliquely spiral threads. (32 mm)
Distribution: Very rare. Pam Piombino found the figured specimen on a hotel beach in Hurghada.

Turridrupa sp.
Endemic
5–21.5 mm. → Spiral cord with single line of strong dark brown dots or dashes alternating with spaces of the body color (beige or white). Siphonal canal short. (21.5 mm)
Distribution: Rare, Hurghada–Safaga area, quiet bays farther south.
Notes: Apparently in more southern parts of the Red Sea there is a violet stain on the aperture or the siphonal canal, but that does not usually occur on Egyptian specimens. The species is known by many different names. It appears that it is having an identity crisis and may be referred to as simply *Turridrupa* sp. Research is ongoing.

Turris garnonsii Reeve, 1845
31 mm. → Very long spindle, spiral sculpture at broadest point is triangular in profile, with another similar but weaker cord above it but still below the suture. Larger dots than any other Red Sea turrid. (31 mm)
Distribution: Rare, Gulf of Aqaba.

actual size

x2

Lophiotoma cingulifera erythraea

actual size

x3

Tritonoturris cumingi

Lophiotoma indica

x2

actual size

Turridrupa sp.

actual size

x2

Turris garnonsii

Family TEREBRIDAE

Terebrids, like cones and turrids, have a poisonous gland. They use it to paralyze their prey. They usually live buried in the sand except for the tip of their long shell. They in turn are the prey of larger creatures, and it is very common to find shells that have been damaged by a predator but the animal inside survived and has lived to repair its shell. The shells are long and narrow, usually with a shiny surface, and most are very pretty.

Please resist the temptation to pick them up. The animal is capable of retreating a long way inside the shell, and there is no operculum (solid door), so it appears empty. It is impossible to keep them alive in your resort room, they smell terrible when they die, and it is extremely difficult to remove the dead animal. So the dead animal and shell end up in the rubbish instead of continuing its natural life in the sea.

Acus crenulata (Linnaeus, 1758)
31–97 mm. → Spiral row of widely spaced white nodules just below the suture, short brown axial lines between the nodules. (94 mm)
Distribution: Uncommon, Gulf of Aqaba to Shams Alam.

Acus dimidiata (Linnaeus, 1758)
91–120 mm. → Distinctive orange and white pattern. (110 mm)
Distribution: Rare, Gulf of Aqaba, Hurghada to Wadi Lahmi.
Notes: Prior to the development of coastal resorts in Egypt it was not uncommon to see these beautiful creatures on the seabed in calm areas. Humans walking on the seabed are the biggest threat to all terebrids as our feet dislodge them, thus exposing them to natual predators and unthinking human collecting. I have not seen a specimen *A. dimidiata* since 1996.

Acus maculata (Linnaeus, 1758)
48–170 mm. → Large, and very heavy for its size, light brown with white lines and very dark brown spots. (160 mm)
Distribution: Uncommon, offshore reefs from Hurghada to Wadi Lahmi.
Notes: Dead shells of *Acus maculata* under water are always occupied by a certain large species of hermit crab with its own role to play in its environment. Do not disturb it.

Cinguloterebra insalli (Bratcher & R. D. Burch, 1976)
Endemic
43 mm. Very slim, elongate, yellow-orange color. → Strong band of fused pale beads just below suture. Below it a band of smaller separate beads, then two spiral rows of flat rectangles and just above the suture a band of tiny beads. Intersections of axial and spiral grooves punctuate. (43 mm)
Distribution: Very rare, offshore reefs out of Hurghada.

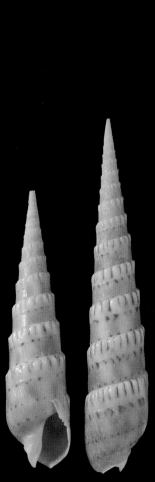

Acus crenulata

Acus dimidiata

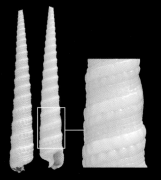

Cinguloterebra insalli

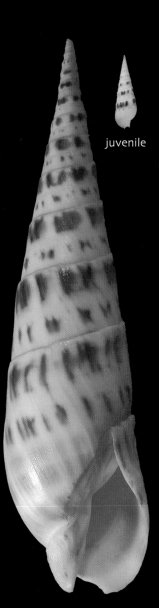

juvenile

Acus maculata

Duplicaria duplicata (Linnaeus, 1758)
9–43 mm. → Upper whorls look like duplicates of each other: each whorl is composed of two sections of raised axial ribs separated by an incised spiral line. (39 mm)
Distribution: Locally and intermittently common in the Hurghada–Safaga area.

Hastula albula (Menke, 1843)
16–18.5 mm. Slender, glossy shell with ribbed white subsutural band. Axial ribs on the upper whorls only. (18.5 mm)
Distribution: Rare, Hurghada–Safaga area.

Impages hectica (Linnaeus, 1758)
28–58 mm. → No axial ribs at all. Spiral bands of varying shades of brown, separated by a white band at the suture. Colors 'bleed' into each other. (58 mm)
Distribution: Generally uncommon, known primarily from Quseir to Ras Banas. Very rare in the Gulf of Aqaba, never in the Gulf of Suez.

Myurella affinis (Gray, 1834)
15–52 mm. Glossy, with slightly stepped straight-sided whorls. → Straight smooth-feeling axial ribs. Interstices between the ribs often brown, even in white areas of the shell. The aperture is usually white, never orange, and in some specimens the brown axial lines of the interstices show through. (48 mm)
Distribution: Rare in the Gulf of Aqaba, not found in the Gulf of Suez, moderately common from Hurghada south.
Notes: Confusion often arises between *M. nebulosa* and *M. affinis.* The latter is usually glossy and the former dull. *M. affinis* never has an orange aperture and *M. nebulosa* usually does. *M. nebulosa* never has brown interstices. *M. affinis* is a little more common.

Myurella columellaris (Hinds, 1844)
24–27 mm. Elongate, one spiral row of lighter colored beads, straight flat-topped axial ribs, → relatively wide interstices with numerous white spiral threads in them. Pale yellow-orange including the columella and aperture. (27 mm)
Distribution: Very rare, Safaga to Wadi Gimaal.
Notes: Never strongly colored, weak micro-cancellate sculpture on ribs, each rib fading to nearly white centrally, edges and interstices slightly darker. Ribs of *M. kilburni* are curved, not straight. *T. amanda* has two rows of beads below the suture. *M. affinis* has no spiral threads.

Myurella kilburni (R.D. Burch, 1965)
25–35 mm. → Numerous small but strong spiral threads in the orange spaces between the glossy white curved axial ribs. (35 mm)
Distribution: Very rare, Hurghada–Safaga area.
Notes: Interstices darker and proportionately wider than in *M. nebulosa* (see page 140).

Duplicaria duplicata

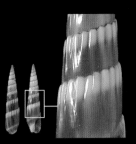

Hastula albula

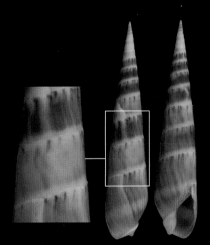

Impages hectica

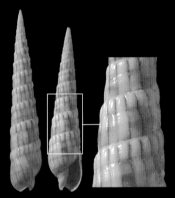

Myurella affinis

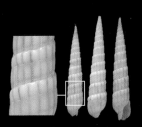

Myurella columellaris

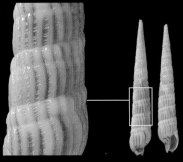

Myurella kilburni

Myurella nebulosa (Sowerby I, 1825)
11–55 mm. → Dull clouded surface; with a good imagination you can see orange clouds on a white sky. Subsutural band cut into square blocks by incised lines. Axial ribs separated by slightly curved interstices that are never darker than the ribs next to them. Small spiral threads and striae cross the axial ribs. → The aperture and columella are usually glossy orange. (50. 5 mm)
Distribution: Never common, most likely to be found in the Hurghada–Safaga area, also found offshore South Sinai.

Perirhoe cerithina (Lamarck, 1822)
36–42.5 mm. Elongate curved outline. One strong incised spiral line below the suture, sutural band not raised. Overall axial pattern of chestnut and white, without darker spirals or spots. (42 mm)
Distribution: Very rare, Hurghada to Wadi Lahmi.
Notes: P. cerithina never has the extended recurved siphonal canal of the *Rhinoclavis* species.

Terebra amanda Hinds, 1844
32.5–40 mm. → Two spiral rows of beads on each whorl, upper row more prominent. Elongate, slightly stepped, straight-sided whorls. Three fine spiral grooves, ribs not raised. Fine, irregularly spaced axial grooves. Various shades of orange, often mixed with axial bars of soft white. (40 mm)
Distribution: Uncommon, Gulf of Aqaba, Hurghada to Marsa Alam.

Terebra babylonia Lamarck, 1822
16.5–52 mm. → Subsutural band of white blocks, curved axial ribs cut by two incised spiral lines. On the body whorl the axial ribs terminate well before the basal curve begins. Basal area, aperture and columella orange. Entire shell may fade to white. (42 mm)
Distribution: All areas but always uncommon.
Notes: → Axial incised lines curve in one direction through the subsutural band and in the opposite direction through the whorl producing a unique sinuous effect.

Terebra castigata Cooke, 1885
Endemic
20.5 mm. Glossy, mushroom gray, strong axial ribs, raised sutural band of light gray and chestnut beads. (20.5 mm)
Distribution: Rare, South Sinai, Hurghada–Safaga area.
Notes: Henk Dekker found the pictured specimen.

Terebra consobrina Deshayes, 1859
Endemic
33–96 mm. → Three rows of spots on the body whorl, two rows on all the others. (92 mm)
Distribution: Uncommon, sandy silty areas, Gulf of Aqaba, Hurghada to Wadi Lahmi.
Notes: Some specimens have an incised line below the suture.

Myurella nebulosa

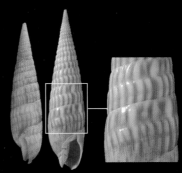

Perirhoe cerithina

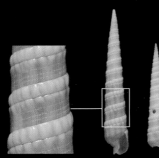

Terebra amanda

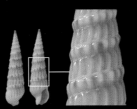

Terebra castigata

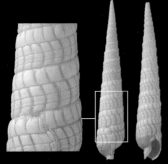

Terebra babylonia

Terebra consobrina

The next two families, Architectonicidae and Pyramidellidae, are grouped together as heterobranchs on the basis of anatomical features of the animal.

Family ARCHITECTONICIDAE

These shells are quite circular in outline with a domed or nearly flat spire. The most interesting feature is that you can see up inside the umbilicus. The space gets narrower and you can see the inner edge of the whorls. It is like looking up the inside of a spiral staircase. The common name for them is sundial shells.

Heliacus areola (Gmelin, 1791)

10–19 mm. → Spire raised, dome shaped. Body whorl with four spiral cords plus peripheral cord. Two cords in umbilicus. (15 mm)
Distribution: Rare, Safaga and south.

Heliacus implexus (Mighels, 1845)

7–10 mm. → Spire very weakly domed. Four minutely beaded spiral cords per whorl, plus a large beaded cord at the periphery. One strong and one weak corrugated cord spiraling into open umbilicus. (7 mm)
Distribution: Rare, northern Gulf of Aqaba, Hurghada–Safaga area, Wadi Lahmi.
Notes: Finer sculpture than the other members of its genus.

Heliacus variegatus (Gmelin, 1791)

6–10 mm. → Rough, nearly flat spire, three spiral cords per whorl, plus a large beaded cord at the periphery, finely cut by oblique grooves. Two cords in umbilicus. (6.5 mm)
Distribution: Rare, northern Gulf of Aqaba, Hurghada–Safaga area, Wadi Lahmi.
Notes: In the Red Sea *H. variegatus* is very flat spired.

Psilaxis oxytropis (A. Adams, 1855)

7–12 mm. → Smooth and silky feeling to the touch, spire slightly domed. Faint spiral sculpture, no cords on spire. → Only one cord at periphery and inside umbilicus. (12 mm)
Distribution: Rare, northern Gulf of Aqaba, Hurghada–Safaga area, Wadi Lahmi.

actual size

x3

Heliacus areola

actual size

x3

Heliacus variegatus

actual size

x3

Heliacus implexus

actual size

x3

Psilaxis oxytropis

Family PYRAMIDELLIDAE

As the name suggests, these shells are somewhat pyramidal in shape. They are often glossy white or off-white with beige, tan, and brown markings. Large species have folds on the columella. Certain species have some individuals with teeth on the inside of the lip and others without. The animals are parasitic and live by sucking blood from other animal hosts.

The majority of Pyramidellidae shells are quite small and many species strongly resemble each other. The really tiny ones are usually very elongate and highly sculptured but exceedingly difficult to identify. Only a few larger ones are presented here.

Longchaeus halaibensis (Sturany, 1903)
Halaib Pyramid Shell

10.5 mm. → Moderately elongate, upper spire curves inward toward apex. Spiral groove at the periphery of the body whorl, sutures incised. Shell glossy white with single spiral row of brown dots. → Two rows on the body whorl, one above the incised line and one below. (10.5 mm)

Distribution: Rare, Gulf of Aqaba and far south.

Notes: The most reliable difference between this shell and *L. teres* is the difference in the outline of the spires. *L. haliabensis* is slightly curved and *L. teres* is completely straight sided and has more whorls. This shell is named for the town of Halaib in the far south of Egypt near which Sturany found the type specimen.

Longchaeus maculosus (Lamarck, 1822)
Synonym *Pyramidella sulcata* (A. Adams in Sowerby, 1854)

12–30 mm. Glossy, moderately elongate pyramid, sharp apex. → Each whorl slightly rounded, sutures indented. White with brown and tan spots, usually occurring as axial bars, randomly and widely spaced on the individual whorls. (25 mm)

Distribution: Moderately common in the Gulf of Aqaba, common from Marsa Alam south. Not found in the Gulf of Suez.

Notes: Occasionally a specimen with teeth on the inside of the lip will be found.

Longchaeus teres (A. Adams in Sowerby, 1854)

10–27 mm → Glossy, elongate pyramid, absolutely straight sides, sharp apex. Incised line on the body whorl, from the top of aperture around to the middle of the outer lip. Glossy white with numerous medium and light brown axial bars on whorls. These may be single or double, straight or wavy. → Two spiral rows of squarish dots below the incised line on base of body whorl. (13 mm)

Distribution: Rare, but known from all areas.

Notes: See *L. halaibensis* (above).

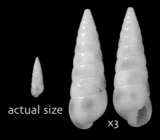

actual size

x3

Longchaeus halaibensis

actual size

x3

Longchaeus maculosus

actual size

x3

Longchaeus teres

Monotigma lauta (A. Adams, 1853)
Leucotina gratiosa Melvill, 1898 of authors
8–13 mm. Elongate white shell with numerous regularly spaced spiral grooves. Columella straight. No teeth or folds.
Distribution: Uncommon, northern Gulf of Suez.

Otopleura mitralis (A. Adams in Sowerby, 1854)
10–20 mm. → Stubby shell, spiral threadlets, interrupted by axial ribs. Columella with folds. Inner part of lip plain or with denticles. Gray-brown cloud-like smudges of color on white shell, darker on the lower whorls. (17 mm)
Distribution: Locally and occasionally abundant, especially south of Marsa Alam. Moderately common in the northern Gulf of Aqaba, but quite unpredictable.

Otopleura sp.
14–20 mm. → Glossy, moderately elongate, axial rib interstices with small pits. Columella with folds. Body whorl near the aperture thin, translucent, without ribs, with → reticulate pattern of little craters on this area; without magnification it just appears slightly rough. Pentultimate whorl thicker. Body whorl with white band without any colored blotches. (20 mm)
Distribution: Rare in all areas, but when found there may be many specimens.
Notes: Occasionally in the northern Gulf of Aqaba there are specimens with the stubbier shape of *O. mitralis* and the light caramel blotches and basal white band of *Otopleura* sp.

Pyramidella dolabrata (Linnaeus, 1758)
9–15 mm. → Glossy, broad-based, elegant shell with one brown line on each whorl and four on the body whorl. (10 mm)
Distribution: Very rare, Hurghada–Safaga area only.
Notes: *P. terebelloides* (A. Adams in Sowerby, 1845) is smaller, narrower and has only three lines on the body whorl. Not illustrated.

actual size   x3

Monotigma lauta

actual size

x3

Otopleura mitralis

x3   actual size

Otopleura sp.

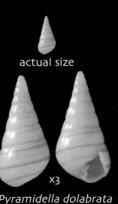

actual size

x3

Pyramidella dolabrata

Opisthobranchia

The next seven families—Acteonidae, Bullidae, Cylichnidae, Hydatinidae, Haminoeidae, Philinidae, and Ringiculidae—are grouped under the name opisthobranchs, referring to the relationship of the animal's mantle to its shell. Many of the animals are larger than their shell. Nudibranchs, or sea slugs, are also in this group, but are not included here as they have no shells.

Scientific classification of this group is constantly undergoing revision, and the following order is not intended as a contribution to that discussion. The families are presented alphabetically.

Family ACTEONIDAE
Pupa affinis (A. Adams, 1855)
4–14.5 mm. Dark or light brown dashes → axially aligned leaving axial white areas. (13 mm)
Distribution: Uncommon but found in all areas.

Pupa solidula (Linnaeus, 1758)
11–14 mm. Dark brown spiral dashes not axially aligned. (13 mm)
Distribution: Rare, northern Gulf of Aqaba.

Family BULLIDAE
Bulla ampulla Linnaeus, 1758
10–50 mm. Mottled brown shell with → large white aperture. When the carnivorous animal is alive it is bigger than the shell. (34 mm)
Distribution: Common, all regions.

Family CYLICHNIDAE
Acteocina simplex (A. Adams, 1850)
4.5–6 mm. This little white shell has absolutely straight parallel sides and a raised stepped spire. With magnification you can see that the shoulders of each whorl are very sharp and the suture is deeply sunken below them. The protoconch coils over itself, perpendicular to the axis of the shell. (6 mm)
Distribution: Locally abundant in the northern Gulf of Suez.

Family HYDATINIDAE
Hydatina physis (Linnaeus, 1758)
11 mm. Very light unmistakable striped shell. (11 mm)
Distribution: Very rare, Hurghada.

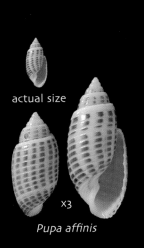

actual size

x3

Pupa affinis

actual size

x3

Pupa solidula

actual size

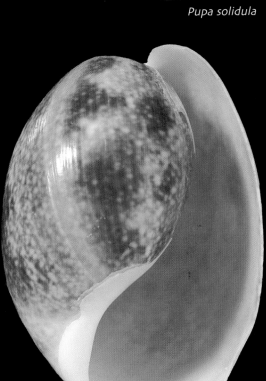

x3

Bulla ampulla

x3

actual size

Acteocina simplex

x3

actual size

x3

Hydatina physis

Family HAMINOEIDAE
Atys cylindricus (Helbling, 1779)
6–15 mm. Cylindrical, but slightly rounded, narrows at upper end. → Sharp channeled protrusion between intorted spire and top of lip, clearly present even on juveniles. Striae at upper and lower thirds only. (15 mm)
Distribution: All areas, common to abundant.
Notes: Shells from south of Marsa Alam are likely to be larger, stronger, and more opaque and more complexly sculptured than those from farther north. Shells from Suez are especially thin—nearly transparent. Cylindrical specimens without the protrusion and with striae on the entire shell may be *Liloa curta* (see below).

Atys ehrenbergi (Issel, 1869)
Atys naucum (Linnaeus, 1758) of some authors
10–21 mm. Nearly transparent fragile shell, globose. Outer lip rises well above the deeply sunken spire. Columella straight. The outer lip forms a long smooth arc. → There are fine incised lines at the upper and lower thirds of the shell only. (21 mm)
Distribution: Rare, Gulf of Aqaba and Safaga.

Diniatys dentifer (A. Adams in Sowerby, 1850)
3–6 mm. Semi-transparent, fragile, globose shell. Flat or sunken spire. No spiral sculpture. → Sharp tooth at base of aperture. Color always white. (6 mm)
Distribution: Uncommon, northern Gulf of Aqaba, far south.

Haminoea pemphis (Philippi, 1847)
4–14 mm. Slightly elongated globose shape. → No incised spiral lines. The outer lip extends from the sunken spire almost straight across before descending in a smooth arc. Columella smoothly curved, with thin shield of opaque white. This contrasts with the nearly transparent, usually beige or white body of the shell. (12 mm)
Distribution: Common south of Marsa Alam, occasional elsewhere.

Liloa curta (A. Adams in Sowerby, 1850)
5–12.5 mm. Cylindrical, straight-sided, sunken spire, nearly flat topped, → spiral striae on entire shell. (12.5 mm)
Distribution: Infrequent, all areas. Locally common in shell grit.
Notes: *L. curta* never has a spout-like protrusion at the top of the lip. *Atys cylindricus* never has striae in the middle section.

Ventomnestia girardi (Audouin, 1826)
Synonym *Bulla bizona* A. Adams, 1850
3.5–5 mm. Very slender profile. Fresh specimens tan with a white spiral band near each end. (5 mm)
Distribution: Rare, northern Gulf of Suez.

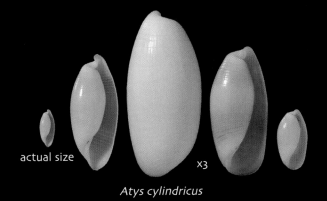

actual size   x3

Atys cylindricus

actual size

actual size

x3

x3

Atys ehrenbergi

x3   actual size

Diniatys dentifer

x3   actual size

Haminoea pemphis

x3   actual size

Liloa curta

x3   actual size

Ventomnestia girardi

Family PHILINIDAE
Philine vaillanti (Issel, 1869)
Philine aperta of some authors
Endemic
12–24 mm. → Nearly transparent white shell, huge aperture, single whorl. The carnivorous animal is much larger than the shell and completely covers it. It lives offshore in sand. (20 mm)
Distribution: Occasional. Usually found only after storms, most common in the Gulf of Suez.
Notes: May be conspecific with the Mediterranean *P. aperta.* Research is ongoing.

Family RINGICULIDAE
Ringicula acuta Philippi, 1849
Synonym *Ringicula savignyi* Morlet, 1878
3–5 mm. Very sharply pointed spire, two strong teeth on columella, strongly thickened lip. (5 mm)
Distribution: All sandy areas, common in fine shell grit, abundant in the northern Gulf of Suez.

Pulmonata
The following two families, Siphonariidae and Ellobiidae, include animals which breathe air and are referred to as pulmonates—they have lungs.

Family SIPHONARIIDAE
The shells of this family and the behavior of the animals that inhabit them are similar to those of true limpets (Patellidae and Nacellidae). They are flattish, cling tightly to rocks, and graze on algae. However, the animals are radically different. Siphonariidae have a siphon through which they breathe air; limpets do not.

Siphonaria crenata (Blainville, 1827)
4–22 mm. → Strong ridge on one side for the siphon, extends beyond the outline of the shell. Variable number of additional ridges or ribs. (21 mm)
Distribution: Common in all regions.
Notes: This species exhibits quite a range of height, color, and pattern. The strong siphonal ridge is consistent and distinctive.

actual size

Philine vaillanti

x3

x3

actual size

Ringicula acuta

actual size

x3

Siphonaria crenata

Siphonaria sp. 1

8–14 mm. Broadly ovate, peak nearly central, fine dark brown and white radial ribs. Strong shell. Inside brown. (11 mm)
Distribution: Rare, Hurghada–Safaga area.

Siphonaria sp. 2

2–4 mm. → Peak close to the end and to one side. Thin shell. Brown with white rays or the reverse. (4 mm)
Distribution: Intermittently common, northern Gulf of Suez to Wadi Gimaal.

Family ELLOBIIDAE

Some species live in seaweed tossed up on shore. Some specialists consider them land snails.

Allochroa layardi (H. & A. Adams, 1855)

5–6 mm. → Outline smooth, whorls not stepped. Spiral threadlets evenly covering the shell. → Columella with a deep rounded notch above lowest tooth. Teeth on columella thin, plate-like. Usually brown with a white spiral. (6 mm)
Distribution: Rare, all areas.

Melampus lividus (Deshayes, 1830)

5–7 mm. Cone shaped, but → with teeth and a large notch on columella. Aperture lirate. (7 mm)
Distribution: Uncommon, South Sinai, Quseir, Wadi Gimaal.

Pedipes granum (Morelet, 1872)

3–10 mm. Whorls lightly stepped and slightly rounded, sutures somewhat indented. Spiral cords evenly covering the shell. → Aperture with very strong teeth on the columella, gap or notch below uppermost tooth. Interior of outer lip with or without teeth or raised lirations. Usually without contrasting color spiral. (9mm)
Distribution: Uncommon, all areas.

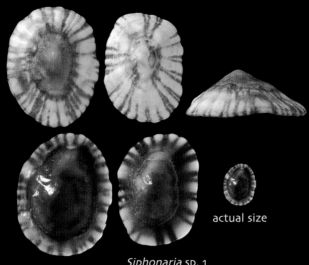

actual size

Siphonaria sp. 1

actual size

x3

Siphonaria sp. 2

actual size

x3

Allochroa layardi

x3   actual size

Melampus lividus

actual size

x3

Pedipes granum

Scaphopoda

These curved tube-like shells are grouped together under the heading Scaphopoda. Included here are the families Dentaliidae, Laevidentaliidae, and Gadilinidae, often called the Tusk Shells because of their resemblance to elephants' tusks. There is an opening at each end: the apex is narrower and allows for water to flow in and out; the wider aperture is where the animal's foot comes out. The animals live in both deep and shallow water buried almost entirely in the sand. Only the tip of the apex is normally above the sand.

Family DENTALIIDAE

Dentalium clavus Cooke, 1885

28–43 mm. → Strong, tusk-shaped shell with strong longitudinal ribs, usually eleven, becoming obsolete near broader end. In perfect specimens (extremely rare) there is a tiny 'pipe' projecting from the apex. (40 mm)

Distribution: Usually common from Hurghada–Safaga area. Rare elsewhere.

Dentalium reevei P. Fischer, 1871

38–44 mm. → Light shell, nine ribs with fine riblets in the interstices extending all the way to the broader end. (41 mm)

Distribution: Rare, Hurghada–Safaga area.

Notes: Apical (top) end narrower and more curved than that of *D. clavus*.

Family LAEVIDENTALIIDAE

Laevidentalium longitrorsum (Reeve, 1842)

62–75 mm. → Large, glossy, tusk shell. Translucent white or beige. (75 mm)

Distribution: Rare, Gulf of Suez and south of Marsa Alam.

Family GADILINIDAE

Episiphon subtorquatum (P. Fischer, 1871)

Synonym *Dentalium sewelli* Ludbrook, 1954

5–19 mm. → Delicate, narrow, glossy, very weak curve, apex a sharp point. Featureless appearance. Magnification shows tightly spaced spiral lines, stronger at narrow end. (15 mm)

Distribution: Common locally and intermittently in the Gulf of Suez.

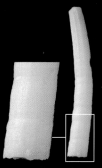

Dentalium clavus

Dentalium reevei

Laevidentalium longitrorsum

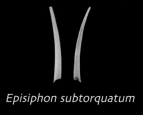

Episiphon subtorquatum

Class Bivalvia—The Bivalves

The animal is enclosed by two shells which are called 'valves.' These protect the soft-bodied animal and can open slightly and close tightly. Most burrow into the sand or mud with a blade-like foot. Others attach themselves to solid surfaces such as rocks, coral, other shells, or wood. A few species are free-living and can swim by snapping their valves shut, expelling water and thus using a low-grade, natural, marine form of jet propulsion.

Family ARCIDAE

These shells always have numerous fine teeth arranged more or less vertically along the straight hinge line. The ligament grooves are oblique markings on the dorsal area and join under the beaks to form inverted chevrons.

Acar plicata (Dillwyn, 1817)

8.5–28 mm. Strong cancellate sculpture. → Adductor muscle scars usually thickened and opaque milky white. Shell usually white but some individuals have a yellow, pink, or light orange blush. Some may have a line of sharp scales along the posterior carina. (20 mm)
Distribution: Common, all regions.
Notes: See *Striarca erythraea*, pages 166–67.

Anadara antiquata (Linnaeus, 1758)

Antique Ark Shell
20–64 mm. Weakly nodulose ribs, narrow interstices. → Anterior ribs with a single groove down the middle. (50 mm)
Distribution: Common from Marsa Alam south, occasional in South Sinai area and Gulf of Aqaba. Never in the Gulf of Suez.
Notes: A. uropigimelana (see below) looks quite similar to this shell: both have very narrow interspaces. In *A. uropigimelana* the anterior ribs have several striae, *A. antiquata* has only one. In juveniles it may be difficult to tell if the ribs are striate or bisected. However *A. antiquata* is usually more elongate and has bumpier ribs. Use your fingernail to test them.

X2

Acar plicata

actual size

X2

actual size

Anadara antiquata

Anadara ehrenbergi (Dunker, 1868)

12–62 mm. → Elongate, flat-topped ribs, strong straight cross bars on top and in the interstices. → Only the outer chevron of the ligament is visible. Very short vertical teeth. (62 mm)

Distribution: Occasional in the Gulf of Suez. Rarely found elsewhere.

Notes: Juveniles resemble *A. pygmaea* (H. Adams, 1872) which is apparently not found in the Egyptian Red Sea.

Anadara natalensis (Krauss, 1848)

16–63 mm. Squarish light shell. → Ribs smooth, well separated. Interspaces almost as wide as the ribs. (63 mm)

Distribution: Rare, Gulf of Suez.

Notes: A similar-looking subfossil shell is very common in the Ras Sudr area. It is heavier, beige, and always very worn.

Anadara uropigimelana (Bory de St. Vincent, 1824)

12–60 mm. → Smooth-feeling surface, multiple fine striae running down the anterior ribs. Narrow interstices, weak densely spaced, extremely fine concentric striae across ribs. (36 mm)

Distribution: Locally common in the northern Gulf of Aqaba and muddy areas just north of Hurghada and in the far south. Not found in the Gulf of Suez.

Notes: Sometimes the most central of the striae is deeper than the others, which can cause confusion with *A. antiquata. A. uropigimelana* is always smoother, and never has strong nodulose cross bars on and between the ribs.

Anadara ehrenbergi

Anadara natalensis

Anadara uropigimelana

Arca avellana Lamarck, 1819

15–62 mm. → At least one oblique ligament mark can be found posterior to the triangle of marks under the beaks. Ligament itself covers entire dorsal area. Anterior white or at least lighter than the brown posterior. (41 mm)

Distribution: Common in the Gulf of Suez. Occasional in the far south.

Notes: See *Arca ventricosa* below.

Arca navicularis Bruguière, 1789

25–59 mm. → Elongate shell, neat regular sculpture. Ribs much broader than in either of the other two Egyptian Red Sea *Arcas*. (40 mm)

Distribution: Rare, Gulf of Suez.

Arca ventricosa Lamarck, 1819

19–64 mm. Decussate sculpture, irregularly arranged. Posterior dorsal area with big strong ribs. May have a large ventral sulcus. → Posterior and dorsal area with dark brown patterns of lines. (50 mm)

Distribution: Never common, all areas. Seems to prefer habitats with living corals.

Notes: To distinguish *A. avellana* (above) and *A. ventricosa* look for ligament marks on the dorsal area. → *A. ventricosa* has marks only in a triangle under the beaks. Good specimens have brown stripes crossing the dorsal area and others on the outside of the shell. *A. avellana* may have ligament marks anywhere on the dorsal area, never has stripes or pattern.

Arca avellana

Arca navicularis

Arca ventricosa   juvenile

Barbatia amygdalumtostum (Röding, 1798)
Dusky Ark Shell
12–58 mm. Very fine regular riblets, stronger posteriorly. Shell brown, → two white rays going out from umbo; these sometimes more visible from inside. Rays more evident on juveniles than adults, beak always white. (50 mm)
Distribution: Common from Marsa Alam south, occasional in the Hurghada Reefs and South Sinai. Rare in the Gulf of Suez.

Barbatia foliata (Forsskål in Niebuhr, 1775)
Leafy Ark Shell
10–90 mm. → 'Leafy' lamellose pericostracum, coarse decussate sculpture. Shell white. Inhabits living hard corals and develops irregular shapes, some subtrigonal, some sub-rectangular. (90 mm)
Distribution: Common from Marsa Alam south, occasional in the Hurghada Reefs, South Sinai, and Dahab.
Notes: Easily confused with *B. trapezina*, but differs in having coarser and more knobby radial ribs. Specimens with pericostracum are easily distinguished as *B. foliata* never has radial lines of spiny hairs.

Barbatia parva (Sowerby, 1833)
Little Pink-nosed Ark
7–17 mm. Fragile. Unusually fine sculpture. → Beaks always pinkish, shell brown. (14 mm)
Distribution: Occasional in the Gulf of Aqaba, intermittently common Hurghada–Safaga area.

Barbatia reticulata (Gmelin, 1791)
Synonym *Arca sulcata* Lamarck, 1819
10–26 mm. → Ribs relatively few and large, about twenty-seven. Usually one or more secondaries between primaries. No concentric rings or ridges. → Usually with a small sulcus in middle of the ventral margin, which makes it look pinched or squeezed in the middle. Adductor muscle scars are never raised or colored differently from the rest of the shell. (24 mm)
Distribution: Rare. Wadi Gimaal area, Hurghada–Safaga area.

subadult

Barbatia amygdalumtostum

Barbatia foliata

Barbatia parva

Barbatia reticulata

Barbatia setigera (Reeve, 1844)

17–55 mm. → Widely spaced rows of strong bristles, especially along the posterior carina. Even when all the pericostracum is worn off, the indented lines where the bristles were remain visible as lighter radial lines. Shell brown, often white umbonally. (51 mm)
Distribution: Very common in the Gulf of Suez and south to Safaga. Occasional in the far south.

Barbatia trapezina (Lamarck, 1819)

Synonym *Byssoarca decussata* Sowerby, 1833
10–48 mm. → Fine, spiky, pericostracum in closely spaced radial lines, decussate sculpture. Anterior outline rounded. Shell white. (41 mm)
Distribution: Very common in all areas except the Gulf of Suez.
Notes: → Without the pericostracum it is not always possible to definitively distinguish between the shells of *B. trapezina* and the subrectangular specimens of *B. foliata* (see above).

Family NOETIIDAE

Striarca erythraea (Issel, 1869)

Endemic
4.5–13 mm. → Very fine sculpture of riblets and concentric rings. Ligament lines in the dorsal area are vertical, not in chevrons. (11 mm)
Distribution: Locally common, northern Gulf of Suez.
Notes: Some specimens are quite tumid and others are not. Much finer sculpture than *Acar plicata*.

Barbatia setigera

Barbatia trapezina

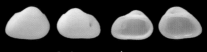

Striarca erythraea

Family GLYCYMERIDIDAE

Shells in this family are usually nearly round. They always have a curved hinge with numerous teeth similar to those of the Arcidae. The sculpture may be radial or smooth. They live in sand.

Glycymeris arabica (H. Adams, 1871)

7–20 mm. Small strong shell with strong radial ribs. Color and pattern variations of brown and white. (19 mm)

Distribution: Abundant in the Gulf of Suez, common in the Gulf of Aqaba and south to Safaga. Only occasionally found south of Marsa Alam.

Glycymeris livida (Reeve, 1843)

16–67 mm. → Smooth exterior. Large nearly round shell, light brown. Inside may be brown or white or some of both. (58 mm)

Distribution: Common in the northern Gulf of Aqaba. Less common in the Gulfs of Aqaba and Suez and across South Sinai. Infrequent south of Hurghada.

Tucetona audouini Matsukuma, 1984

Glycymeris pectunculus (Linnaeus, 1758) of authors

15–51 mm. → Strong radial ribbing, strong pattern of irregular lateral bands of dark and pale brown. (25 mm)

Distribution: Common in both the Gulfs of Aqaba and Suez. Rare elsewhere.

Family LIMOPSIDAE

Limopsis multistriata (Forsskål in Niebuhr, 1775)

17–30 mm. → Much flatter than any similar shell. Many narrow radial ribs. Pericostracum of long dense off-white hairs. (25 mm)

Distribution: Common only around Ras Sudr in the Gulf of Suez. Rare in the Gulf of Aqaba. Very rare south of Hurghada.

Notes: Very similar to shells in the family Glycymerididae but has a triangular ligament pit.

Glycymeris arabica

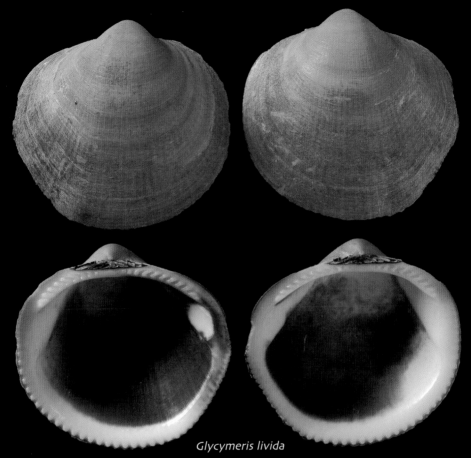

Glycymeris livida

Tucetona audouini

Limopsis multistriata

Family MYTILIDAE

All the shells commonly referred to in English as mussels belong to this family. All are elongate with the beak either at or very near the anterior end. They never have strong teeth. Most produce threads called byssus. Depending on the species, they attach themselves to rocks, pebbles, pilings, or other materials using the byssus threads. Some species bury themselves in sand or mud and make protective nests. Others live inside other marine creatures such as sea squirts; still others bore holes in other shells or stones.

In presenting these shells I am using the subfamily groupings because they relate to obvious shell characteristics even a beginner can appreciate.

Subfamily MYTILINAE

Members of this subfamily have beaks at the absolute anterior end of the shell.

Brachidontes pharaonis (P. Fischer, 1870)
Synonym *Brachidontes variabilis* (Krauss, 1848)
10–36 mm. → Shell entirely covered with numerous narrow ribs. Elongate or wedge shaped, brown, white, or a mix. Wide range of habitat: attached to piers, rocks (above and just below the sand), and inside several species of sponges. (22 mm)
Distribution: Common in the Gulf of Suez, occasional elsewhere.
Notes: Occasionally large groups may be seen covering the entire surface of intertidal rocks.

Septifer forskali (Dunker, 1855)
8–10 mm. → Usually a wonderful jade or turquoise green color, sometimes red. Fine tightly spaced riblets cut co-marginally by micro incised lines. Beak very far to anterior. Interior with a very small shelf, a septum, connecting the dorsal and ventral margins where they join at the pointed anterior of the shell. Tiny teeth all along the dorsal margin. (8.5 mm)
Distribution: Uncommon, northern Gulf of Aqaba, Hurghada. Rare in the Gulf of Suez and south of Hurghada.

Subfamily CRENELLINAE

Small shells, 19 mm or less, with ribs except on the medial area. Margin crenulate corresponding to the ribs.

Gregariella ehrenbergi (Issel, 1869)
5–14 mm. Irregularly elongate. Ventral margin is straight, the ends rounded, and dorsal margin distinctly peaked. Rounded umbonal carina, a few weak riblets anteriorly, many posteriorly, and none medially. Numerous very small teeth. Beached shells are usually white with brown areas. (14 mm)
Distribution: Uncommon, the Gulf of Suez only.

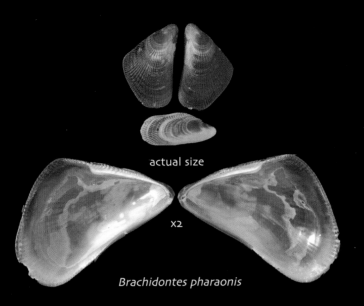

actual size

x2

Brachidontes pharaonis

actual size

x2

Septifer forskali

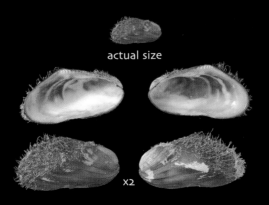

actual size

x2

Gregariella ehrenbergi

Modiolarca coenobita (Vaillant, 1865)

6–17 mm. → Thin, fragile shell with many anterior ribs (more than eight, usually between nine and fourteen). Medial section without ribs, posterior and dorsal areas covered with numerous small fine ribs. Shell can be greenish, coral colored, brown, or cream, with or without fine zigzag lines. It lives in tunicates (sea squirts), a squishy roundish marine invertebrate. (14 mm)

Distribution: Locally common, Gulf of Suez only.

Notes: Another species, *Modiolarca cumingiana* (Reeve, 1857), is also reported from the Gulf of Suez, but I have never seen one. It never has more than eight anterior ribs.

Musculista senhousia (Benson in Cantor, 1842)

8–14 mm. Fragile, pericostracum transparent green with red-brown mostly concentric markings. Four very weak anterior ribs, numerous very weak small teeth along the dorsal margin. (14 mm)

Distribution: Highly localized, common on Suez City beaches, rare if ever elsewhere.

Musculista perfragilis (Dunker, 1857)

20–30 mm. Fragile, pericostracum translucent red with white radial rays posteriorly. Numerous tiny weak teeth along dorsal margin. (30 mm)

Distribution: Very rare, highly localized, Suez City beaches, and other sites in the far north of the Gulf of Suez.

Notes: Presumably lives in deeper water, found beached only after unusually strong storms.

Subfamily MODIOLINAE

Members of this group are often called horse mussels. The sculpture is smooth and may show concentric growth lines. The shell never has ribs. The pericostracum is usually hairy in life, but has often worn off on beached shells.

Modiolus auriculatus (Krauss, 1848)

Ear Mussel

10–46 mm. → Large, no ribs. Ventral margin straight. Dorsal margin slants up to a rounded peak, then dips downward, then rises up again a little. Posterior dorsal margin nearly parallel to ventral. Mostly dark purple color, ventral area often nearly white. (42 mm)

Distribution: Very common, all regions.

Notes: This is one of the most commonly found shell on the beaches of the Egyptian Red Sea. A very careful observer will notice some specimens appear a little different in color and shape (see uppermost figured specimens). Until more research is completed, these are generally considered unnamed variations of the species.

Modiolarca coenobita

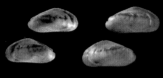

Musculista senhousia

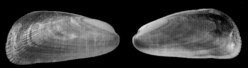

Musculista perfragilis

Modiolus auriculatus

Modiolus sp.
Red Sea Bearded Mussel
19–38 mm. → Worn beach specimens bright coral orange. Fresh specimens dark brown with rough hairs on the posterior end, may have sand grains stuck to them. → Dorsal margin always smoothly rounded. (35 mm)
Distribution: Uncommon, Gulf of Suez only.
Notes: The best way to distinguish this mussel from the ubiquitous *M. auriculatus* is by the shape of the dorsal margin. In the present species this always forms a smooth slightly arched convex curve. *M. auriculatus* always has at least a slight concavity posterior to the highest point, although in very small specimens it may appear nearly straight. *M. barbatus* (Linnaeus, 1758) is a Mediterranean species. The shell found in the Gulf of Suez is very similar but does not yet have its own name.

Modiolus ligneus (Reeve, 1858)
18–36 mm. → Anterior broadly rounded. Pericostracum shiny chestnut brown, often peels off in big flakes. Shell white or white and reddish-purple. *M. ligneus* makes a nest under the sand. (28 mm)
Distribution: Sandy areas, uncommon. Dahab Lagoon and northern Gulf of Suez.

Family PTERIIDAE
The common name for this family is wing oysters. The hinge line is always straight. There are no teeth. The nacreous area is larger on the LV. The non-nacreous margins become very brittle and fragile when dry. In the genus *Pteria* the dorsal margin usually forms a long narrow extension. The *Pinctada* species were the source of natural pearls and their nacreous area is still used commercially as mother-of-pearl.

Electroma alacorvi (Dillwyn, 1817)
25–43 mm. → Obliquely ovoid, no dorsal extension. Nearly flat, thin, shiny, very dark brown shell. No teeth or pits in the hinge. (43 mm)
Distribution: Very rare, near reefs in Gubal Straits and Gulf of Suez.
Note: The unlined specimens of *Crenatula picta* (see page 182) have a similar exterior but as members of the Isognomonidae they have numerous ligament pits in the hinge.

Modiolus sp.

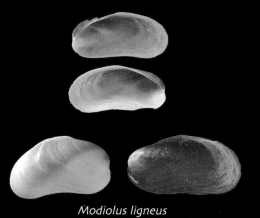

Modiolus ligneus

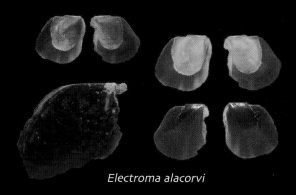

Electroma alacorvi

Pinctada margaritifera (Linnaeus, 1758)
15–140 mm. → Gray-green color, white radial rays. Appressed and sometimes extended lamellae cover the surface. (140 mm)
Distribution: Uncommon, all regions.
Notes: The name means 'bearer of pearls.'

Pinctada margaritifera

Pinctada vulgaris (Schumacher, 1817)

Pinctada radiata (Leach, 1814) of some authors

Common Pinctada

10–74 mm. → The exterior is rough with short appressed lamellae. Usually plain brownish straw color, some with dull reddish or yellow radial rays. Interior shiny, slightly iridescent. Nacreous area of LV large, on RV smaller, sometimes used as mother-of-pearl. *Distribution:* Common in all regions. (69 mm)

Note: This shell is widely known as *P. radiata* (Leach, 1814), but the original specimen described (the type specimen) of that species was from the Caribbean Sea and the east coast of the United States. Thus it is unlikely to be the same species.

Pteria aegyptiaca (Dillwyn, 1817)

Endemic

30–80 mm. → Brown and gold zigzags usually on LV only. Posterior 'wing' very long. LV inflated, RV quite flat. Interior iridescent. Non-nacreous margin very fragile. (78 mm)

Distribution: Uncommon, seen mostly at offshore reefs near South Sinai and Hurghada.

Notes: The 'wing' of the shells found in Egypt is much longer than depicted in other works. These exotic-looking animals attach themselves firmly with byssus threads to certain corals and man-made wire structures. They are rarely found on the beach. If you see one while diving, observe it from a distance, downcurrent so that you will not be carried too close and risk damaging the coral. Do not touch it or attempt to dislodge it. Although this species is uncommon, it is the most often seen of the *Pteria* species living in the Egyptian Red Sea.

Pteria macroptera (Lamarck, 1819)

58–64 mm. → Strong, widely separated, dark concentric lines, these stronger on LV. On beached shells the nacre may be pink. Non-nacreous margin very fragile. (63 mm)

Distribution: Rare, reefs in Gubal Straits.

Notes: Shell thicker and heavier than *P. aegyptiaca*, but wing disproportionately shorter. The fragile non-nacreous margin is missing on the illustrated specimen.

juvenile

actual size

x0.5

Pinctada vulgaris

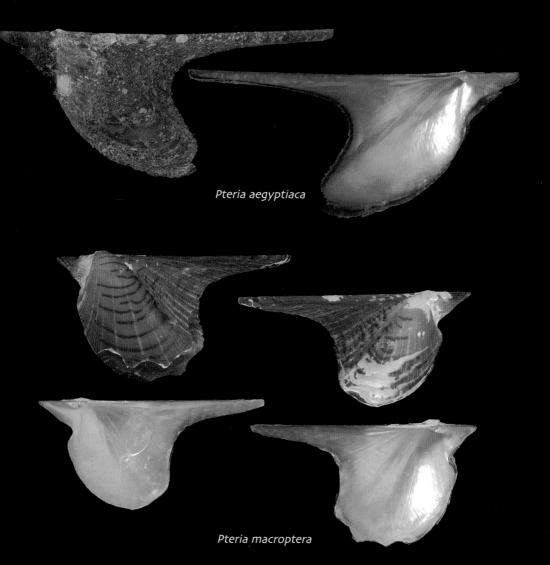

Pteria aegyptiaca

Pteria macroptera

Family MALLEIDAE

The common name is hammer shells, but the species in our area lack the extended wings that resemble a hammer. They are related to the Pteriidae and the Isognomonidae. Some Malleidae attach themselves to rock or coral and others live inside sponges. They are not common but are most likely to be found in the northern part of the Gulf of Suez.

Malvufundus regulus (Forsskål in Niebuhr, 1775)

18–63 mm. → Flat irregular shell, usually long and narrow, often distorted and warped. Sometimes the outer layers of the shell seem to be blistered and peeling off. Extremely variable in shape and color, so it is not immediately obvious what Forsskål had in mind when calling it 'regulus.' It lives attached to rocks or coral debris and seems to prefer quiet shallow waters. (63 mm)
Distribution: Rare, very localized, northern Gulf of Suez only.

Vulsella fornicata (Forsskål in Niebuhr, 1775)

6–66 mm. → Elongate or ovoid. → Hinge with large spoon-like resilifer, obvious even in juveniles. The bottom edges of the resilifer are connected by the ligament but the beaks grow farther and farther away from each other. Beaks coil in the plane toward anterior, separated from each other by the deeply excavated diamond-shaped cavity formed by the resilifer. The anterodorsal margin rises higher than the posterodorsal, forming a little peak or bulge anterior to the resilifer. Honey beige, many specimens with brown radial lines. Inhabits a fine-grained sponge. (65 mm)
Distribution: Somewhat common in the northern Gulf of Suez, usually found still inside clumps of sponge torn away by storms.

Vulsella vulsella (Linnaeus, 1758)

18–29 mm. Ovoid, resilifer a small sunken crescent, beaks not widely separated. Anterior shoulder never rising above top of ligament. Light beige, with or without fine radial line. Inhabits a coarse-grained, spiky-surfaced sponge. (25 mm)
Distribution: Very rare, northern Gulf of Suez.
Notes: The resilifer is much less conspicuous in *V. vulsella* than in *V. fornicata*. It is easier to distinguish the Gulf of Suez specimens of these two species on the basis of the size and shape of the resilifer than by other features.

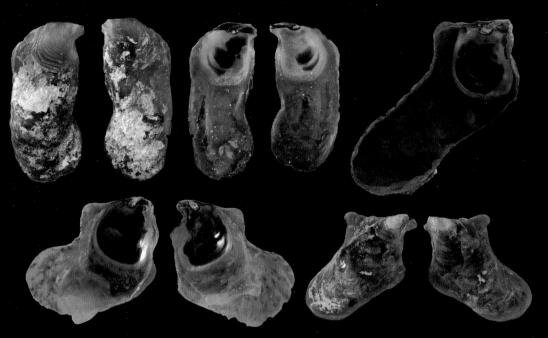

Malvufundus regulus

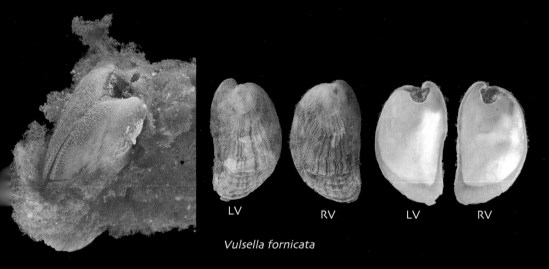

LV   RV   LV   RV

Vulsella fornicata

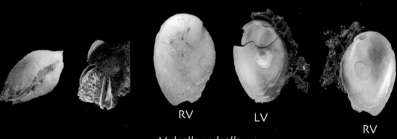

RV   LV   RV

Vulsella vulsella

Family ISOGNOMONIDAE

In the species found in the Egyptian Red Sea, the hinge line is always straight and has small pits where the ligament sits. The animal attaches itself to a solid surface with byssal threads.

Crenatula picta (Gmelin, 1791)

50–67 mm. → Irregularly ovoid, thin, flat, fragile shell with smooth regular margins. Brown to black with light brown to white irregular radial lines. Some specimens lack these lines altogether. The animal lives commensally with sponges. (67 mm)

Distribution: Common on the beaches of Ras Sudr (northeast Gulf of Suez) after winter storms. I have never seen it outside the Gulf of Suez. The sponges are commonly referred to as Finger Sponges and are clearly different from those inhabited by *Vulsella fornicata* and *V. vulsella.*

Notes: The specimens without lines resemble *Electroma alacorvi* from the exterior, but one look at the hinge distinguishes them: *C. picta* has about ten strong regular ligament pits; *E. alacorvi* has none.

Isognomon legumen (Gmelin, 1791)

23–48 mm. → Fragile shell, often in flake-like layers. Irregular shapes. Ligament pits obvious. White, tan, or lavender with small nacreous area. (48 mm)

Distribution: Uncommon, South Sinai, reefs in the Gobal Straits and south of Marsa Alam.

Isognomon nucleus (Lamarck, 1819)

9–23 mm. → Small shell, sometimes pear shaped. Ligament pits small, few. Surface smooth or with many appressed lamellae. Light or dark purple or ivory with traces of purplish color. (9 mm)

Distribution: Moderately common, all areas.

Notes: Sometimes may be seen attached to intertidal rocks.

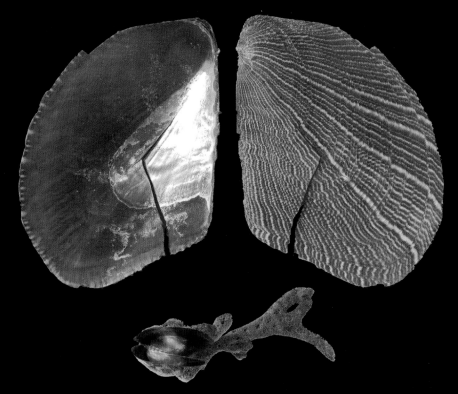

Crenatula picta

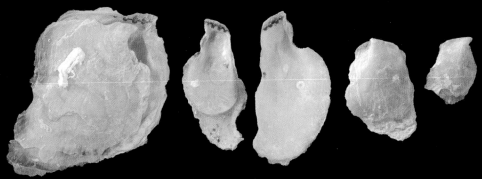

Isognomon legumen

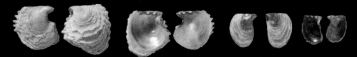

Isognomon nucleus

Family PINNIDAE

The common name for this family is pen shells, due to their fancied resemblance to old-style quill pens. They are very fragile, and usually only broken specimens are seen on the beach.

Pinna muricata Linnaeus, 1758

30–116 mm. → Very elongated triangular shape, nearly transparent. Extremely fragile, shell rarely found intact. Each valve has a lengthwise seam down the middle of it. A few scales near the wider end. Juveniles are all white. Mature specimens may show irregular muddy-looking areas. (116 mm)

Distribution: Moderately common, all regions.

Notes: Sometimes one finds broken bits of a much heavier similar shell. These may be subfossil remains of a species no longer found in the northern part of the Red Sea, *Pinna bicolor* Linnaeus, 1758.

Streptopinna saccata (Linnaeus, 1758)

35–111 mm. → Translucent purple, caramel or white, broad and irregularly shaped, often with a bend in the outline of the shell. Strong undulating ribs. The end opposite the beak gapes widely, usually encrusted with white growth. (93 mm)

Distribution: Uncommon, Gulf of Aqaba, Safaga area, and south of Marsa Alam.

juvenile

Pinna muricata

Streptopinna saccata

Family LIMIDAE

Limas, or file shells, are unusual among bivalves because they are able to swim freely. They squeeze their shells together and thus expel water and move themselves ahead.

Ctenoides annulata (Lamarck, 1819)

11–30 mm. Ovoid, fragile, often translucent white, very small ears, → smooth anterior byssal gape with developed edges, like lips. Weak, barely visible radial threads covering the shell, numerous tiny semi-erect pointed scales.(27.5 mm)
Distribution: Uncommon in Gulf of Suez, South Sinai. Moderately common south of Hughada. Rarely found on beaches.

Lima paucicostata (Sowerby II, 1843)

Few Ribbed Lima or File Shell
Endemic
30–60 mm. → Strong, flat, white shells, obliquely ovoid, with between ten and fifteen broad ribs. Shells in good condition with strong arched erect scales on the ribs. Worn specimens with scars where the scales were attached. Juveniles as miniature adults. (57 mm)
Distribution: All areas but never common.

Limaria fragilis (Gmelin, 1791)

Fragile Lima
20–25 mm. → Posterior margin nearly straight, anterior margin with a bend. → Almost the entire area above the bend gapes. Sharply pointed auricles at the ends of the hinge area. Narrow acute radial ribs, without scales, strongest at the ventral margin. (20 mm)
Distribution: Rare, South Sinai and associated reefs.
Notes: Due to the similarity in shape, this shell could be confused with *Limatulella viali* (see below).

Limatulella viali (Jousseaume in Lamy, 1920)

9–14 mm. Anterior margin bent, posterior straight, sharp ribs medially. → No anterior gape. (9 mm)
Distribution: Very rare, northern Gulf of Aqaba, Hurghada–Safaga area.
Notes: The obvious difference, easily discernable at the beach by placing the shell on any flat surface, between *Limaria fragilis* and *Limatulella viali* is that the former always gapes above the bend on the anterior side and the latter never does.

Ctenoides annulata

Lima paucicostata

Limaria fragilis

Limatulella viali

The Gryphaeidae and the Ostreidae are the two families of true oysters. They have no teeth and only one adductor scar. They all attach themselves firmly to rock or coral or other shells with a kind of cement. Individuals may vary considerably within species. Precise identification can be vexing.

Family GRYPHAEIDAE

Shells in this family always have a porous-looking shell structure. They have tiny dense bars (vermiculate chomata) on the margin on both sides of the hinge. The adductor scar is subcircular but not kidney shaped. The appearance varies greatly from one individual to another.

Hyotissa numisma (Lamarck, 1819)
Coin Oyster
10–43 mm. Variable. RV (the upper one) usually subcircular, flattish. LV cemented to rocks, low raised margins, never deeply cup shaped. Toothless ligament area may be obscure. Exterior usually encrusted. Surf-scrubbed specimens white to pale orange or pink. Interior white, gray, brown, or a mixture. (43 mm)
Distribution: Common from South Sinai to Wadi Lahmi.
Notes: The margins are not sharply plicate, though they may be irregular or undulating. Plicate honeycombed shells with hollow spines are *H. hyotis* (Linnaeus, 1758) which is known from deeper waters. I have never found a well-developed recognizable specimen on the beach.

Family OSTREIDAE

The single muscle scar in shells of this family is kidney shaped or has an indented dorsal margin. UV is usually plicate. The shell structure is not porous.

Alectryonella crenulifera (Sowerby, 1871)
10–34 mm. → Green or white inside. Usually found attached to other shells. → A few weak nodular chomata, only near the ligament. UV flat or plicate, exterior often red. (31 mm)
Distribution: Common in the northern Gulf of Suez, occasional near the reefs off Hurghada.
Notes: A much less common species, *Nanostrea exigua*, has stronger chomata all the way around the margin (see below).

Nanostrea exigua Harry, 1985
Ostrea deformis Lamarck, 1819 of some authors
16–25 mm. Attachment area extensive. Margins form a little raised edge all around the shell, smooth or weakly plicate. UV flat, no sculpture, not plicate. → Large chomata protruding on the UV and sunken on the lower, usually all the way around the shell on the inner margin. (20 mm)
Distribution: Uncommon, northern Gulf of Suez.
Notes: Most commonly found inside the aperture of large, long-dead gastropod shells, especially *Semicassis faurotis*. See *Alectryonella crenulifera* above.

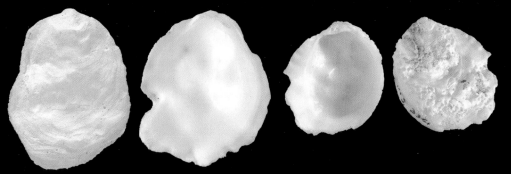

Hyotissa numisma

Alectryonella crenulifera

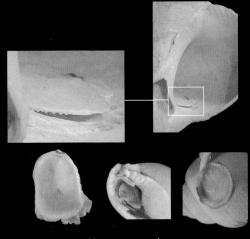

Nanostrea exigua

Saccostrea cuccullata (Born, 1778)

15–60 mm. → Large heavy shell, variable shape, margins of the bottom valve turned up, strong sharp plicate edges. UV fits snugly down into the lower one. Nodular chomata usually only on the dorsal half of the margin. Margins often dark purple-black, may be white. Exterior RV white with or without two or three dark reddish-purple rays. May have hyote spines. Attached to rocks in the intertidal zone, often in clumps of several individuals together with younger shells attached to the top shells of older ones—a little like multi-generational apartment buildings! (57 mm)

Distribution: Very common in the Gulf of Aqaba, occasional elsewhere in rocky areas. Subfossil specimens common in the Gulf of Suez and embedded in shoreline rocks in South Sinai. Painful to step on with bare feet.

Notes: If the muscle scar is darker than the surrounding area you can be sure it is *Saccostrea cuccullata.*

Family PLICATULIDAE

These shells always have folds, or pleats, in the upper valve and sometimes the lower. The Plicatulidae have crural teeth in the hinge area. These are two ridges on the hinge of the upper valve arranged in an inverted 'V' shape, usually with a smaller projection in between. These fit into slots on the lower valve. The teeth are usually brown or chestnut; the hinge brownish or white. The rest of the interior is primarily plain white. There is only one adductor muscle scar. Plicatulidae usually attach themselves to rocks or coral or other shells.

Plicatula australis Lamarck, 1819

5–31 mm. → LV thin, entirely attached to and conforming to substrate, usually inside other shells. No chomata. UV light beige with light chestnut markings. Exterior surface featureless or with divergent ribs and/or a few small hollow spines. (31 mm)

Distribution: Rarely found, all regions.

Notes: Nanostrea exigua and *Alectryonella crenulifera* are also sometimes attached to shells. These other species are oysters, have chomata and never have crural teeth.

Plicatula plicata (Linnaeus, 1767)

15–54 mm. → Thick, subcircular, or slightly fan-shaped shells with eight to twelve strong irregular ribs or folds (plications). Lower valve attaches near the umbo to the substrate. UV with large or small smooth umbonal disk, not to be confused with the attachment area of the lower valve. Cream color with short fine radial lines of orange to red. (40 mm)

Distribution: Abundant in the Gulf of Suez. Rare elsewhere.

Notes: Some specimens have many more than the expected number of ribs, even up to 34. These usually, but not always, have a very large attachment area. This may be an undescribed species or a very rugged form of *P. australis*. Or *P. plicata* may exhibit more variation than previously recognized. Other specimens have steep angular ribs.

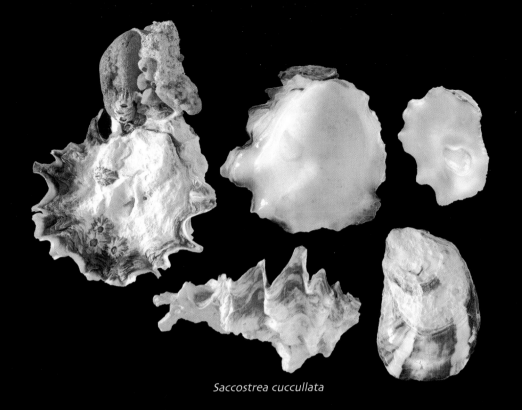

Saccostrea cuccullata

Plicatula australis

Plicatula plicata

Family PECTINIDAE

This family contains some of the most beautiful shells in the world. The common name in English is scallops. Their adductor muscles often appear on the menu in seafood restaurants. The sculpture is usually stronger on one valve than the other; which valve depends on the species. In a few species the color is also quite different between the valves. The auricles vary not only from valve to valve but also between the anterior and posterior ears of the same valve. Color may also vary within a species. Most Pectinidae attach themselves to the substrate by means of byssal threads, but some are free living and can swim.

Decatopecten plica (Linnaeus, 1758)

24–41 mm. → Five to seven broad, low, smoothly undulating ribs with fine raised closely spaced riblets, no scales. Both ears small, anterior like an equilateral triangle, posterior with long lateral margin. Ventral margin sometimes compressed. LV and RV may have very different colors, RV whiter, LV more colored. Many solid shades of red-brown, coral, cream, and white, as well as patterns of these. (37 mm)

Distribution: Common in the Gulf of Suez. Rare elsewhere.

Notes: This species is usually described as having five to nine ribs, but I have never seen a specimen with more than seven. The variation in tumidity is greater among individuals than between valves of the same individual.

Excellichlamys spectabilis (Reeve, 1853)

Spectacular Scallop

13–30 mm. → LV almost flat, ribs alternating in height, occasionally in color too—usually pink and white. RV slightly convex with around eleven evenly raised, rounded, closely spaced ribs. Scales of very thin, very closely packed concentric lamellae. The overall effect is rather neat and tidy. Light cream or white color with a few small dots of pink, red, red-brown, or a combination. Exterior surface feels like fine sandpaper, not rough. (27 mm)

Distribution: Uncommon, South Sinai, and from Hurghada to Shalatein.

Notes: The only species likely to be initially confused with this is *Gloripallium maculosum* in which LV is convex, not flat, so there can be no mistake. *G. maculosum* RV has fewer ribs, and larger, more untidy scales. Its interspaces are wider. The general effect is more robust and coarser.

Gloripallium maculosum (Forsskål in Niebuhr, 1775)

Synonym *Ostrea sanguinolenta* Gmelin, 1791

Mottled Scallop

Endemic

15–56 mm. → Strong red and white patterns, around ten strong, high, round ribs. Interspaces wide and deep with one to three scaly riblets in them. Tops of the ribs rough to the touch. (41.5 mm)

Distribution: Common in all regions.

Notes: See *Excellichlamys spectabilis* above.

Decatopecten plica

Excellichlamys spectabilis

Gloripallium maculosum

Juxtamusium maldivensis (E.A. Smith, 1903)
Maldives Scallop
11–16 mm. → Small, fragile shell, around 30 small undulating ribs. No scales, smooth feeling. White, pink, or orange, plain or flecked. (16 mm)
Distribution: Rare, Gulf of Aqaba, Hurghada Reefs.

Laevichlamys rubromaculata (Sowerby II, 1842)
Red-spotted Scallop
8–35 mm. Small- to medium-sized fragile shell, yellow or white, left valve with red spots. LV with relatively large triangular anterior ear. RV not usually spotted, with a more rectangular anterior ear with five or six very closely spaced riblets. The ribs on the RV are more numerous, narrower, more densely spaced, and more similar to each other. (26 mm)
Distribution: Common around reefs in the Hurghada–Safaga area and farther south.
Notes: Of the specimens I have seen in Egypt, the smaller shells are usually yellow, larger ones usually white, and mid-size either color.

Laevichlamys ruschenbergerii (Tryon, 1869)
9–45 mm. → Plain maroon shell with numerous narrow ribs and very narrow tall erect scales the same maroon color as the shell. The scales never extend across the entire breadth of the ribs. Umbonal area may be white. Juveniles bright orange. (48 mm)
Distribution: Rare. Gulf of Aqaba and Safaga.
Notes: Most specimens have a stylized lotus pattern on the umbo that appears to be made of tiny cracks. Magnification may be needed to see it. *Laevichlamys ruschenbergerii* always has more and narrower ribs than *L. superficialis*. It may have an occasional white scale, but they are almost always dark maroon. See below.

Juxtamusium maldivensis

Laevichlamys rubromaculata

juvenile

Laevichlamys ruschenbergerii

Laevichlamys superficialis (Forsskål in Niebuhr, 1775)

17–63 mm. → RV with around 20 to 25 flat ribs, the broadest with low broad white scales. The anterior ear is large and shaped like a wobbly rectangle with a rounded bay at the base next to the body. LV very similar but fewer of the ribs with scales. LV anterior ear much larger than the posterior but shaped like an equilateral triangle. Various colors: usually mottled fulvous or orange with lighter or darker rays, occasionally all white or yellow. (53 mm)

Distribution: Common in the Gulf of Suez and around reefs in the Straits of Gubal to Safaga. Occasional in Shalatein and the Gulf of Aqaba.

Notes: Some specimens of *L. superficialis* can be difficult to separate from *L. ruschenbergerii.* This latter is rarely found, so the specimen is more likely to be *L. superficialis.* The ribs on *L. superficialis* are flat and broad, scales are low, broad, and white. On *L. ruschenbergerii* the ribs are narrower and the scales are maroon, very narrow, and much taller.

Mimachlamys andamanica (Preston, 1908)

9–17 mm. → A huge number of fine, regular ribs (45 to 70) covered with very tiny scales. Rough to the touch. The ears seem disproportionately large for such a small shell. Bright orange or pink. (17 mm)

Distribution: Rare, northern Gulf of Aqaba, Hurghada Reefs.

Notes: The rough feel of this species makes it easy to separate from the similar-sized but smooth-feeling *Juxtamusium maldivensis.*

Mimachlamys sanguinea (Linnaeus, 1758)

Synonyms *Ostrea senatoria* and *Ostrea porphyrea* Gmelin, 1791

20–66 mm. → Narrow, evenly shaped, and tightly spaced rounded ribs with deep narrow interstices. Colors strong: white, orange, red, brown, or a mixture. Inside color usually similar to the outside. (54 mm)

Distribution: Moderately common in the Gulf of Suez. Not found elsewhere.

Laevichlamys superficialis

Mimachlamys andamanica

Mimachlamys sanguinea

Mirapecten yaroni Dijkstra & Knudsen, 1998
Mirapecten rastellum of authors non Lamarck, 1819
Yaron's Scallop
Endemic
14–57 mm. RV nine ribs somewhat angular. Scales strong at the top edge of the ears and on the lateral ribs, weak and narrow on medial ribs. LV eight rounded, undulating ribs. No scales at the top of the ears. Scales strong and broad on ribs, weaker on laterals. Many different colors and patterns of different colors on the same shell: red, pink, brownish-purple, orange, yellow, and white. Interior brightly colored. (45 mm)
Distribution: Common in the Gulf of Aqaba, South Sinai, and around reefs from Hurghada south. Very rare in the Gulf of Suez.

Pecten erythraeensis Sowerby II, 1842
Red Sea Pecten
Endemic
13–78 mm. RV very tumid. LV nearly flat, but slightly concave—near the umbo it pushes up into the body area. RV usually white, cream, or beige with a few markings in orange-beige or red. LV often plain dark red inside, reddish patterns outside. (57 mm)
Distribution: Common, the Gulf of Suez and Great Bitter Lake only.

Mirapecten yaroni

juvenile

Pecten erythraeensis

Semipallium crouchi (E.A. Smith, 1892)
11–43 mm. → Anterior lateral margin only half the length of the posterior one. Rather flat, eight to eleven low, rolling ribs. Interspaces similar. → Radial threads, usually stronger near the ventral margin. Reticulate microsculpture, → no scales. Lighter and darker loosely concentric bands of yellow-orange with a few slightly darker ones, either plain or mottled. (42 mm)
Distribution: Rare, associated with coral reefs from the Gubal Straits to Marsa Alam.
Notes: Unfortunately the auricles are missing from the right valve specimen.

Family SPONDYLIDAE
The teeth of the Spondylidae are unique to this family, and easy to recognize. Each valve has two strong teeth and two big pits. The shape and sculpture vary considerably within some species. Color plays a larger role in identification of the spondylids than in most families, but even this it not absolute. Because of this different authors have used different names over the years and discussion continues to the present.

Spondylus candidus Lamarck, 1819
22–43 mm. → Bright coral color. Specimens range from all coral to white with just a little bit of coral or any combination in between. Few to many raised ribs, fine radial threads in between, very few spines. Shape unusually constant with the ventral margin longer than the dorsal. (30 mm)
Distribution: Uncommon, most likely to be found across South Sinai to Hurghada and south to just north of Marsa Alam.

Spondylus hystrix Röding, 1798
Synonym *Spondylus nicobaricus* Schreibers, 1793
16–36 mm. White with small dark purple markings, spines and ribs sharp and fine. Inner margin white or colored. (35 mm)
Distribution: Occasional in South Sinai and the Gulf of Suez, common around offshore reefs from Hurghada to Marsa Alam.

Semipallium crouchi

Spondylus candidus

Spondylus hystrix

Spondylus marisrubri Röding, 1798

Synonym *Spondylus spinosus* Schreibers, 1793

25–75 mm. Extremely variable, inside and out. Usually shades of red, purple, or yellow-orange; ribs, riblets, and spines the same color or white, usually heavy, coarse. Interior usually white, with a yellow, orange, red, or purple dry-looking margin, with or without a glossy caramel or brown band. (73 mm)

Distribution: Abundant in the Gulf of Suez. Found in all areas.

Notes: Any *Spondylus* not fitting one of the other species given here is probably *S. marisrubri*.

Spondylus marisrubri

Spondylus smytheae Lamprell, 1998

47–54 mm. → Oblique ovate shape with short spines resembling rose thorns. Usually only the posterior side of the UV with spines, normally three or four ribs of them. Spines very short, the same color as the shell, usually orange or purple. The crenulations on the inner margin are distinctive: strong, neat, straight, and nearly parallel to each other. Inner margin the same color as the shell. (50 mm)

Distribution: All regions but rare.

Notes: Some specialists consider this species to be conspecific with *Spondylus fauroti* Jousseaume in Lamy, 1927. However, that species always has a distinctive black line. I have never seen a black-lined specimen in the northern Red Sea.

Family ANOMIIDAE

The common name for shells in this family is jingle shells. They make a nice jingle sound when dropped on a very hard surface. The lower valve attaches itself to the substrate by a calcified plug of byssal threads passing through an opening, the foramen.

Anomia achaeus Gray, 1850

10–22 mm. → Thin shell, irregularly shaped, lustrous, and sometimes translucent. → UV ligament not on the margin of the shell, but a little inside the body cavity. Scarified roughly oval area having within it a kidney-shaped scar and two very small fused roundish scars. → Lower valve with foramen (see the translucent white image opposite). Quite variable in color and form. Never with chomata. (21 mm)

Distribution: Rare.

Notes: Beginners may initially encounter difficulty in distinguishing the UVs of Anomiidae from Ostreidae. Anomiidae never have chomata, Ostreidae always do. To definitively separate the UVs of *A. achaeus* and *Pododesmus caelata* you must be able to see the scars. In both species small scars are located inside a somewhat irregular ovoid scar near the hinge. *A. achaeus* has one medium-sized scar and two vary small ones, which may be fused together. *P. caelata* has one large oval scar and a tiny rounded one which is fused to the base of the oval zone. However, these scars are often obscure. But in the Egyptian Red Sea we are fortunate because *Anomia achaeus* is always lustrous and without a pattern. And *Pododesmus caelata* always has some kind of pattern or markings and irregular margins.

Pododesmus caelata (Reeve, 1859)

21–23 mm. → Ligament placement as in *Anomia achaeus* (above). UV usually somewhat corrugated. Exterior usually encrusted, interior glossy coral color or beige with reddish veins, looking a little like a small elongate crinkly fall leaf. (23 mm)

Distribution: Very rare, Hurghada–Safaga area, South Sinai.

Notes: See *Anomia achaeus* above.

Spondylus smytheae

actual size

Anomia achaeus

x3

Pododesmus caelata

Family CHAMIDAE

Recognizing a shell that belongs to the Chamidae family is quite easy. The umbonal area is always coiled. The lower valve (LV) coil may be quite large. One large slanting tooth and slot on each valve. The more intensely colored side of each valve is the posterior. LV deep, cements itself to rocks, coral, or other shells underwater. When the animal dies this shell usually remains in place. The upper valve (UV) is more commonly found on the beach.

There are two genera in the Red Sea. Use these tips to identify them:

1. LV somewhat bowl shaped, with an attachment area.

• Hold the shell as if it were still attached to a rock, the inside facing you and the umbo at the top or pointing away.

• Look at the coil of the umbo. Follow the apparent direction of the coil from the margin to the apex. If this structure appears to come up from the left-hand side of the shell and move to the right, you are holding the left valve of the animal, the margin to your right is the anterior, and the genus is *Chama*. Most shells you find will be in this genus.

• If the coil seems to come up from the right-hand side of the shell and to continue across to the left and wind around back on top of itself this is the right valve, the anterior is to your left, and the genus is *Pseudochama*.

2. UV relatively flat.

• Hold the shell with the inside facing you and the umbo pointing up or away. Now tilt the umbonal end slightly upward toward you.

• Look at the coil of the umbo. If the coil on the upper valve winds from the right side of the shell upward and left it is in the genus *Chama* and the anterior is to your left.

• If it winds from left to right it is *Pseudochama* and the anterior is to your right.

Chama asperella Lamarck, 1819

13–24 mm. A small white shell. Inner margins very finely crenulate. UV → Pink area umbonally, either inside or outside or both. → Very fine, relatively densely spaced, erect half-tubular spines. No posterior sulcus. (24 mm)
Distribution: Infrequent in all areas.
Notes: Many specimens found in Egypt and attributable to this species on the basis of the scales lack the characteristic pink umbonal patch. Some may have a fine pink line.

Chama aspersa Reeve, 1846

14–26 mm. Small white or coral-colored shell with → chestnut rays, or tiny dots, or a broad posterior band. Color strong or weak, internally and/or externally, always on posterior side only. Inner margin finely crenulate. UV usually quite flat, scales if present not erect. LV exterior often without scales, may have low concentric lamellae, ruffled or fluted to form small low subtubular spines, a bit stronger on the posterior side, sometimes with chestnut color. Coil usually strong, protuberant. (21 mm)
Distribution: Very common in the Gulfs of Aqaba and Suez. Rare elsewhere. The coral-colored ones are common in the Gulf of Suez.
Notes: Some *C. aspersa* are pure white. The shells are rarely encrusted.

x2

actual size

Chama asperella

x2

actual size

Chama aspersa

Chama fragum Reeve, 1846
Chama brassica Reeve, 1847 of some authors
40–50 mm. → UV radial red lines on the underside the scales, smooth internal margin. Moderately large, heavy shell. Usually white, may be pale rose or orange. (37 mm)
Distribution: Rare, Marsa Alam area and south only.
Notes: May be confused with *C. limbula* but that never has colored lines on the underside of the scales. Some specimens may lack this characteristic. If the scales are intact but not colored, look for low radial ribs on the scales; if present it is *C. fragum.*

Chama lazarus Linnaeus, 1758
31 mm. → UV Strong, widely spaced lamellae, yellow area near the umbo and one or more strong purple-red curving radial rays. (31 mm)
Distribution: Very rarely found as it inhabits deeper water. Gulf of Aqaba only.

Chama limbula Lamarck, 1819
15–60 mm. → Thick, heavy shell, usually eroded smooth and white. Subtriangular or subcircular. UV with posterior sulcus and scales; these usually removed by erosion. Strong colorless adductor muscle scars. Dark purplish-red ring around the smooth interior margin, rarely any color except on the margin. Margin smooth, not crenulate. (42 mm)
Distribution: All regions, very common.
Notes: Pseudochama corbieri has similar shape and color, but coils in the opposite direction (see pages 210–11).

Chama pacifica Broderip, 1834
26–67 mm. → Brick red exterior, numerous white ribs. Usually stubby remains of heavy white scales or spines. → White rays all emanate from the upper umbonal area, spread out lengthwise over the shell. Interior mostly white. Postero-ventral margins and adjoining area usually purple red. Inner margin crenulate. (67 mm)
Distribution: Common in the Gulf of Suez. Rare elsewhere.
Notes: The external color and pattern of the white rays are good field identification characteristics. *C. pacifica* is always brick red to burnt orange; *C. savignyi* (pages 210–11) is always purple-red. In *C. pacifica* the white rays start near the white umbo and run the length of the shell; in *C. savignyi* they start from an unmarked spot in the center of the shell and radiate out toward the margins.

Chama fragum

Chama lazarus

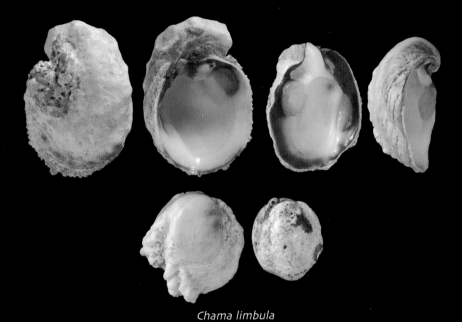

Chama limbula

Chama pacifica

Chama savignyi Jousseaume in Lamy, 1921
Synonym *Chama plinthota* Cox, 1927
25–55 mm. Strong, solid shell, often elongate and pointed. → Purple-red and white rays on both the UVs and LVs. → UV Rays radiate from the center of the shell, not from the umbo. UVs from ideal environments have two very strong ridges on the exterior left (posterior) side. → Inner margin smooth. (53 mm)
Distribution: Moderately common, all areas, but rare in northern Gulf of Suez.
Notes: For contrast with *C. pacifica* see above. *C. limbula* (above) is similar in color, sulcus, and smooth margin but never has purple and white rays.

Chama yaroni Delsaerdt, 1986
Endemic
22–35 mm. Very similar to *C. savignyi* (above) but → orange in color instead of purple. Two strong ridges of → broad scales. (17 mm)
Distribution: Moderately common in the Gulf of Aqaba, infrequent in the Gulf of Suez to Safaga.
Notes: Some specialists consider this simply a color variation of *C. savignyi*; others regard it as a separate species. Of the specimens I have seen a higher proportion of orange shells are subcircular. The purple ones are more likely to be elongate with a pointed tip, but both colors occur in both shapes.

Pseudochama corbieri (Jonas, 1846)
20–42 mm. Subcircular to subtrigonal, LV coil often large. White with red-violet inside, sometimes concentric lines of color show near the ventral margin on the outside. UV flat. Coiling flat but visible. White with deep red-violet. → Inner margin smooth. (30 mm)
Distribution: Common in the Gulf of Suez. Rare if ever elsewhere.
Notes: *P. corbieri* may be entirely purple inside, color usually more reddish and UV coil more visible than in *Chama limbula*.

Pseudochama rianae Delsaerdt, 1986
Pseudochama radians of some authors
Endemic
16–41 mm. Shell usually not encrusted, appears clean. Delicate sculpture of small riblets, short spines and scales. → UV interior often with a red ray and a yellow ray, or other patterns and combinations of those colors. → Inner margin crenulate. (31 mm)
Distribution: Rare to occasional in the Gulf of Suez, rare to never in other areas.
Notes: This species has a very thin, lightweight shell compared to *P. corbieri*. Surprisingly it is often found with both valves still together.

Chama savignyi

Chama yaroni

Pseudochama corbieri

Pseudochama rianae

Family LUCINIDAE

Shells in this family are usually quite circular in outline and white in color. Most Red Sea Lucines have interesting, distinguishing sculpture and denticulate margins, with the notable exception of the genus *Andontia*. Most of the nearly circular 'little white clams' found on the beach are members of either the Lucinidae family or the related family, the Ungulinidae.

Anodontia kora Taylor & Glover, 2005
Anodontia edentula (Linnaeus, 1758) of some authors
8.5–60 mm. → No teeth at all. → Large, tumid. Sculpture of weak growth lines only, smooth feeling. Pallial line entire with a secondary line of attachment scars to the interior, anterior side only. (47 mm)
Distribution: Common, occasionally abundant, all regions. Prefers fine sand, silt, and sea grass.
Notes: A. edentula (Linnaeus, 1758) was the name commonly used for most spherical, plain white, toothless circum-Arabian lucines for many years, even though various taxonomists such as Reeve had long ago identified several different species. Taylor and Glover did a review of all recent *Anodontia* and separated them into numerous different species in 2005, reviving some old names and describing some new species as appropriate. The genus name means 'without teeth'—an aptly descriptive name. This species' name, *kora*, means 'ball' in Arabic, a reference to its ball-like shape.

Anodontia ovulum (Reeve, 1850)
Anodontia edentula (Linnaeus, 1758) of some authors
10–24 mm. Extremely tumid small shell. Beak large for size of shell, anterior may be extended. Pallial line discontinuous. (10 mm)
Distribution: Uncommon, most likely south of Marsa Alam.
Notes: Smaller at maturity and proportionately much more tumid than other Red Sea *Anodontia.*

Anodontia ovum (Reeve, 1850)
Anodontia edentula (Linnaeus, 1758) of some authors
10–32 mm. Moderately tumid, small beak. May have small glittering dots on the internal surface. Pallial line continuous, not broken, close to shell margin. (31 mm)
Distribution: Moderately common, found in all areas.
Notes: Differs from *A. kora* in being smaller, less tumid, more circular, and having the pallial line closer to the ventral margin.

Cardiolucina semperiana (Issel, 1869)
4–9 mm. → Small, strong shell with strong cancellate sculpture. Concentric ridges somewhat stronger than the radial. Posterior sulcate, subtruncate. (8 mm)
Distribution: Very common in the Gulf of Suez, locally and occasionally common elsewhere.
Notes: Because the size, shape, and color are similar, a beginner could confuse this shell with *Fragum sueziensis* (Cardiidae family), but that shell has strong radial ribs with tiny scales.

Anodontia kora

Anodontia ovulum

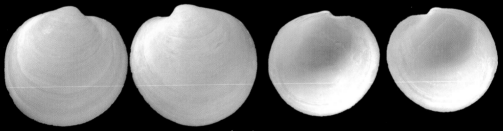

Anodontia ovum

actual size   x2

Cardiolucina semperiana

Cavilucina fieldingi (H. Adams, 1871)
Endemic
9–18 mm. Outline subcircular, anterior end protruding. → Fine concentric ridges, rough to the touch. → Pallial sinus large extending downward from above the posterior adductor scar to a point lower than the base of the anterior scar, nearly reaching it. (18 mm) *Distribution:* Locally common, Hurghada–Safaga area. Occasional farther south and in the Gulf of Suez. Rare if ever in Gulf of Aqaba.

Chavania erythraea (Issel, 1869)
8–11 mm. → Exterior with a matte finish composed of micro-cancellate sculpture. Feels like fine emery paper if you run your fingernail over it. Long, strong, slanting resilifer, entirely internal. Weak sulcus on each side of the beak. Inner margin minutely denticulate, more easily felt with the fingernail than seen. (11 mm) *Distribution:* Very common in the Gulf of Suez down to Safaga. Also found in Shalatein and Dahab, but rare elsewhere.

Codakia paytenorum (Iredale, 1937)
13–47 mm. Inside light or intense yellow with a pink or purple ring around the margin. Exterior white with → fine incised radial lines, very weak medially. Surface relatively smooth to the touch. Seems to prefer deeper sandy areas near offshore reefs and is only rarely found on the beach. Please leave it lying there for others to enjoy! (45 mm) *Distribution:* Moderately common near reefs from Hurghada south.
Notes: See *Codakia tigerina* (below).

Codakia tigerina (Linnaeus, 1758)
14–80 mm. Large, thick, and heavy. Its sculpture is a very good example of the term 'cancellate': the concentric and radial ridges are of nearly equal strength and spacing. A little peak forms where the two ridges cross each other. It has a rough feel to the touch. Interior white or yellow, usually with strong pink at the hinge or sometimes all around the inner margin. (76 mm)
Distribution: Common south of Marsa Alam and in the Gulf of Aqaba and Straits of Tiran. Very rare north of Zafarana in the Gulf of Suez.
Notes: The color pattern is nearly identical to that of *C. payentorum.* To distinguish the two species pay close attention to the sculpture. *C. paytenorum* has weak sculpture with incised radial lines; *C. tigerina* has rough raised cancellate sculpture all over.

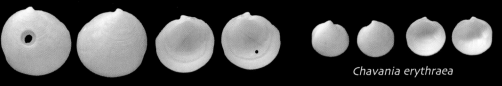

Cavilucina fieldingi

Chavania erythraea

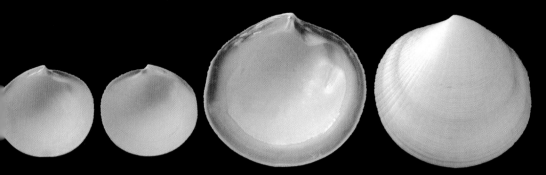

Codakia paytenorum

Codakia tigerina

Ctena divergens (Philippi, 1850)
Divergent Lucine
8–25 mm. Many narrow radial ribs, spreading out (diverging) as the shell gets wider. Toward the ventral margin some of the ribs split into two ribs. Usually all white, sometimes all yellow. (19 mm)
Distribution: Abundant from Hurghada south, occasional in Gulf of Suez. Uncommon in the Gulf of Aqaba.

Divalinga arabica Dekker & Goud, 1994
Egracina ornata (Reeve, 1850) of some authors
6–35 mm. Thin, light shell. → Finely incised lines forming inverted chevrons. Each chevron crossing the entire shell. Points of the chevrons (upside-down 'V's) not exactly in the middle of the shell, but a little over toward the anterior side. (17 mm)
Distribution: Common in the Gulf of Suez, moderately common in the Gulf of Aqaba, occasional farther south.

Divaricella macandreae (H. Adams, 1871)
Endemic
10–18 mm. Circular in shape with acute ribs forming chevrons. Ribs extend beyond the margin of the shell giving spiky look. Prefers gentle waters and sandy, silty bottoms. (18 mm)
Distribution: Occasional Hurghada to Shalatein, rare north of Hurghada.

Lamellolucina dentifera (Jonas, 1846)
12–28 mm. Exquisite sculpture of strong concentric lamellae. Posterior lamellae extend beyond outline forming the 'teeth' for which it is named. Sulcus on both sides of beaks. Lives in sand in quiet areas, both silty and clean. It needs calm water to grow and preserve its beautiful ornamentation. (26 mm)
Distribution: All regions, usually uncommon, but occasionally common in the Hurghada–Safaga area.

Pillucina vietnamica (Zorina, 1978)
Synonym *Pillucina fischeriana* (Issel, 1869)
8–14 mm. → Numerous faint undulating ribs, most noticeable at lateral margins. Concentric ridges undulating along with the ribs visible with magnification. Sculpture quite variable. (14 mm)
Distribution: Common in the Gulf of Suez and all the way to Shalatein.

Rasta lamyi (Abrard, 1942)
Endemic
20–27 mm. Irregular shapes. Beak tilted to the anterior, short straight anterodorsal slope. Weak irregular concentric sculpture. → Distinctive sharp radial or vertical indentations or creases may be present. (27 mm)
Distribution: Rare, offshore between Hurghada and Wadi Gimaal, shallow silty coral reef areas.

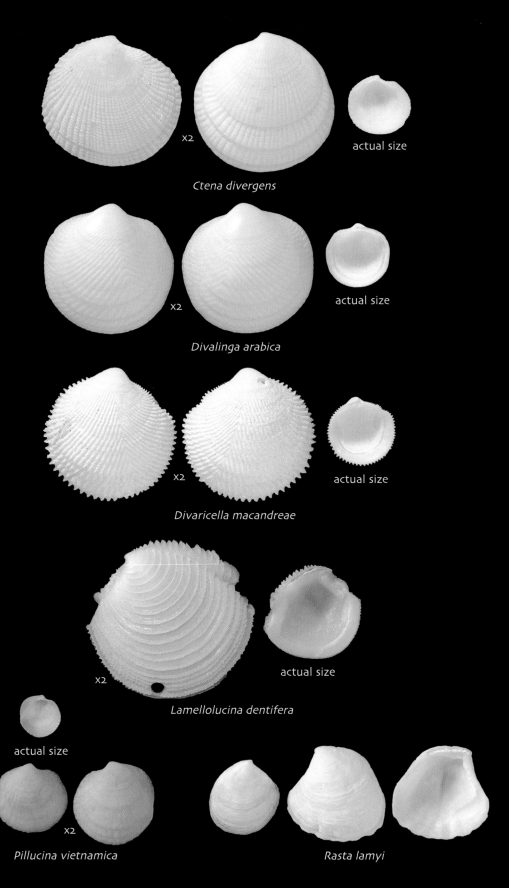

x2

actual size

Ctena divergens

x2

actual size

Divalinga arabica

x2

actual size

Divaricella macandreae

x2

actual size

Lamellolucina dentifera

actual size

x2

Pillucina vietnamica

Rasta lamyi

Family UNGULINIDAE, Genus *Diplodonta*

All these subcircular white shells have two small distinct cardinal teeth. The shells vary from rather flat to tumid or nearly spherical. The inner margins are always smooth and the sculpture is mostly concentric but very weak.

Diplodonta bogii Van Aartsen, 2004

5–7 mm. Small, thin shell, nearly circular, weakly tumid, beak small and tilted.
Distribution: Rare, northern Gulf of Suez. (7 mm)

Diplodonta globosa (Forsskål in Niebuhr, 1775)

28–25 mm. → Strongly globose shape, strong shell and teeth. Ligament partially internal. (33 mm)
Distribution: Erratically uncommon, northern Gulf of Suez, Shalatein.
Notes: Anodontia species, which are very common, are similar in size, shape, and color, but have absolutely no teeth and have thinner shells. The presence of *Diplodonta globosa* is wildly unpredictable. I searched for it for ten years without finding a single one, and then found three specimens on the same day at a beach I had visited at least 20 times before.

Diplodonta raveyensis Sturany, 1899

7–13 mm. → Strong and heavy for its small size. Beak pronounced, tilted toward anterior. Shell quite tumid. (12 mm)
Distribution: Uncommon, northern Gulf of Suez to Wadi Lahmi.

actual size

x3

Diplodonta bogii

Diplodonta globosa

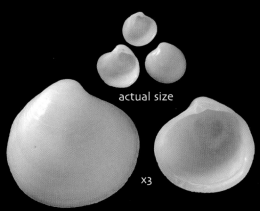

actual size

x3

Diplodonta raveyensis

Diplodonta subrotunda (Issel, 1869)

(*D. subrotundata* is a common misspelling referring to the same shell.)

9–21 mm. → Ligament entirely external, sits on nearly flat little plates. These bordered by a fine incised line. No lunule. (19 mm)

Distribution: Abundant in all sandy areas except the northern Gulf of Aqaba.

Notes: There are at least three all-white, thin-shelled, very similar species of the genus *Diplodonta* living in the Egyptian Red Sea. They can be differentiated only by closely examining the hinge area and the resilifer, preferably with magnification. *D. subrotunda* is the only one with external plates for the ligament.

Diplodonta sp. 1

8.5–18 mm. Hinge line straight, not curved, both sides slant downward very lightly from beak. → Anterior and posterior portions of the hinge area are much more like each other in height in this species than in any of the others in its genus. Postero-dorsal hinge area does not extend into the shell cavity at all. Upper edge of the resilifer slants downward but the lower edge remains horizontal. Ligament both internal and external. Broad lunule area, weakly incised. (17 mm)

Distribution: Uncommon, northern Gulf of Suez, Safaga, and south of Berenice. Occasionally locally common.

Diplodonta sp. 2

8–22 mm. Posterior dorsal area has a long, thick, high (relatively speaking) space for carrying the ligament. → Posterior dorsal margin is about twice as high as the anterior, usually about 1 mm, remaining almost equally high along its length from the beak to its end. Difference between the anterior and posterior readily observable without magnification. → Lower posterior end of this area protrudes significantly into body cavity area of the shell. Resilifer midway between the top and bottom of this area, long and narrow, slanting downwards from the beak to the posterior end, almost reaching the body cavity. → Ligament primarily internal. Beak small, not inflated. (20 mm)

Distribution: Moderately common, northern Gulf of Suez to Safaga.

X3   actual size

Diplodonta subrotunda

X3   actual size

Diplodonta sp. 1

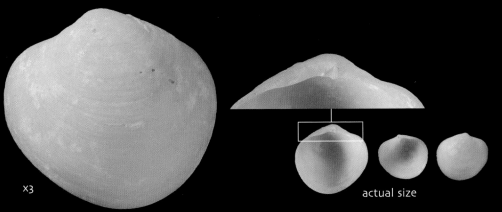

X3   actual size

Diplodonta sp. 2

Family SPORTELLIDAE

Very little is known about this family. The shells are usually rhomboidal in shape, varying within each species as to exact proportions (squarish vs. elongate), and surprisingly strong for their small size.

Basterotia angulata (H. Adams, 1871)
Endemic
6.5–12 mm. → Strong angular carina, sharply pointed posterior, weak concentric growth marks. → Shell covered with tiny irregular pustules. (12 mm)
Distribution: Rare, Dahab, Hurghada and south to Wadi Gimaal.
Notes: Corbula sulculosa is similar in size and shape but never has pustules or granules and always has strong, even concentric sculpture.

Basterotia arcula Melvill, 1898
Synonyms *Basterotia djiboutiensis* H. Fisher, 1901,
10 mm. → Extraordinarily produced beak. Strong angular carina. Rough pustulose surface. (10 mm)
Distribution: Very rare, Hurghada.
Notes: Specialists disagree about the identity of this species. Some believe it is simply an overgrown form of *B. angulata*.

Basterotia borbonica (Deshayes, 1863)
4–12 mm. → Weak, rounded carina. Shape more rounded than the other two species. Surface primarily smooth, irregular concentric growth marks, some specimens slightly pustulose. (12 mm)
Distribution: Always uncommon, all areas.

actual size

x3

Basterotia angulata

actual size

x3

Basterotia arcula

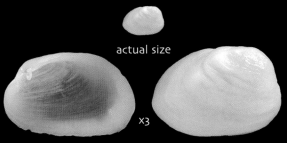

actual size

x3

Basterotia borbonica

Family CARDITIDAE

The shells in this family are sometimes mistakenly called cockles due to their superficial resemblance. The Carditidae never have strongly developed lateral teeth, whereas the true cockles, Cardiidae, do. The rounder species live buried in sand. The modioliform ones, like the mussels they resemble in shape, live attached by byssus threads to rocks.

Cardita variegata Bruguière, 1792

11–34 mm. → White with caramel, brown, or almost black spots. Modioliform. About twelve large, curving ribs plus six very small ones near the anterior. White or brown inside. They live attached to rocks by byssal threads. (27 mm)
Distribution: Common in all regions.

Cardites akabana (Sturany, 1899)

6–16 mm. → About fifteen regular tuberculate ribs. Subcircular. Plain white or with a few light brown markings. (10 mm)
Distribution: Locally and occasionally common, Gulf of Aqaba, Hurghada–Safaga area.

Cardites rufa (Deshayes in Laborde, 1834)

Endemic
12–50 mm. → About twenty broad flat-topped ribs, with or without cross bars. Posterior ribs narrower and more rounded. In cross section the ribs are always broader than high. Off-white to orange-brown or a mixture of both. (50 mm)
Distribution: Excellent specimens are common in the Gulf of Aqaba; worn ones in the northern Gulf of Suez. Occasional near Hurghada. Rare further south.
Notes: The rib shape prevents confusion of white juveniles of *C. rufa* with *C. akabana* whose ribs are proportionately narrower and more rounded.

Family CARDIIDAE

The common name for all the Cardiidae is cockles or cockle shells. The umbos and lateral teeth are pronounced. The shells usually have radial ribs and a crenulated ventral margin. They can be thick or thin.

Acrosterigma biradiatum (Bruguière, 1789)

24–55 mm. → Inside milky white with two dramatic coral-colored rays. Exterior surface smoother than most. Requires fine coral sand and quiet water. (43 mm)
Distribution: Never common, all regions.

Acrosterigma maculosum (W. Wood, 1815)

17–39 mm. → Pinkish light brown spots on the outside, red violet spots on the inside. Regular ovoid outline. More than forty-five smooth, rounded, narrow, radial ribs. (30 mm)
Distribution: Common in the Gulf of Suez, occasional to rare elsewhere.

Cardita variegata

Cardites akabana

Cardites rufa

Acrosterigma biradiatum

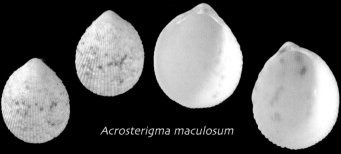

Acrosterigma maculosum

Afrocardium richardi (Audouin, 1826)
8–15 mm. Modioliform with many narrow ribs. Posterior ribs with strong upright scales giving it a rough, raspy feel. All white, or posterior area may be mottled red-brown, color showing more strongly on the interior. (15 mm)
Distribution: Locally common in the northern Gulf of Suez, occasional near Hurghada and Wadi Lahmi.

Cerastoderma glauca (Bruguière, 1789)
14–33 mm. Shape variable, around twenty ribs. Thin white shell, posterior often dark, → rich chestnut inside. (26 mm)
Distribution: Common in brackish water, Port of Suez, Birket Qaroun in Fayoum Oasis.
Notes: Subfossil shells of this and possibly several species of cockles are commonly found on the beaches of the Gulf of Suez.

Ctenocardia fornicata (Sowerby II, 1840)
10–21 mm. → Quadrate (squarish) posterior, sharp carina, many narrow closely spaced ribs. White or white with red spots, white or rose interior. (21 mm)
Distribution: Common in the Gulf of Suez, occasional in all other regions.

Fragum nivale (Reeve, 1845)
9–26 mm. → Heart-shaped, lightweight shell. Posterior straight, carina sharp, posterior slope very steep. Ribs numerous and narrow with small arched scales, often absent in juveniles and beached shells. (23 mm)
Distribution: Common in all regions.
Notes: The scales are stronger, larger, and more persistent on shells south of Marsa Alam.

Fragum sueziensis (Issel, 1869)
3.5–6 mm. → Tiny but typical cockle shell with strong teeth, many ribs with arched scales across them and grooves between. White, sometimes with pink markings. (5 mm)
Distribution: Common, all regions.
Notes: This tiny cockle was originally known from the Gulf of Suez; hence its name. It is the only cockle shell in the Red Sea that is mature at this size. Take care not to confuse this with *Cardiolucina semperiana*, which is similar in size and color but lacks the strong lateral teeth and has cancellate sculpture with strong concentric ridges.

Afrocardium richardi

subfossil

Cerastoderma glauca

Ctenocardia fornicata

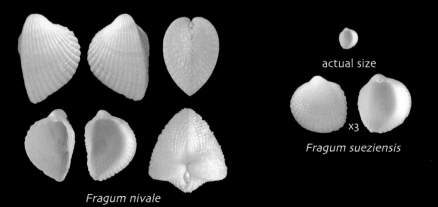

actual size

x3

Fragum sueziensis

Fragum nivale

Fulvia australis (Sowerby, 1834)

8–41 mm. Shiny, thin, light shells, stronger than they look, with a great number of fine ribs, stronger laterally. Cardinal and lateral teeth prominent. Pale cream, with freckles or other markings of beige to pink. Color more intense on the inside, where posterior area may be yellow, but never red. (40 mm)

Distribution: Throughout the Egyptian Red Sea but only in areas of fine sand or mud. Most common in the Gulf of Suez.

Notes: The animal lives buried in fine sand and mud. In winter storms many juveniles are often torn from the substrate by the waves and carried onto the shore. Juveniles are rounder, adults become higher than broad. See *F. fragilis* (below).

Fulvia fragilis (Forsskål in Niebuhr, 1775)

11–67 mm. → Strong dark red-violet coloring on the inside posterior. Very fragile when young, as the name indicates, becoming strong at maturity. (52 mm)

Distribution: All regions, in fine sand or mud only, most common in the northern end of the Gulf of Suez. Thrives in sewage-polluted water.

Notes: Perhaps less common than *F. australis*. Although the specimens shown are easy to distinguish from *F. australis*, some specimens found on the beach can be quite difficult to separate. If it is smaller than 20 mm and does not have the red marking inside even the experts content themselves with just calling it *Fulvia* sp.

Lunulicardia auricula (Niebuhr, 1775)

Endemic

12–51 mm. → Lunule extends deep into the body cavity. (43 mm)

Distribution: Common in the Gulf of Suez.

Notes: This is one of the very first shells from the Red Sea to be named. Niebuhr accompanied Forsskål on his expedition from Denmark to the Red Sea (1761–67) and was the only one to return alive (the others all died of malaria and/or dysentery). Juveniles are relatively broader than adults. On some specimens the lunule is shallower, but these are still considered to be the same species. On the shallow lunule specimens the posterior slope is nearly vertical and the anterior much more flared. The shallow lunule form is less common overall and more likely to be found south of Marsa Alam. Barbara Rusmore found the complete specimen, pictured on the far right, dead on the shore.

Fulvia australis

subadult

Fulvia fragilis

subadult

shallow lunule

juvenile

Lunulicardia auricula

Lyrocardium anaxium Oliver and Chesney, 1997

22–40 mm. → Raised oblique lines on the anterior, very fine ribs on the posterior.
Exterior glossy, rose pink and white with delicate chestnut patterning. Interior white with
an umbonal blush ranging from apricot yellow to deep coral pink. (40 mm)
Distribution: Rare, Hurghada–Safaga area, Marsa Alam.

Vasticardium marerubrum (Voskuil & Onverwagt, 1991)

Trachycardium enode (Sowerby, 1834) of some authors
Endemic
20–71 mm. → Large, heavy, scaly shell with about 28 to 34 large, rounded ribs. White
with brown, purple, or yellow marks or spots. Interior white, some with a rich yellow
band along the inside posterior margin. Juveniles are more rounded in shape and may
have dark purple spots showing in the interior. (71 mm)
Distribution: Common in the Gulf of Aqaba, across South Sinai, and down the coast
to Shalatein.
Notes: None of the other large Indo-Pacific cockles are found in Egyptian waters.

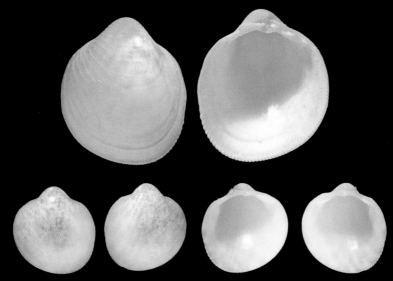

Lyrocardium anaxium

juvenile

Vasticardium marerubrum

Subfamily TRIDACNINAE

The giant clams are now considered a subfamily of the Cardiidae rather than their own family. They live nestled into spaces among the coral both on the top of the reef plate and in deeper water. If you snorkel very quietly and slowly you might see one. Tridacnids have a brightly colored mantle, usually turquoise blue or purple with dark spots, sometimes beige with black spots. This fleshy mantle contains algae which convert sunlight into energy. The clam waits with its valves separated to catch the sunlight—a natural example of converting sunlight into sugars. Never try to touch one or drop anything into the open clam.

Their greatest predators are human beings. Any damage to the reef (such as that from dynamite, pollution by fresh water or sewage from hotels, or sand kicked up by waders) endangers the clam. In addition, the people who have traditionally lived here in harmony with the desert and the reef depend on the tridacnids (and other molluscs and fish) for protein. As the reefs become less healthy or even destroyed, and the people's right of access to the reefs is taken away by the construction of hotels, there is the danger that juvenile clams will be harvested as a vital source of protein. In the 1980s it was not uncommon to find *Tridacna maxima* reaching 300 mm; now it is rare to see one over 150 mm.

Tridacna maxima (Röding, 1798)
Giant Clam

14–118 mm. Outline variable, both long and short specimens are found. → Broad low scales crowded together: many scales very closely spaced on each rib, ribs close to each other. Shell white inside and out, a few with yellow or apricot band on interior margin. (104 mm)
Distribution: Moderately common, all areas except the Gulf of Suez, where rare.
Notes: Although related to the Giant Clam of Australia, this is not the same species and never grows as large. The scales on *T. maxima* are broader and more rounded than those of *T.* sp. (below).

Tridacna sp.
Tridacna squamosa Lamarck, 1810 of some authors

33–110 mm. → Valves inequilateral. Shell elongate. Narrow erect scales, distinctly separate, few scales per rib, distant from each other on the rib, ribs widely spaced. Underside of scales with cancellate sculpture. (69 mm)
Distribution: Occasional in the Gulf of Aqaba. Rare elsewhere.
Notes: T. squamosa has equilateral valves, that is, the distance from the beak to the posterior margin is the same as from the beak to the anterior margin. I have never found any specimens of *Tridacna squamosa* in Egypt. The shell featured in this book seems to be unnamed.

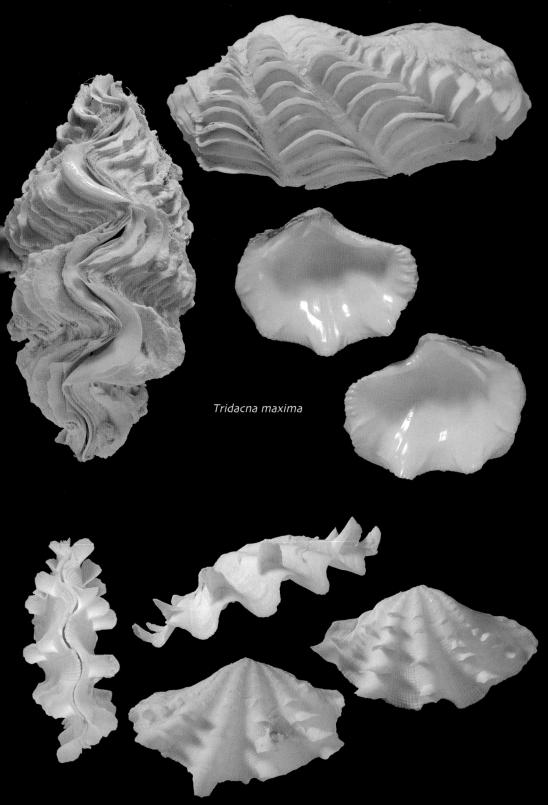

Tridacna maxima

Tridacna sp.

Family MACTRIDAE

Trigonal shells (shaped a bit like a triangle with rounded corners). Ligament always internal. The cardinal teeth of Mactridae are narrow, and arranged like an inverted 'V.' Shells in the genus *Mactra* have long sharp lateral teeth, both anterior and posterior, one of each in the left valve and two in the right valve.

Mactra achatina Holten, 1802

20–48 mm. If it looks like a pretty colored *Mactra* (look for the long lateral teeth inside) with caramel and white rays and has small blurry white spots, it is *M. achatina*. Sometimes there is a tinge of red on it as well. (43 mm)
Distribution: Occasional in the Gulf of Aqaba, rare in the Gulf of Suez and south of Marsa Alam.

Mactra lilacea Lamarck, 1818

12–43 mm. Slightly trigonal, with long lateral teeth. → Beak always with a tiny dark spot. Exterior usually a yellowish-beige, with or without darker and lighter rays, some with a touch of lilac, some quite plain. Interior usually with violet. Some specimens pure white. (28 mm)
Distribution: Rare in the Gulfs of Suez and Aqaba, common in the Wadi Lahmi area in the south, occasional between Marsa Alam and Shalatein.
Notes: The color of this species varies considerably but it always has a very small dark dot right on the beak. *M. olorina* never has this dot.

Mactra olorina Philippi, 1846
Endemic

19–60 mm. Strong lateral teeth. Pale in color, even plain white, some with pale tan rays. Some specimens with purplish-brown markings on the dorsal areas on one or both sides of the umbo, but never with a tiny dark dot on the beak. Interior usually plain white. (55 mm)
Distribution: Occasional in the Gulf of Aqaba. Abundant in the Gulf of Suez. Usually not found south of Safaga.

Mactra achatina

x2

actual size

Mactra lilacea

Mactra olorina

Meropesta solanderi (Gray, 1837)

22–42 mm. Usually inequilaterally ovate, but can be quite deformed. → Sharp, narrow riblets. The last riblet to the posterior, the longer end in this species, is higher and stronger than the rest. Shell all white. (42 mm)

Distribution: Occasional in the Gulf of Suez, especially around Ras Sudr. Rare to never elsewhere.

Notes: The ribs might at first remind one of the similar-looking Psammobid *Asaphis violascens* (pages 261-262). That shell is much heavier and coarser, with at least a little purple near the hinge or posterior.

Meropesta nicobarica (Gmelin, 1791)

40–55 mm. Elongate ovoid outline, beaks far to the anterior. More than forty low, closely spaced ribs. (40 mm)

Distribution: Very rare, Hurghada area, Shalatein.

Notes: Shells found in the Egyptian Red Sea seem to be subfossils. The animal may be extinct in these waters.

Raeta pellicula (Deshayes, 1855)

70 mm. Large fragile shell, acute posterior, concentric lamellations, spoon-like resilifer. Lives offshore in deeper water in fine sand or mud substrates, rarely found on beaches. (70 mm)

Distribution: Very rare, south.

Notes: One quick look at the resilifer will eliminate confusion with the venerid *Clementia papyracea* which has a similar shape. This beached specimen was found by Pamela Piombino and is the only one I have seen in Egypt.

Meropesta solanderi

Meropesta nicobarica

Raeta pellicula

Family MESODESMATIDAE
Atactodea striata (Gmelin, 1791)
Synonym *Mactra glabrata* Gmelin, 1791
Surf Clam
7–31 mm. Triagonal, strong and heavy for the size, hinge area is very thick, concentric ridges and lines (striations, thus *striata*). (28 mm)
Distribution: Very common in all regions.
Notes: Their genius lies not in their beauty, but in their suitability to their habitat. If you see a live one at the edge of the water, watch how quickly it can dig itself back in under the sand. This is essential for it to survive in areas of surf. Its chief predators are the moon snails (Naticidae) which wrap their big foot around the clam and bore a little round beveled hole in it.

Donacilla sp.
5.5–7 mm. → Shape resembles a right triangle with rounded corners, beaks at anterior, base nearly twice the height. Ligament internal. Hinge thick, with very strong curving teeth. RV with two anterior cardinals, one posterior cardinal, and one very long strong posterior lateral. LV with two anterior cardinal teeth; the more anterior very strong, the weaker next to the ligament. One slanting posterior cardinal, and one very long strong posterior cardinal. Exterior glossy with faint growth lines. White, pinkish-beige or white and pink with variable patterns of fine rays or a checkerboard effect. Interior white or pinkish-beige. Interior margin smooth. (7 mm)
Distribution: Northern Gulf of Aqaba, rarely found but occasionally locally common.
Notes: This species is not well known and does not have its own name yet.

The shells in the next two families, Solenidae and Pharidae, are long and thin. Most of the shells in both families are commonly called razor clams after their resemblance to old-style razors.

Family SOLENIDAE
Solen lischkeanus Dunker, 1865
24–47 mm. → Ventral margin slightly curved. Anteroventral angle sharp, anterior margin a straight line set at an oblique angle, posterior slightly rounded. Translucent white or palest pink, not spotted. (47 mm)
Distribution: Uncommon, northern Gulf of Suez.

Family PHARIDAE
Ensiculus cultellus (Linnaeus, 1758)
60–72 mm. → Elongate, rounded on both ends. Hinge very close to anterior end with small, sharp, distinctive teeth. Color ivory mottled with light chestnut and red spots. Very fragile, rarely found intact, but even the fragments are unmistakable. (71 mm)
Distribution: Rare, northern Gulf of Suez.

Atactodea striata

actual size

x2

Donacilla sp.

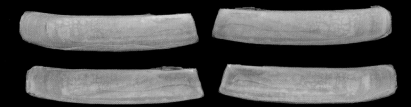

Solen lischkeanus

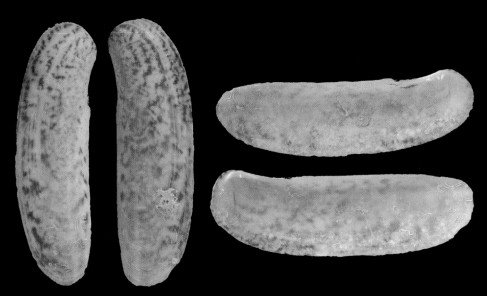

Ensiculus cultellus

Family TELLINIDAE

Most members of this family have at least a small deviation from the plane at the posterior of the shell, often called a 'posterior twist to the right.' If you hold one of these shells with the umbo toward you and the ventral margin away from you, you will see this feature relatively easily. The photo of *Quidnipagus palatam* on page 245 shows this clearly.

Arcopaginula inflata (Gmelin, 1791)

19–51 mm. Anterior a broad smooth continuous curve. → Posterior acute. Lateral teeth strong in RV, weak in LV. Shell surface of a special smooth quality, texture of fine silk. (46 mm)

Distribution: Very common locally in the northern Gulf of Suez; rare if ever elsewhere.
Notes: The presence of lateral teeth prevents any confusion with specimens of the subfamily Macominae.

Arcopella isseli (H. Adams, 1871)

8–12 mm. Small, white, equilateral shell with surprisingly strong, widely spaced, raised concentric ridges. It may have faintly colored rays. (12 mm)

Distribution: Rare, northern Gulf of Suez.
Notes: The shape is similar to *Pinguitellina pinguis*, but that species never has strong concentric ridges.

Clathrotellina sp.

17 mm. → Fine cancellate sculpture, apricot color. (17 mm)
Distribution: Very rare, Hurghada–Safaga area.

Elliptotellina pulchella (H. Adams, 1870)

Endemic
6–9.2 mm. → Elliptical shape. Medial area with concentric ridges. Ends with neatly arranged small knobby scales, stronger posteriorly. (9.2 mm)
Distribution: Uncommon, all areas south to Wadi Gimaal.

Moerella lactea (H. Adams, 1871)

5–7 mm. → Beak very far to the posterior. Anterior dorsal and ventral margins almost parallel. → Clear regular incised concentric lines, RV with strong lateral teeth. Milky white—*lactea* is Latin for milky—or light or dark pink, or yellow. (6.8 mm)

Distribution: Locally common in the northern Gulf of Suez, extremely rare to never elsewhere.
Notes: When comparing the plain white left valves of *M. lactea* and *E. triradiata*, with good light and a hand lens, one can see that the concentric sculpture of *M. lactea* is more regular, crisper, and denser than that of *E. triradiata*.

Arcopaginula inflata

Arcopella isseli

Clathrotellina sp.

actual size

×3

Elliptotellina pulchella

actual size

×3

Moerella lactea

Comparison between *Moerella lactea*, *Exotica triradiata*, and *Loxoglypta clathrata*

	Size in mm.	Sculpture, dentition	Color	Red rays	RV w. laterals	Locality	Frequency
M. lactea	7 or smaller	Concentric, cardinals, RV strong laterals	White, pink, yellow	Very rarely	Always	Northern Gulf of Suez	Locally common
Exotica. triradiata (Macominae)	12 or smaller	Concentric, cardinals, no laterals	White	Sometimes	Never	Gulf of Aqaba, Far South, Suez	Rare
L. clathrata (Macominae)	13–18	Scissulate, cardinals, no laterals	White	Sometimes	Never	All	Moderately common

Obtellina sericata (Melvill, 1898)

6–21 mm. → Posterior dorsal margin serrated. Anterior rounded, extended. (19 mm)
Distribution: Uncommon, Gulf of Aqaba and reefs in the Hurghada–Safaga region.
More likely to be seen by divers than on the beach.
Notes: O. sericata is a favorite food of moon snails (Naticidae), and many specimens
have the characteristic beveled hole drilled into them.

Pharaonella pharaonis (Hanley, 1844)

40–80 mm. → Elongate shell with a uniquely narrow extended posterior. BV with coarse
concentric sculpture, stronger on RV. RV pink, LV white. (79 mm)
Distribution: Moderately common in the northern Gulf of Suez.
Notes: RV and LV of this species are so different to each other in color and sculpture it
is hard to believe they both come from the same animal. This species more elongate,
larger, coarser, and more common than *P. semilaevis* (below).

Pharaonella semilaevis (Von Martens, 1865)

35–73 mm. Elongate shell with slightly extended posterior. RV with very closely spaced,
fine, concentric ridges. It feels like fine sandpaper. LV feels the same at the anterior, but
is very smooth feeling in the middle. Both valves same shiny color—white or pink or yellow. → Umbo usually with three or four red rays—sometimes they reach the posterior
end of the ventral margin. Inside often with egg-yolk yellow area or rays as well as red
rays. (40 mm)
Distribution: Uncommon, Dahab, South Sinai, Hurghada, Safaga, and south.
Notes: Sculpture is twice as dense as that of *P. pharaonis*, but smoother, less rough to the
touch. Posterior much shorter.

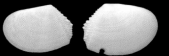

Obtellina sericata

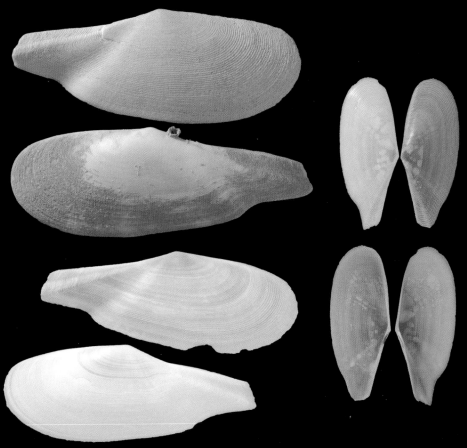

Pharaonella pharaonis

Pharaonella semilaevis

Pinguitellina pinguis (Hanley, 1844)
5–10 mm. Unusually strong and shiny for such a small shell. → Small weak point to the posterior margin. Very weak concentric lines, hard to see without magnification. Some specimens with a bit of yellow, usually all white. (8.5 mm)
Distribution: Uncommon, found in all areas except the Gulf of Suez.
Notes: Arcopella isseli (pages 240–41) is very similar in shape and only slightly larger, but its concentric sculpture is much stronger and can easily be seen without magnification.

Pistris capsoides (Lamarck, 1818)
35–54 mm. Strong, rough feeling → continuous concentric ridges, very weak, fine radial sculpture underneath. (38 mm)
Distribution: Rare, most likely in the Hurghada–Safaga area. Also known from Dahab Lagoon and central Gulf of Suez.
Notes: P. capsoides has smooth, concentric, continuous ridges, *Quidnipagus palatam* (below) has discontinuous wobbly ones.

Quidnipagus palatam Iredale, 1929
Rough Ridged Tellin
10–66 mm. → Rough, wiggly, often discontinuous, concentric raised ridges. (62 mm)
Distribution: Abundant from Safaga to Shalatein, occasional in the Gulf of Aqaba.

actual size   x2

Pinguitellina pinguis

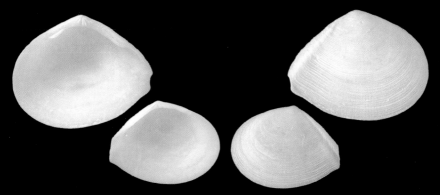

Pistris capsoides

Quidnipagus palatam

Scutarcopagia delicatula (Selli, 1974)
Endemic
Scutarcopagia scobinata (Linnaeus, 1758) of some authors
20–65 mm. → Nearly round shape, finely scaly surface, sculpture slightly discrepant between valves. (60 mm)
Distribution: Common from Safaga south and around the reefs from Hurghada across South Sinai and the Straits of Tiran. Rarely found in the gulfs.
Notes: The endemic Red Sea species has finer sculpture than the widespread Indo-Pacific *S.scobinata.*

Tellidora lamellosa (Issel, 1869)
Endemic
5–7 mm. → Very small thin triangular shell with concentric ridges, stronger at posterior margin. (7 mm)
Distribution: Rare. Found in shell grit in the northern Gulf of Suez and Safaga.

Scutarcopagia delicatula

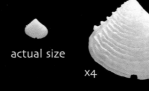

actual size

x4

Tellidora lamellosa

The next three species are placed by some in the genus *Angulus*. I follow Oliver (1992) in keeping the original genus, *Tellina*.

Tellina arsinoensis Issel, 1869
6.5–19 mm. Very thin, anterior broadly rounded, → posterior slopes sharply to a dull point. Translucent, shiny. Soft white, light or dark apricot, or colorless. Quite a lovely shell, especially when the light is shining through it. (19 mm)
Distribution: Locally common in the northern Gulf of Suez and in Shalatein Harbor. Requires shallow, silty habitat.
Notes: The more pointed shape of the posterior easily separates this shell from other thin pastel-colored Red Sea species. *Tellin flacca* Römer, 1871 (not illustrated), with its yellowish color and oblique subtruncate posterior, is reported by others from the Gulf of Suez but I have never seen one.

Tellina valtonis Hanley, 1844
6–20 mm. Slightly elongate, RV with anterior lateral tooth fused to anterior cardinal. Usually pink to dark pink with some whitish rays posteriorly. (16 mm)
Distribution: Common in the northern Gulf of Suez. Occasional in the far south.
Note: Darker in color, more elongate than *A. vernalis* (below).

Tellina vernalis Hanley, 1844
12–20 mm. Pink, white, or both and may have one or two whitish rays posteriorly.
Distribution: Uncommon, far northwest Gulf of Suez only. (20 mm)
Notes: Less elongate, higher in proportion to length and paler in color than *T. valtonis* (above).

Tellinella adamsi (Bertin, 1878)
16–24 mm. Ovoid. Fine, closely spaced, regular raised concentric ridges, stronger on posterior area. Several narrow red radial rays, usually faded. (24 mm)
Distribution: Common in the Hurghada–Safaga area, also found near Zafarana, Dahab Lagoon, and Shalatein.

Tellinella asperrima (Hanley, 1844)
42–48 mm. → Covered with short, broad, knobby scales. Cream colored with many narrow dark red rays, stronger at the ventral margin. (43 mm)
Distribution: Very rare, Gulf of Aqaba.

Tellina arsinoensis

Tellina valtonis

Tellina vernalis

Tellinella adamsi

Tellinella asperrima

Tellinella crucigera (Lamarck, 1818)

14–51 mm. → Elongate. Posterior pointed, flexes to the right. Fine closely spaced concentric ridges. Cream color with numerous narrow unevenly colored, weak red rays usually visible only near the ventral margin. Color variants may be orange or purple. (42 mm)

Distribution: Moderately common, all areas, especially near Safaga, in the Dahab Lagoon, and south of Marsa Alam.

Notes: Similar in shape and color to the rare, larger, heavier, and more strongly sculpted *T. philippii* (below).

Tellinella philippii (Anton in Philippi, 1844)

Synonym *Tellina rastellum* Hanley, 1844

62–83 mm. → Large, heavy, scratchy shell. Posterior sculpture very strong: RV with lamellate scales toward posterior, then strong raised concentric lamellations over the posterior slope. (83 mm)

Distribution: Uncommon, Gulf of Aqaba and South Sinai.

Notes: This shell is stronger in every way than *T. crucigera*, which it resembles in shape. Compared to *T. staurella* (below), *T. philippii* is more elongate, more rostrate, and has much stronger sculpture.

Tellinella crucigera

Tellinella philippii

Tellinella staurella (Lamarck, 1818)

27–65 mm. Subovate shell with concentric ridges. Juveniles slightly more elongate. Pattern variable. May be all white, with or without short red rays umbonally, or strong red and white rays extending from red or white umbo to ventral margin. (60 mm)

Distribution: Occasional from Hurghada across South Sinai to Dahab Lagoon and the Straits of Tiran. Common from Safaga to Wadi Gimaal.

Notes: T. crucigera is more elongate with posterior more rostrate, rays weaker, intermittent and fading toward umbo.

Tellinella sulcata (W. Wood, 1815)

18–56 mm. → Strong posterior sulcus, remarkably regular concentric ridges becoming stronger over posterior sulcus on both valves. → Underlying sculpture of fine incised radial lines and slightly raised ribs. (41 mm)

Distribution: All along the eastern coast of Egypt, from Suez to Shalatein. Moderately common, more so in the south.

Notes: T. sulcata is less elongate and much more sulcate than *T. crucigera*. It is less round, more sulcate, more strongly ridged, and much more common than *Pistris capsoides*.

Tellinides ovalis (Sowerby I, 1825)

19–41 mm. → Almost perfectly oval shell. Pink with white rays. (38 mm)

Distribution: Occasional, the Gulf of Suez and Wadi Lahmi.

Tellinella staurella

Tellinella sulcata

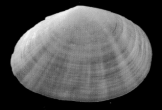

Tellinides ovalis

Subfamily MACOMINAE
The subfamily Macominae differs from the rest of the Tellinidae in having no lateral teeth.

Exotica triradiata (H. Adams, 1871)
8–11 mm. Elongate white shell, may have one to three broad or narrow red rays. Weak irregular concentric sculpture. Strong cardinals but never with lateral teeth. (11 mm)
Distribution: Always rare, but most likely in northern Gulf of Suez, also known from Gulf of Aqaba and the far south.
Notes: Confusion possible with *Loxoglypta clathrata* and *Moerella lactea*. See table on page 242.

Loxoglypta clathrata (Deshayes, 1835)
Synonym *Tellina rhomboides* (Quoy & Gaimard, 1835; non Gmelin, 1791)
12.5–19 mm. About four light red broken rays, often brighter on the inside. → Scissulate sculpture with the oblique lines very straight and very close together. (18 mm)
Distribution: Widespread but only occasionally common.
Notes: Red rays often completely faded away. See also *L. secunda* (below).

Loxoglypta secunda (Berlin, 1878)
13.5–22 mm. Fragile. Very similar to *L. clathrata*, but never with any colored markings. → Weak scissulate sculpture, somewhat irregular. (17 mm)
Distribution: Locally abundant in very quiet, non-muddy lagoons south of Ras Banas. Rare north of Ras Banas.
Notes: A good hand lens or microscope is required to distinguish any reliable difference between *L. secunda* and non-rayed specimens of *L. clathrata*. Scissulate lines of *L. secunda* are spaced farther apart and tend to get off track where they cross the concentric sculpture. At the posterior of the area with oblique sculpture the lines terminate randomly. On the RV the sculpture of the posterior slope is likely to be quite strong. In *L. clathrata* the lines are more densely spaced. Their terminal points fall in an imaginary straight line down from the dorsum to the ventral margin.

Loxoglypta subpallida (E. A. Smith, 1891)
Endemic
14–27 mm. → Rather broadly wedge-shaped anterior, long straight anterior dorsal margin. Scissulate sculpture reasonably visible without magnification, lines not tightly spaced. (21 mm)
Distribution: Infrequent, most likely in Shalatein Harbor and northern Gulf of Suez.
Notes: Stronger and relatively higher (thus less elongate) than the other two species of Red Sea *Loxoglypta*.

actual size

x2

Exotica triradiata

Loxoglypta clathrata

Loxoglypta secunda

Loxoglypta subpallida

Pseudometis dubia (Deshayes, 1855)
Synonym *Tellina coxa* Jousseaume, 1894
10.5–40 mm. → Smoothly rounded arch of the ventral side of the hinge line. Small triangular resilifer, external portion occupying one quarter of length of dorsum. (37 mm)
Distribution: Common, northern Gulf of Suez.
Notes: This species has been called by several names but recent research on the type specimens in Paris (*T. coxa* Jousseaume) and London (*T. dubia* Deshayes) concludes this is the correct name. The outline of the shell varies with growth and among individuals.

Pseudometis sp.
Pseudometris praerupta (Salisbury, 1934), *Psammotreta edentula* (Spengler, 1798) of authors
20–58 mm. → Outline of the body cavity below the hinge area comes to a blunt point under the beak. → External resilifer unusually large, both long and wide, bordered by incised line. Resilifer occupies nearly half the length of posterodorsal margin. (55 mm)
Distribution: Occasional, northern Gulf of Suez.
Notes: This species and *P. dubia* are both found in the same places, are white and lack distinctive sculpture. The difference between the resilifers is definitive and eliminates confusion between these two species in the northern Red Sea. The correct name for this species is still unclear.

Family SEMELIDAE
All Red Sea members of this family have a sunken, slanting resilifer.

Cumingia striata (Reeve, 1853)
4–18 mm. Irregularly shaped due to its habit of living in or among rocks and coral. Ventral margin may be sinuous. Concentric lamellae, long, slanting resilifer. White, yellow, or both. Usually dirty looking and in poor condition. (14 mm)
Distribution: Uncommon, northern Gulf of Suez only.
Notes: The venerid *Irus macrophylla* has a similar lifestyle and sculpture. It has typical strong venerid teeth: three cardinals in each valve. *C. striata* has strong lateral teeth, but not strong cardinals.

Ervilia purpurea (Lamy, 1914)
4–10 mm. Elliptical with narrow rounded ends, beaks toward the posterior. Mature and fully colored specimens pink, with brownish or reddish color and marks. Long beached specimens are all white. External surface smooth and shining. (10 mm)
Distribution: Locally abundant in shell grit in the northern Gulf of Suez.
Notes: A similar but smaller species, less than 3.5 mm. in length, *Ervilia scaliola* (Issel, 1869), has a more equilateral outline and a more pointed posterior. Never with darker rays or spots. Pink, white or both. Often found together with *E. purpurea* in the northern Gulf of Suez. Not pictured.

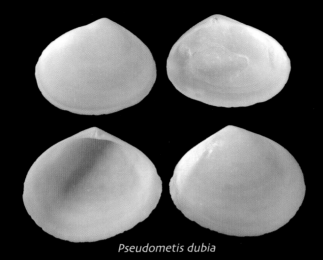

Pseudometis dubia

Pseudometis sp.

Cumingia striata

Ervilia purpurea

Iacra kallima (Salisbury, 1934)

Synonym *Tellina speciosa* Deshayes, 1856; non Edwards

13–24 mm. → Oblique sculpture in the medial area. → Resilifer short, narrow, → RV only has strong concentric ridges at both ends and strong lateral teeth. Very well developed specimens have lamellae in the medial area as well. LV all teeth weak, no lamellae. (24 mm)

Distribution: Common in sandy areas south of Marsa Alam. Found in other areas on sandy beaches but only rarely.

Notes: Confusion is possible with *I. seychellarum* as both have oblique sculpture medially and the same dentition, but the latter never has lamellae. In *I. kallima* the resilifer is small and never descends into the body cavity.

Iacra seychellarum A. Adams, 1856

9–21 mm. → Oblique sculpture in external medial area, RV strong lateral teeth. → BV with large oblique resilifer extending into body, this stronger in RV. (19 mm)

Distribution: Abundant in northern Gulf of Suez, locally common south of Marsa Alam, rare if ever in the Gulf of Aqaba.

Notes: The length and strength of the resilifers definitively distinguish *I. seychellarum* from *I. kallima* (above).

Leptomya subrostrata (Issel, 1869)

12–32 mm. Exact shape may vary but is quite distinctive: tumid and rounded anteriorly, extended and pointed posteriorly. → Slanting, protruding resilifer. Regular incised concentric lines. Yellow, white, or both. (23 mm)

Distribution: Never common, most likely in the Hurghada–Safaga area. Occasional in the Gulf of Aqaba.

Notes: Noting the hinge with its large oblique resilifer will prevent any confusion with tellinids.

Semele lamellosa (Sowerby I, 1833)

Semele carnicolor (Hanley, 1845) of authors

30–32 mm. Strong concentric lamellae and the characteristic semelid slanting resilifer. Dirty beige color. (32 mm)

Distribution: Very rare, south of Marsa Alam only.

juvenile

Iacra kallima

Iacra seychellarum

Leptomya subrostrata

Semele lamellosa

Family PSAMMOBIIDAE

Shells in this family are usually somewhat oblong in shape. The posterior is generally more expanded than the anterior. The ligament is usually attached to a small flange, the nymph, that extends above the outline of the shell just posterior to the beaks. Many species in this family have strong sculpture and bright colors.

Asaphis violascens (Forsskål in Niebuhr, 1775)

14–70 mm. → Strong coarse radial ribs, a variety of different dusty colors. Inside with lovely shiny colors: pink, apricot, yellow, white, or purple. Usually only one main color per shell with a bit of purple near the hinge, and sometimes also at the posterior end. Rarely a specimen will have radial rays of both purple and orange. (55 mm)
Distribution: Common in all regions, but prefers coarse sand rather than fine.

Gari insignis (Deshayes, 1855)

Synonym *Gari bicarinata* (Deshayes, 1855)
Endemic
9–27 mm. RV with up to six riblets, usually scaly or nodulose, in the posterior area. LV without riblets, or with weak, smooth ones. Many possible colors and combinations: bright pink, orange, purple, or beige and may have rays of a contrasting color. (17 mm)
Distribution: Uncommon. Most likely to be found in areas of fine sand, known from all regions.
Notes: G. *insignis* is a good example of a species whose RV and LV are so different in sculpture that it was once considered to be two different species.

Gari pallida (Deshayes, 1855)

Synonym *Gari weinkauffi* (Crosse, 1864)
24–40 mm. → Moderately spaced, moderately strong, oblique incised lines on the medial part of the shell. When newly dead, it is glossy with light brown and beige concentric bands and pale cream radial rays. (33 mm)
Distribution: Rare overall, but occasionally common in the northern Gulf of Suez; also known from sandy lagoons south of Berenice.
Notes: The strong oblique sculpture distinguishes this shell from the plain-surfaced G. *sharabatiae* (see below). The latter is also more inequilateral with the beaks very far to the posterior.

Asaphis violascens

Gari insignis

Gari pallida

Gari pennata (Deshayes, 1855)

Synonym *Gari dispar* (Deshayes, 1855)

18–25 mm. → Distinct diverging ribs on the posterior end, oblique sculpture on the rest. Usually very colorful: purple, coral, pink, beige. Each specimen usually has two or three different colors on it with freckles and rays of different colors. The pattern shows through on the shiny interior. (25 mm)

Distribution: Rare and irregular, Gulf of Aqaba and reefs off of Hurghada.

Notes: My experience with *Gari pennata* illustrates the difficulty of stating the likely locality of intermittently found species. I found one specimen on fine sand at the base of a reef off Hurghada in 1998 and, in 2000, three others all on the same beach on the same day in the northern Gulf of Aqaba. Despite numerous subsequent visits to both sites, I've never found another specimen.

Gari sharabatiae Rusmore-Villaume, 2005

Endemic to the Gulf of Suez

14–25.5 mm.→ Thin, compressed, broadly elliptical shell. Although unusual for a *Gari*, the anterior is slightly higher. LV nearly flat, RV slightly inflated. Beaks strongly to the posterior, at about one-third of the length of the shell. If both valves are together and closed, a small posterior gape is apparent. RV with two cardinal teeth; posterior slightly bifed, anterior simple and narrow. LV anterior cardinal faintly bifed, posterior cardinal becoming obsolete. No lateral teeth. No particular sculpture on the posterior slope. Entire shell with very faint concentric growth marks, but overall appears smooth. Fresh specimens are olivaceous tan with soft golden rays. (21.5 mm)

Distribution: Uncommon, restricted primarily to the Ein Sukhna area of the Gulf of Suez.

Heteroglypta contraria (Deshayes, 1863)

12 mm. → Thin, fragile shell with complicated sculpture. Anterior with fine oblique ribs, medial area with fine, widely spaced radial ridges, posterior with short, heavier, widely spaced divaricate ribs. Small chestnut stain posterior to the hinge. (12 mm)

Distribution: Very rare, prefers fine sand. Dahab.

Soletellina ruppelliana (Reeve, 1857)

20–78 mm. → Bright amethyst color, both inside and out. Somewhat elliptical flattish shell, exact outline somewhat varible. Strong raised nymph. Weak concentric growth marks. Fresh specimens have a thin olivaceous pericostracum. (63 mm)

Distribution: Abundant in the Gulf of Suez, common in Shalatein Harbor. Not found in the Gulf of Aqaba.

Gari pennata

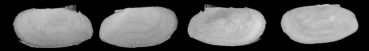

Gari sharabatiae

Heteroglypta contraria

Soletellina ruppelliana

Family SOLECURTIDAE
Azorinus coarctatus (Gmelin, 1791)
35–37 mm. → Dorsal and ventral margins straight and strikingly parallel. Ends rounded and gaping. Beak much closer to the anterior. Strong curved peg-like teeth. Fine concentric growth marks. (37 mm)
Distribution: Rare, muddy areas, far south only.

Solecurtus subcandidus Sturany, 1899
Endemic
33–65 mm. → Square ends, parallel margins. Beaks near the anterior. → Interesting sculpture of fine incised lines in various directions and angles. Soft pink color with two white rays medially. (57 mm)
Distribution: Common in the Gulf of Suez. Rare elsewhere.

Family DONACIDAE
The shells in this family are wedge shaped and live buried in sandy beaches with good surf action.

Donax biradiatus Forsskål in Niebuhr, 1775
Synonym *Donax veneriformis* Lamarck, 1818
Endemic
15–24 mm. Shape almost equilateral triangle, rather flat. → Many beautiful different colors and color combinations, including purple, rose, yellow, and orange, with two or more radial rays of contrasting color. (19 mm)
Distribution: Occasional, Marsa Alam south to Shalatein. Sometimes locally common. Never found north of Marsa Alam.

Donax semistriatus Poli, 1795
15 mm. Very elongate shell with faint radial and concentric incised lines, serrate margin, finely lirate inner margin. Light fulvous or purple radial rays are visible on both the exterior and the interior. (15 mm)
Distribution: Rare, the Gulf of Suez.
Notes: Shells of this edible Mediterranean species are occasionally found in the Gulf of Suez. Some think they may have been discarded after a meal. This juvenile is the only specimen I have ever seen.

Azorinus coarctatus

Solecurtus subcandidus

Donax biradiatus

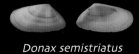

Donax semistriatus

Family TRAPEZIIDAE

Shells in this family are notable for their extremely strong teeth, both cardinal and lateral. In most species the dorsal and ventral margins are nearly parallel but the ends are irregular. The shape gives rise to the family name.

Glossocardia obesa (Reeve, 1843)

18–71 mm. → Tumid shell, angular posterior outline, weakly angular carina, and light concentric growth sculpture. → Never with radial sculpture. A startling feature against the white shell is the bright red ligament. (58 mm)

Distribution: Occasional in all regions, common around Safaga reefs and south of Marsa Alam.

Notes: Like *Trapezium oblongum* (below) it is more likely to be seen by divers than beachcombers. Both species are often found in the same locations. The angular posterior and absence of radial sculpture clearly distinguish *G. obesa* from that species. The shell of *G. obesa* seems to be a less favorable habitat for encrustations.

Trapezium oblongum (Linnaeus, 1758)

14–61 mm. Trapezoidal in shape, anterior blunt, posterior rounded. Softly rounded carina and rough irregular concentric growth ridges. → Numerous weak narrow radial ribs producing crenulate margin. Shell white, sometimes with pink blush posteriorly.

Distribution: All areas but much more common south of Marsa Alam. (62 mm)

Notes: Mature shells are usually encrusted with algal and coralline growth. Immature specimens have a shaper carina, a more extended anterior margin and a more expanded posterior margin than adults.

Glossocardia obesa

immature

juvenile

Trapezium oblongum

Family VENERIDAE

The English name clams is broadly used for all bivalves but more deliberately for this family. The clams on the menu in Egyptian restaurants are of this family. The Veneridae comprise more species in the Egyptian Red Sea than any other bivalve family. Many of them are abundantly present on the beaches, especially *Circenita callipyga* and, in the Gulf of Suez, *Callista florida*. These and several others are quite attractive and readily identifiable. This makes the Veneridae a good starting point for the novice conchologist. Most are roundly triangular or oval in shape and have thick hinges and strong teeth, usually three cardinals on each valve. Most burrow in sand or mud, a few attach themselves to rocks, and others use an acid secretion to excavate a home in rock or coral. It would be an unusual day at the beach if you saw no Veneridae.

Callista florida (Lamarck, 1818)

10–45 mm. → Strong, shiny shell with moderately spaced incised concentric lines. Pattern of both radial rays and concentric bands of mottled fulvous colors on white. Inside white and fulvous. The colors fade quickly on the beach. (41 mm)
Distribution: Abundant in the Gulf of Suez, occasional in all other regions.

Circe crocea (Gray, 1838)

Endemic

14–50 mm. → Heavy shell, large strong hinge area, weak concentric sculpture. Low divaricating ridges in umbonal area, these often more visible as raised bars near the escutcheon. Inner margin finely crenulate. Pale colored, with or without red or fulvous rays or blotch umbonally. Inside may be all white or flushed with yellow, apricot, or even red and yellow. (50 mm)
Distribution: Very common in the Gulfs of Suez and Aqaba. Moderately common in all areas.
Notes: C. rugifera always has strong umbonal and concentric sculpture and fine brown lines across the lunule and escutcheon. In *C. crocea* the escutcheon and lunule may be darker than the rest of the shell, but never have fine dark lines in them.

Circe rugifera (Lamarck, 1818)

Circe corrugata of some authors

15–54 mm. → Strong divaricating ridges in the umbonal area, strong concentric ridges. Very finely crenulate inner margins, easier to feel with your fingernail than to see. Exterior with fine brown lines. These may fade completely on the body of the shell, but always remain across the lunule and escutcheon. Inside fulvous, yellow, or brown. (40 mm)
Distribution: Very common in the northern part of the Gulf of Suez. Occasional to rare elsewhere. Not reported south of Safaga.
Notes: See *C. crocea* (above).

Callista florida

Circe crocea

Circe rugifera

Circe scripta (Linnaeus, 1758)

41 mm. → Fine weak divaricate ridges unbonally. Fine low concentric ridges, smooth inner margin. (41 mm)
Distribution: Very rare, Gulf of Suez.
Notes: This species is the only *Circe* in the Red Sea with smooth inner margins.

Circenita callipyga (Born, 1778)

Endemic
12–45 mm. Strong shell, hinge area thick, sculpture of simple concentric ridges, stronger posteriorly. Some variation of shape occurs during growth, probably due to crowded or cramped living conditions. Amazing diversity of patterns in white, beige, tan, orange, and brown. Inside white or coral, usually with some purple near the posterior. (35 mm)
Distribution: Abundant, all regions.
Notes: C. callipyga is the second-most frequently found species in the Egyptian Red Sea. The mussel *Modiolus auriculatus* is the most common.

Circe scripta

Circenita callipyga

Dosinia alta (Dunker, 1848)

11–22 mm.→ Lunule never domed, shell white. (20 mm)
Distribution: Rare, most likely to be found in the south near Wadi Lahmi.
Notes: The straight line of the edge of the lunule prevents confusion with pale specimens of *D. hepatica.*

Dosinia erythraea Römer, 1860

11–62 mm. → Strongly raised concentric ridges, no escutcheon. Umbo and a few radial rays may be purple or fulvous. (45 mm)
Distribution: Abundant in the Gulf of Suez and the sandy spit and lagoon at Dahab. Rare if ever elsewhere.
Notes: The absence of the escutcheon distinguishes small worn specimens with no color pattern from *D. histrio,* which has a small escutcheon.

Dosinia hepatica (Lamarck, 1818)

11–21 mm. Very fine, tightly spaced, smooth concentric ridges. Lunule dome shaped. The Latin name for this species means 'liver colored,' but the colors and patterns vary. Exterior usually plain shade of dusty violet or yellow, sometimes with violet rays or bands. Inside all or partially purple or brownish-purple. (19 mm)
Distribution: Locally common just north of Hurghada and in Shalatein Harbor. Rare elsewhere.
Notes: Color always more intense south of Marsa Alam. This shell tends to look unusually beautiful while wet and extremely plain and dusty when dry. Resist the temptation to take it home—it will be very disappointing later on.

Dosinia histrio (Gmelin, 1791)

10–27 mm. Sharp, raised concentric lamellae, dark brown zigzags. Small escutcheon has small ridges on RV but smooth on LV. Sometimes the beak is pink. (24 mm)
Distribution: Moderately common in the Gulf of Aqaba, occasional in the Gulf of Suez and south to Shalatein.
Notes: Checking for the presence of the escutcheon can eliminate possible confusion between this species and *D. erythraea* (above).

Dosinia alta

Dosinia erythraea

Dosinia hepatica

Dosinia histrio

Gafrarium pectinatum (Linnaeus, 1758)

15–55 mm. → Strong nodulose radial ribs. Various patterns in shades of ivory, beige, and brown. Inside white or yellow, usually with dark line on posterior hinge area. (51 mm)
Distribution: Very common in Gulf of Suez. Common from Hurghada to Shalatein. Rare in Gulf of Aqaba.

Globivenus orientalis (Cox, 1930)

Synonym *Globivenus toreuma* of some authors
14–50 mm. Circular outline, tumid, strong concentric sculpture, strong hinge and teeth. (36 mm)
Distribution: Uncommon on beaches, Gulf of Aqaba, south Sinai, and south of Marsa Alam.
Notes: G. orientalis is always tumid or globose. *Dosinia erythraea* is about the same size and sculpture, but is very compressed. Recent research indicates that while *G. toreuma* is widespread in the Indo-Pacific, it is not found in the Red Sea (Dekker, personal communication, 2007).

Irus macrophylla (Deshayes, 1853)

7.5–23 mm. Irregularly oblong, anterior narrow. Four or five distinct lamellate concentric ridges. Very fine (hard to see) tightly spaced radial ridges between the leafy concentric ridges. Usually white, rarely coral-tinged or yellow, some with fine brown lines umbonally. (14 mm)
Distribution: Occasional in all regions.
Notes: See the semelid *Cumingia striata* (pages 256–57) for differences.

Gafrarium pectinatum

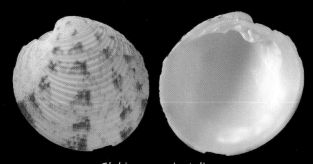

Globivenus orientalis

Irus macrophylla

Note on the genus *Lioconcha*: The pallial sinus is always very weak and small. Shells in the genus *Pitar* may have similar patterns but the pallial sinus is always large and pointed.

Lioconcha cf. *castrensis* (Linnaeus, 1758)

11–52 mm. Glossy white with strong, clear, fine oblique lines of medium to dark brown or purple-brown. On at least the ventral half of the shell these lines form relatively few large tents or mountain shapes. The animal appears to prefer deeper water as the shell is only rarely found beached. (41 mm)

Distribution: Rare on beaches, uncommon in deeper water. Gulf of Aqaba, South Sinai, reefs off Hurghada, Safaga, and south of Marsa Alam.

Notes: L. castrensis is pictured in all the well-known reference books, but the blotchy patterns shown therein are not found in the Egyptian Red Sea. R. Moolenbeek is currently researching the shells shown in these photographs.

Lioconcha ornata (Dillwyn, 1817)

12–37 mm. Strong shell, postero-dorsal line long, nearly straight, sloping to narrow sub truncate posterior. Ligament inset but externally visible, resilifer same width along its length. Pattern of fine brown zigzags and tents on white. Never with radial rays. Inside white. (29 mm)

Distribution: Uncommon, Hurghada to Berenice.

Lioconcha philippinarum (Hanley, 1844)

18 mm. → Strong concentric sculpture. The ridges are raised, smooth, and much broader than the incised line between them. Fine brownish zigzags or mottled rays of cream or white. Interior white or with pinkish fulvous stain centrally. (18 mm)

Distribution: Very rare, Gulf of Aqaba only.

Notes: Although some specimens of *Circenita callipyga* may have the same color pattern, *L. philippinarum* is a more tumid shell, the beaks are more raised and more clearly facing the anterior, and the lunule is broader, almost heart shaped, and not incised.

Lioconcha sp.

19–29 mm. Strong, glossy white shell only slightly inequilateral, beaks slightly to the anterior. Very fine chestnut tenting pattern, sometimes forming radial rays. Interior yellow to apricot. (27.5 mm)

Distribution: Uncommon, fine coral sand around near shore reefs. Hurghada to Wadi Gimaal.

Notes: Pattern typically much finer than that of *L. ornata*. In *Lioconcha* sp. the resilifer is more deeply inset and gradually widens from the anterior toward the posterior end. The shell outline is nearly identical to that of *Pitar hebraea*; much less elongate and truncate than the *L. sulcatina* of reference books. It is usually heavier than *P. hebraea*, from which it is easily distinguished by its very weak pallial sinus.

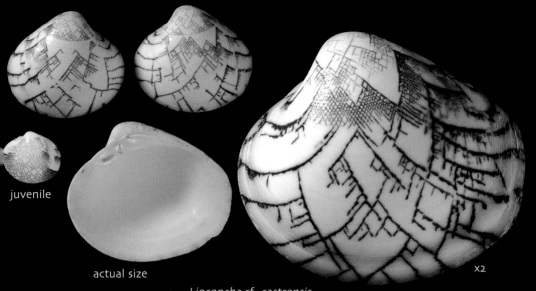

juvenile

actual size

x2

Lioconcha cf. *castrensis*

Lioconcha ornata

Lioconcha philippinarum

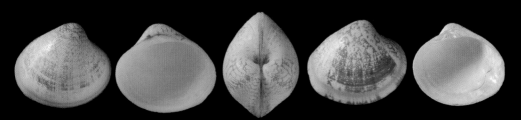

Lioconcha sp.

Paphia textile (Gmelin, 1791)
Paphia undulata (Born, 1778) of authors
32–56 mm. → Very glossy, strong, elongate ovoid, smooth surface. No oblique sculpture. Zigzag pattern in cream and caramel. (50 mm)
Distribution: Common in the far northern part of the Gulf of Suez.
Notes: *P. textile* is one of a handful of species that has migrated north into the Mediterranean Sea. It is often confused in the literature with *P. undulata* probably because the distinction, subtle oblique sculpture on the latter, is usually not visible in photographs. I have never found any specimens of *P. undulata* in the Red Sea.

Periglypta aff. *reticulata* (Linnaeus, 1758)
65–70 mm. Strong, heavy shell. → Strong rough sculpture of clearly separated radial riblets crossed by strong lamellae forming peaks where they cross the radial ribs. Off-white with random or radial pattern of small brown squares or oblongs (defined by the ribs and the lamellae). Interior all white, never with purple blotches. (50 mm)
Distribution: Occasional in the Gulf of Aqaba. Locally common between Marsa Alam and Wadi Lahmi.
Notes: Usually darker brown than *P. crispata*. On the umbonal area there is an observable sunken oblong space between each rib and the next. On *P. crispata* there is only an incised groove. The exact name of this shell is still under discussion among taxonomists.

Periglypta crispata (Deshayes, 1853)
45–71 mm. Strong, heavy shell. → Delicate sculpture of low radial riblets separated by a fine incised line and crossed by fine concentric lamellae rising and falling depending on the underlying radial rays. White to beige with light brown irregular patches, often arranged in radial rays. Interior white with some light yellow blush. (71 mm)
Distribution: Common around the reefs of the Straits of Gubal and Straits of Tiran. Occasional in the Gulf of Aqaba, and around southern reefs. Uncommon on beaches from Hurghada to Shalatein.
Notes: Both of these *Periglypta* have crispate concentric lamellae, but overall *P. crispata* is more delicate looking. Both seem to be a favorite food of some larger creature, perhaps the Titan Triggerfish. Divers often find one intact valve with the broken remains of the other still attached.

Paphia textile

Periglypta aff. *reticulata*

Periglypta crispata

Pitar hebraea (Lamarck, 1818)

10–32 mm. Usually thin, lightweight. Sculpture of growth lirations only. Beige with light brown zigzags and tents, quite variable. Some specimens have a ray of the background beige with no markings in the ray. → Pattern always continues to the posterior edge. Deep pallial sinus. Interior light beige, occasionally with a radial fulvous streak near the umbo. (31 mm)

Distribution: Common in all regions with fine sand, clean or muddy.

Notes: Lioconcha ornata often has a similar pattern, but *P. hebraea* has a strong deep pallial sinus and is lighter in weight. The infrequent *L. ornata* has a very shallow pallial sinus and a longer, straighter, posterodorsal margin.

Pitar spoori Lamprell & Whitehead, 1990

17–31 mm. Usually thin, lightweight. Sculpture of growth lirations only. Beige with light brown zigzags and tents. → Posterior area with solid light brown patch. (31 mm)

Distribution: Uncommon, all regions.

Notes: Confusion with *P. hebraea* (above) or any *Lioconcha* is avoided by noticing the diagnostic unpatterned solid color posterior of *P. spoori.*

Redicirce sulcata (Gray, 1838)

7–21 mm. Subcircular, compressed, with very fine concentric ridges covering the outside of the shell. Lunule sunken, shell outline next to the lunule somewhat straightened. No umbonal disc. White or with irregular brown or colored areas. (12 mm)

Distribution: Very uncommon, found in both gulfs and south to Safaga.

Ruditapes decussatus (Linnaeus, 1758)

33–50 mm. → Sculpture primarily of radial threads. On the anterior the radial and concentric incised sculpture are nearly equally strong and form little squares or diamonds. This pattern is called 'decussate,' and is the reason for its name. (50 mm)

Distribution: Rare, Suez Canal and northern Gulf of Suez only.

Notes: Common in the Mediterranean, widely used as food. It is not certain that it actually lives and reproduces in the Gulf of Suez; the shells found here may be the remnants of someone's meal.

Samarangia quadrangularis (A. Adams & Reeve, 1850)

68–75 mm. Large, heavy shell, smooth and white on the inside, thickly covered with sand grains on the outside. Each valve with three raised curving lines of sand grains running from the beak along the entire posterior of the shell. (68 mm)

Distribution: Rare, deeper water near offshore reefs, Straits of Tiran.

Notes: Likely to be seen only by very alert divers. The exterior of the pictured shell appears to have been raked by a predator's teeth. Some specialists consider this to be a different species than that found elsewhere, but no name has yet been published.

Pitar hebraea

Pitar spoori

Redicirce sulcata

Ruditapes decussatus

Samarangia quadrangularis

Tapes deshayesii (Hanley, 1844)
15–43 mm. → Elongate ovoid, flat concentric ridges arranged almost like very low steps one above the other, stronger and broader posteriorly. Off-white with brown markings, sometimes with broken rays. Inside white or yellow, some with a purple stain. (36 mm)
Distribution: Common in sandy areas in all regions. Occasionally abundant.
Notes: Tapes sulcarius (Lamarck, 1818) is a much larger species found in the far south of the Red Sea, not in Egyptian waters.

Timoclea djiboutiensis (Jousseaume, 1894)
Timoclea marica (Linnaeus, 1758) of authors
11–21 mm. Concentric lamellate sculpture, stronger posteriorly. The thin lamellae cross the incised radial grooves undisturbed producing tiny squares or rectangles with raised lines at the top and bottom and incised lines or grooves at both sides. Shell white with loosely radial fulvous markings. Interior usually with fulvous markings right at the margins and under the hinge. (14 mm)
Distribution: Common from Hurghada to Shalatein. Rare to never north of Hurghada.
Notes: Timoclea marica, an Indo-Pacific species, has raised rather than incised radial sculpture.

Timoclea hypopta (Sturany, 1899)
Endemic
11–23 mm. Cancellate sculpture of both radial and concentric incised lines. The resulting blocks are more squarish near the umbo and more oblong near the ventral margin. Color variable: purple, white, or brown, or a rayed or irregular mix. Inside white, purple, or pink, or mixed. (23 mm)
Distribution: Common in the Gulf of Aqaba, occasional in the Gulf of Suez, very rare south of Safaga.

Timoclea roemeriana (Issel, 1869)
Endemic
3–9 mm. → The rough sculpture of this very small shell separates it from all others of its size. Concentric lamellae are more widely spaced than the radial ribs. Shell pink, mauve, or white, never patterned. (9 mm)
Distribution: Common in the northern Gulf of Suez.

Tapes deshayesii

x3

actual size

juvenile

x3

Timoclea djiboutiensis

Timoclea hypopta

x3

actual size

Timoclea roemeriana

Subfamily CLEMENTIINAE
Clementia papyracea (Gray, 1825)
19–76 mm. Large, fragile, white shell, remarkably inequilateral, beaks to anterior. Broad concentric undulations and narrow concentric ridges. Large sharply pointed pallial sinus. (76 mm)
Distribution: Locally and occasionally common in the Gulf of Suez.

Kyrina kyrina Jousseaume, 1894
10–16.5 mm. → Fragile white shell, ovate, slightly tumid, beaks strongly to the anterior, three cardinal teeth in each valve. With magnification its distinctive divarcating threads become visible. All specimens I have seen in Egypt have a tiny red dot on the beak. (16.5 mm)
Distribution: Rare, the Gulf of Suez to Hurghada.

Family PETRICOLIDAE
These rarely found small white shells are notable for having strong cardinal teeth, three in the LV and only two in the RV.

Choristodon hemprichii (Issel, 1869)
9–19 mm. Beaks toward anterior. → Narrow riblets, weak or obsolete at anterior, strong and wiggly at the posterior. Animal burrows into limestone when alive, thus shell often distorted or irregular. (16 mm)
Distribution: Uncommon, far northern Gulf of Suez.

Mysia elegans (H. Adams, 1870)
8–11 mm. Strong venerid teeth, widely spaced and broadly slanting. Slightly rough texture, sculpture composed of tiny nodules arranged in a tight herringbone fashion. Large pointed pallial sinus. All white. (11 mm)
Distribution: Rare, northern Gulf of Suez.
Notes: With a good hand lens you can see the overall tightly spaced divergent bars forming constantly self-replicating chevron patterns. No lucine has this kind of sculpture and no other member of the Petricolidae family in the Red Sea has such fine sculpture.

Clementia papyracea

actual size   x2

Kyrina kyrina

x2

actual size

Choristodon hemprichii

x2

actual size

Mysia elegans

Family MYIDAE
Tugonella decurtata (A. Adams, 1851)
13–26 mm. Somewhat elliptical, posterior looks turned up and chopped off. Radial sculpture extremely weak. LV with large strongly projecting shelf-like resilifer. RV resilifer recessed. Animals bury themselves deeply in soft and silty substrate below the tidal zone in normally quiet waters. (26 mm)
Distribution: Uncommon on beaches due to the rarity of the storms necessary to dislodge them. Gulf of Suez, Wadi Lahmi.
Notes: See *Laternula anatina* (below).

Family CORBULIDAE
Corbula sulculosa H. Adams, 1870
6–9 mm. → Posterodorsal margin long with strong carina and steep posterior slope. RV with sulcate posterior, LV angulate. → Regular concentric sculpture, easy to see even on such a small shell. LV smaller, fits down inside the margins of the RV. Each valve with a peg-like tooth that fits into a corresponding socket on the opposite valve. (8 mm)
Distribution: Uncommon, the Gulf of Suez only.
Notes: This shell can easily be confused with *Basterotia angulata* of the Sportellidae because of the similar size and shape and the strong carina present in both, but *B. angulata* has very weak or obsolete concentric sculpture.

Family LATERNULIDAE
Laternula anatina (Linnaeus, 1758)
28–35 mm. Shell paper thin, transparent, pearly gray-white, covered with tiny pustules, these not always easily visible. → Extended posterior gapes and turns upwards. Projecting process for the ligament in each valve. Natural crack running from the beak down across the umbonal area. (29 mm)
Distribution: Rarely found, the Gulf of Suez only.
Notes: *L. anatina* resembles *Tugonella decurtata* in shape and lifestyle but is much thinner and more transparent.

Family PENICILLIDAE
Brechites attrahens (Lightfoot, 1786)
Watering Pot
98–115 mm. Very fragile and unusual. The siphon is enormous compared to the two valves, and develops a firm chalky exterior like a tube. The animal lives under the sand with the siphonal tube in a vertical position with only the open, ruffled end protruding above the sand. The lower end is dome shaped with small, slightly raised open tubes all over it. Above this inverted dome are the original valves of the shell (note valves in far right image). (98 mm)
Distribution: Uncommon, Gulfs of Aqaba and Suez in sandy areas only.

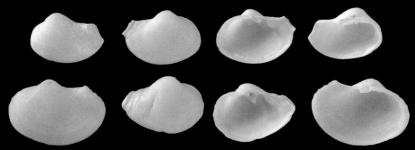

Tugonella decurtata

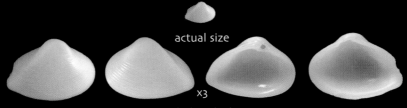

actual size

x3

Corbula sulculosa

Laternula anatina

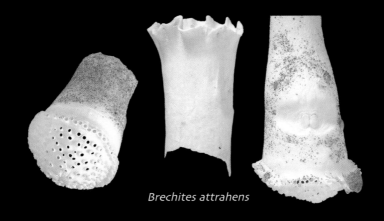

Brechites attrahens

Glossary

This section provides definitions for words which may be used exclusively to describe shells or molluscs. It also includes words whose meanings in this context may be different in other situations. Definitions, like other aspects of science and knowledge, do change with time and usage. Other authors may use other terms and definitions, but in general there should be no cause for confusion.

adductor muscle scars: Scars appearing on the inside of bivalve shells at the point where the muscle was attached to the shell. Most have two scars: one more posterior, the other more anterior. Oysters and related species have only one scar per shell.

anterodorsal: The front end of the upper side of a bivalve shell.

anteroventral: The lower front end of a bivalve shell.

appressed: Refers to scales that lie close to the shell, not erect.

auricle: The 'ear' of pectinid shells, the lateral extension of the umbo. Each valve of a pectinid shell has an anterior and a posterior auricle. Often simply called the ear.

auriculate: Having auricles.

bead: A small usually roundish bump on the surface of a shell. Shells in the genus *Clanculus* have beaded spiral cords—raised spiral lines covered with or composed of beads or tiny round bumps.

beak: The tip of the umbo. The first part of a bivalve shell to form.

bifed: Divided into two by a groove, but still remaining in one piece.

bivalve: The English name for the second-largest class of molluscs. 'Bivalvia' in Latin. Any member of that class. A mollusc having two valves (shells).

byssal gape: An open area, usually defined by the margins of a bivalve, through which the byssal threads pass to secure the animal to the substrate.

byssus: A group of fine strong threads produced by the animal to hold it in place.

calcareous: Made of lime; having a high calcium content.

callus: A deposit of calcareous material. Usually occurs in nassarids and cypraeids near the columella or on theedges. See *Nassarius obvelatus* and *Erosaria nebrites nebrites*.

cancellate: Sculptural elements crossing each other at right, or nearly right, angles.

cardinal teeth: The protruding part of the hinge just below the umbo.

channeled: A suture or spire with one or more deep grooves.

chevron: Ornament or structure having a 'V' shape, may also be upside-down.

chomata: The very small beads, bars, and pits in the margins of oysters.

columella: The structure winding around the imaginary axis of a gastropod, visible in intact shells as the lower part of the inner lip. Its shape, color, and sculpture are often important in determining the correct species identity of a given shell.

commensural: Two or more species living close together, sometimes sharing food. Not to be confused with parasitic.

concentric: Sculpture parallel to the line of growth. May be called axial in gastropods and comarginal in bivalves.

conspecific: Belonging to the same species.

cord: Raised spiral sculpture, thicker than a thread, on a gastropod.

crenulate: Regularly notched sculpture.

crura, crural teeth: Two ridges fitting into two slots on the hinge on the upper and lower valves, respectively, of shells in the family Plicatulidae.

decussate: Sculpture similar to cancellate but meeting obliquely and forming diamond shapes. May also be termed reticulate.

denticle: A small tooth.

denticulate: Having small teeth.

depressed: Low.

discrepant sculpture: Differs on left and right valves.

divaricate: Sculpture that splits or diverges, usually in bivalves.

dorsal: The upper part of a bivalve, the part with the hinge and the umbones.

dorsum: The back side of a gastropod, opposite or behind the aperture.

ear: See auricle.

elliptical: A bivalve outline resembling a compressed circle.

endemic: A species occuring only in a certain geographical area.

entire: Whole; refers to an unbroken pallial line in a bivalve.

equilateral: A bivalve shell that is the same, or nearly the same, on both sides of the umbo. The beak is the same distance from anterior and posterior margins.

escutcheon: Greek for 'shield.' Refers to an area on a bivalve that is posterior to the umbones, related to the ligament, and usually different from the rest of the shell in color or sculpture.

fluted: Usually refers to spines that are becoming tubular.

foliaceous: Leaf-like sculpture, as in the pericostracum of *Barbartia foliata*.

funicle: Specific to the Naticidae, a structure extending from the columella into the umbilicus. Can be important in differentiating species.

fusiform: Spindle shaped, extended at both ends.

gape: The space remaining open when both valves of a bivalve are closed. Serves different purposes in different families and may be located in different places.

granular: Having numerous small beads or grains, usually as in a granular surface.

growth lines: Axial or concentric lines remaining from the former growing edge of the shell.

hinge: Dorsal area of a bivalve where the two valves come together, usually with interlocking sculptural elements called teeth.

hinge plate: Usually flat and smooth, the area on the inner dorsal margin. The cardinal teeth of a bivalve are usually located on the hinge plate.

holotype: The single specimen described in the definition of a species.

inequilateral: Bivalves whose valves are different in size or shape. Most commonly one terminal margin is farther from the beak than the other.

interstices: The spaces between other sculptural elements, especially the ribs of bivalves. Interspaces is a synonym.

intertidal: Relating to the region between the high tide mark and the low tide mark.

keel/keeled: A ridge-like sculptural element.

lamella (pl. lamellae): Thin, very extended ridge, as in the lucine *Lamellolucina dentifera*.

lamellate: Sculpture with lamellae.

lateral teeth: Ridges along the dorsal margin of a bivalve, distant from the beak.

ligament: Flexible, elastic element connecting the two valves. Always situated posterior to the beak.

lip: Edge of the aperture of a gastropod.

lira (pl. lirae): Narrow concentric ridge on a bivalve, a spiral ridge in the aperture of a gastropod.

lirate: Having lirae.

lunule: Depressed or outlined area anterior to the beak on a bivalve.

median or medial: Central area, on or in the middle.

modioliform: Shaped like the shells in the genus *Modiolus*, beaks close to anterior margin.

mytiliform: Shaped like the shells in the subfamily Mytilinae, beaks terminal.

nacre: Mother-of-pearl.

nacreous: Pearly.

nodose: Having small knobs.

nodule: A small knob or bump.

nodulose: having small knobs, nodose, as in the littorid *Echinolittorina marisrubri*.

non: Latin for 'not.' Taxonomists use this to indicate that the species name given, for example '*rastellum* non Lamarck,' does not refer to Lamarck's *rastellum*.

nymph: Small narrow external part of the shell posterior to the beak to which the ligament is attached. Common in the family Psammobiidae.

obsolete: Very weak, almost not present. Absent.

operculum: Hard structure, horny or shelly, atttached to the foot of a gastropod, used to close the aperture and in strombids for locomotion; see *Turbo radiatus*.

ovoid: Egg shaped.

pallial line: Usually slightly shiny line near the ventral margin of a bivalve, where the mantle was attached in life.

pallial sinus: Bulge or indentation of the pallial line where the siphonal retractor muscles were attached in life.

parietal: Having to do with the area posterior to (above) the columella and/or immediately inside and outside the aperture opposite the outer lip. Parietal wall or lip. See *Rhinoclavis fasciata*, *R. sinensis* and *Nassarius obvelatus*.

pericostracum: The outermost layer of a shell, usually missing in dead shells.

plica: Ridge, fold.

plicate: Ridged or folded, having ridges, folds, pleats, wrinkles. Usually used to describe the external sculpture in bivalves *(Plicatula plicata)* or the columella in gastropods *(Vasum turbinellus)*.

posterior: The back end, or toward the back end, of a shell. The end of the aperture opposite the base end and siphonal canal in gastropods; the ligament-containing end of a bivalve.

posterior canal: A notch in the posterior (upper) end of the aperture for the posterior (exhalant) siphon; see *Bursa granularis*.

posterodorsal: The area along the upper margin of a bivalve behind the umbo, may be identified by the presence of the ligament.

posteroventral: The lower back end margin of a bivalve, below the posterodorsal margin.

protoconch: The first shelly part of a gastropod to develop, located above the apex of the spire. Usually glassy and differently sculptured from the rest of the shell.

punctate: Having tiny pits, as if pricked by a pin.

pustule: A small tubercle; like a pimple.

pustulose: Having pustules on the surface of the shell.

recurved: Bending back toward the body, especially as in the siphonal canal of gastropods; see *Rhinoclavis* sps.

resilifer: Small hollowed-out area usually in the hinge plate where the ligament attaches.

reticulate: Having obliquely intersecting sculpture or pattern, a netted pattern, as in the mitrid *Scabricola fissurata*.

rhomboidal: Approximately diamond shaped, but with rounded corners.

rib: in bivalves, the raised radial sculptural element. See the Pectinidae for good examples. In gastropods a raised sculptural element, may be axial or spiral, more commonly used as 'axial ribs.'

riblet: A small rib.

rostrate: Used to describe the outline of a bivalve having a rostrum; see the tellinid *Pharaonella* sps.

rostrum: A beak-like or extended part of a bivalve shell, usually posterior.

rugose: Rough or wrinkled surface, similar to corrugated; see the venerid *Circe rugifera*.

scabrous: Rough-feeling sculpture on a bivalve.

scissulate: Bivalve sculpture that is concentric and changes suddenly to oblique or diagonal, found in the genera *Gari* and *Loxoglypta*.

sculpture: Tangible and usually visible elements on the surface of a shell. Sculptural elements are often critical for differentiating between species, as in the venerid genera *Circe* and *Timoclea*.

secondary: Weaker, later developing sculptural elements, such as secondary ribs between primary ribs, as in the pectinid *Laevichlamys rubromaculata*.

septum: Shelf.

serrated: A margin cut by deep grooves leaving sawtooth-like protrusions; see *Obtellina sericata*.

sinus: Notch, often rounded; see also pallial sinus.

siphon: An anatomical feature through which water or waste enters or leaves a mollusc.

siphonal canal: The notch for the siphon at the anterior of the aperture of a gastropod. May be long and more or less straight as in *Murex forskoehlii*, or short and recurved as in the cerithiid genus *Rhinoclavis*, or barely noticeable as in most gastropods.

spine: A protuberance on a shell, usually long and sharp, like a thorn. In the Spondylidae some spines may be more strap-like.

spiral: Coiling around a central axis.

spire: All the whorls on a gastropod except the first and last.

squamose: Scaly, having numerous scales.

stria (pl. striae): Lines, stripes.

striate: Shell sculpture containing striae, lines.

stromboid notch: Notch or embayment near the lower (anterior) end of the lip through which the eye stalk protrudes. Most common in conches, the Strombidae.

sub-: A prefix indicating the quality is weak or almost or not quite: subcircular = not quite circular.

sublittoral: The near shore area below the low tide level.

sulcate: Grooved or with a trough.

sulcus: Groove or trough, usually not sharp edged. See *Eratoena sulcifera* and *Tellinella sulcata*.

suture: Where two whorls meet, usually visible as a line, often indented.

synonym: A name published later than the original valid name for the same organism or group of organisms. A word with the same meaning.

taxon (pl. taxa): An organism or group of organisms which have been given a scientific name. Names of taxa may be changed for various reasons.

thread: A fine ridge, thinner than a cord.

transverse: At right angles to the main axis.

trapezoidal: Outline of a bivalve having four sides, none parallel to any other.

trigonal: Approximately triangular outline of a bivalve.

truncate: A cut-off or squared-off bivalve outline; see *Tugonella decurtata* in the Myidae.

tubercle: Knob.

tubercular: Knobbed, knobby.

umbilicus: Hole or depression at the base of the central axis of a gastropod shell.

umbo (pl. umbones): Sometimes synonymous with beak. Located between the lunule to its anterior and the escutcheon to its posterior. The area near the beak extending perhaps a quarter of the way to the ventral margin.

umbonal ridge: raised sculptural element running from the umbo to the posteroventral margin.

varix (pl. varices): The remains of a thickened outer lip after the shell has grown on; see *Cymatium marerubrum* of the Ranellidae.

ventral: On bivalves the lower side, on gastropods the apertural side.

whorl: A complete turn of the spirally coiled gastropod shell. The first whorl to form is in the protoconch, the last one is the body whorl.

wing: Angular extension of the dorsal margin, as in the family Pteriidae.

Bibliography

Abbott, R. Tucker and S. Peter Dance. 1986. *Compendium of Seashells.* Burlington, MA: American Malacologists.

Bosch, Donald and Eloise. 1989. *Seashells of Southern Arabia.* Dubai: Motivate Publishing.

Bosch, Donald T., S. Peter Dance (editor), Robert G. Moolenbeek, and P. Graham Oliver. 1995. *Seashells of Eastern Arabia.* Dubai, Abu Dhabi, and London: Motivate Publishing.

Bouchet, P. and J.-P. Rocroi. 2005. "Classification and nomenclator of gastropod families," *Malacologia* 47(1–2): 1–397.

Coan, Eugene V., Paul Valentich Scott, and Frank R. Bernard. 2000. *Bivalve Seashells of Western North America, Marine Bivalve Mollusks from Arctic Alaska to Baja California.* Santa Barbara, CA: Santa Barbara Museum of Natural History.

Dance, S. Peter (editor), 1990. *The Collectors Encyclopedia of Shells.* Secaucus, NJ: Chartwell Books; London: Zachery Kwintner Books.

Dekker, Henk, and Z. Orlin. 2000. "Check-list of Red Sea Mollusca," *Spirula,* 47 (Supplement): 1–46.

Dollfus, P.R., and J. Roman. 1981. *Les échinides de la mer rouge.* Monographie zoologique et paléontologique. Ministère des Universités Comité des Travaux Historiques et Scientifiques, Mémoires de la Section des Sciences. Paris: Bibliothèque Nationale.

Fehse, D., 2005. "Contributions to the knowledge of the Ovulidae (Mollusca: Gastropoda) XIV. A new species in the genus *Prosimnia* Schilder, 1925," *Spixiana* 28(1): 13–16.

Heiman, E.L. 2002. *Cowries of East Sinai.* Jerusalem: Keterpress Enterprises.

Kool, H.H., and Henk Dekker. 2007. "Review of the *Nassarius pauper* complex, Part 2," *Visaya,* August: 62–77.

Lozouet, P. and P. Renard, 1998. "The Coralliophilidae, Gastropoda from the Oligocene and Lower Miocene of the Aquitaine (Southwestern France): systematics and details of coral hosts," Geobios 31(2): 171–84.

Oliver, P. Graham. 1992. *Bivalved Seashells of the Red Sea.* Christa Hemmen, Wiesbaden and National Museum of Wales.

Reid, D.G. 2007. "The genus *Echinolittorina* Habe, 1956 (Gastropoda: Littorinidae) in the Indo-West Pacific Ocean," *Zootaxa* 1420.

Rusmore-Villaume, Mary Lyn. 2005. "*Gari sharabatiae*, a new species from the Gulf of Suez, Red Sea, Egypt," *Gloria Maris* 44 (6): 146–49.

Sharabati, Doreen. 1984. *Red Sea Shells*. London: KPI Limited.

Snyder, M.A. 2006. "A new species of *Fusinus* (Gastropoda: Fasciolariidae) from the Red Sea and the identity of *Fusinus undulatus* (Gmelin, 1791)," *Gloria Maris* 45(5): 104–14.

Taylor, John D. and Emily A. Glover. 2005. "Cryptic diversity of chemosymbiotic bivalves: a systematic revision of worldwide *Anodontia* (Mollusca: Bivalvia: Lucinidae)," *Systematics and Biodiversity* 3 (3): 281–338.

Terryn, Yves. *A Collectors Guide to Recent Terebridae*. 2007. Hackenheim: Conch Books and Natural Art.

Vermeij, G.J. and M.A. Snyder. 2006. "Shell characters and taxonomy of *Latirus* and related fasciolariid groups," *Journal of Molluscan Studies* 72: 413–24.

van Aartsen, J.J. and S. Hori. 2006. "Indo-Pacific migrants into the Mediterranean. 2. *Monotigma lauta* (A. Adams, 1853) and *Leucotina natalensis* Smith, 1910 (Gastropoda, Pyramidellidae)," *Basteria* 70(1–3): 1–6.

Vine, Peter. 1985. *The Red Sea*. London and Jeddah: IMMEL Publishing.

Weil, A., L. Brown, and B. Neville. 1999. *The Wentletrap Book*. Rome: Evolver.

Zuschin, Martin and P. Graham Oliver. 2003. *Bivalves and bivalve habitats in the northern Red Sea*. Vienna: Natural History Museum.

Index

Species and genus names are in *italics*. Genus names begin with a capital letter. Suprageneric Latin names are in ALL CAPS. The images of the species are found on the pages listed in **bold**.